THE CORRESPONDENCE OF
THOMAS CARLYLE AND JOHN RUSKIN

THE CORRESPONDENCE OF

THOMAS CARLYLE

AND

JOHN RUSKIN

EDITED BY GEORGE ALLAN CATE

STANFORD UNIVERSITY PRESS
STANFORD, CALIFORNIA
1982

STANFORD UNIVERSITY PRESS
Stanford, California
© 1982 by the Board of Trustees of the
Leland Stanford Junior University
Printed in the United States of America
ISBN 0-8047-1114-3
LC 81-50784

To Professor Charles Richard Sanders

PREFACE

This is the first edition of the correspondence of Carlyle and Ruskin, and I have tried to make it as complete as possible. I have included every letter (and fragment of letter) that I could find through both public and private sources, and I have attempted to copy the letters with complete accuracy, using the manuscripts as the basis of my text whenever possible. Therefore all of the original repetitions, omissions, abbreviations, and eccentricities of capitalization and punctuation have been retained.

There are 199 letters included in this edition, 114 of which have not yet been published. The actual Carlyle-Ruskin correspondence consists of 154 letters (39 from Carlyle to Ruskin and 115 from Ruskin to Carlyle), of which 80 are hitherto unpublished. The remaining 45 letters are ancillary, forming epistolary tissue vital to the main body. They include six letters from Carlyle to Ruskin's father, John James Ruskin; one letter from Carlyle's brother John to Ruskin; twelve letters from Ruskin to Jane Welsh Carlyle; two letters from Mrs. Carlyle to Ruskin; four letters from Carlyle's niece, Mary Aitken, to Ruskin; and twenty letters from Ruskin to her. Of this group, 34 are hitherto unpublished.

I have made no excisions in the text and have indicated missing parts of letters by brackets and ellipses. Most of the manuscript sources do not have original envelopes or postmarks, but those that do have been noted in the headnotes. Ruskin was careless in dating his own letters, and I have tried to amend silently these errors of omission by placing whole or partial dates within brackets in the letterhead; only significant or unusual dates are discussed in the headnotes. In the headnote to each letter I have indicated my manuscript sources, and in citing previous publications I have thought it best to mention only the earliest ones, unless later ones have been in some way important. Wherever possible, superscript letters have not been brought down to the line, and Carlyle's liberal use of underlining has been faithfully retained. Ruskin's unique use of the apostrophe in common English contractions has been retained without note, as have contemporary spellings of geographical names. These editorial policies have minimized the necessity for frequent use of the word "*sic*" in the text. Wherever a character or characters proved indecipherable, I have indicated this by the use of an ellipsis and a question mark enclosed in brackets. Brackets have also been used to indicate my placement of missing words necessary to clarify meaning, to indicate editorial conjecture on existing words, and to include English translations of foreign expressions that are too minor or too short to require a footnote. Whenever no place of publication is indicated in a note or reference to a published work, London is to be understood.

In order that the reader's steady enjoyment might not be interrupted, I have placed both headnotes and footnotes at the bottom of the page. I have tried to make the footnotes thorough and helpful, but not so extensive as to be ostentatious or burdensome. The most important thing, after all, is that the reader be allowed to read Carlyle and Ruskin in a clean and reliable text. The editor's efforts are to assist in this process and to enrich understanding throughout.

My debts to the owners of the various manuscripts cited throughout this work are all too obvious, as are my debts to the many scholars who have contributed to our knowledge of Carlyle and Ruskin. I am especially indebted to Duke University's Graduate School of Arts and Sciences and to the General Research Board of the University of Maryland for research grants that helped me carry on my work. Dr. Alan Wooley of Duke University and Dr. John D. Howard of the University of Maryland helped me with the classical allusions in the letters. In the difficult and often frustrating task of annotating the letters I was helped by Mrs. Jane Ludington, Mrs. Janet Ray Edwards, Dr. H. Edward Spivey, Mr. Mark H. Watson, Dr. Edwin W. Marrs, Jr., Dr. Harold I. Shapiro, and Dr. Francis A. Burkle-Young. Professor Samuel E. Brown of the University of Maryland has generously allowed me to consult with him on my work and to consult his extensive Ruskin materials. For special help in locating manuscript sources I am grateful to Dr. Robert Hewison, Dr. David DeLaura, Dr. Van Akin Burd, and the late Dr. Helen Gill Viljoen. Editorial assistance, advice, and innumerable acts of friendship have been provided by Dr. K. J. Fielding and Dr. Ian Campbell of the University of Edinburgh, Dr. John Clubbe of the University of Kentucky, and Dr. Ian Ousby of the University of Maryland. Dr. Francis A. Burkle-Young has been of especially valuable assistance in the later stages of the preparation of the manuscript, serving as both research assistant and amanuensis. Mr. James S. Dearden, Curator of the Ruskin Galleries at Bembridge School, Isle of Wight, has been of tremendous help in many ways. He has been especially helpful in providing me with manuscripts for publication, in allowing me access to the extensive collection at the Ruskin Galleries, and in working with me on the many problems that have arisen over the years in the preparation of this book. My greatest debt of gratitude is due to Professor Charles Richard Sanders of Duke University. At his suggestion, I first began this book as a doctoral dissertation under his direction at Duke University. From that time until now he has been unstinting in his cooperation, guidance, and friendship. Without him, this book would simply not have been possible. I offer him my inadequate but sincerest thanks for all that he has been to me.

I am grateful to the following for their permission to publish, and quote from, material in their possession: the Pierpont Morgan Library in New York; the John Rylands University Library of Manchester; the Beinecke Rare Book and Manuscript Library, Yale University Library; the Duke University Library; the Trustees of the National Library of Scotland; Edinburgh University Library; the Henry W. and Albert A. Berg Collection, the New York Public Library, Astor, Lenox and Tilden Foundations; the Folger Shakespeare Library, Washington, D.C.; the Library of the University of California, Santa Cruz; the Alexander Turnbull Library, Wellington, New Zealand; the Library of the Victoria and Albert Museum; the Library of Congress; the Carlyle House, Chelsea; the Ruskin Galleries, Bembridge School, Isle of Wight; Dr. Gordon N. Ray; the Marquess of Northampton; Mr. L. E. Brown; Mr. Luis Gordon and Mr. Charles Gordon, Jr., of Luis Gordon & Sons, Ltd.; the late Dr. Frederick W. Hilles; and the estate of the late Dr. Helen Gill Viljoen. Mr. Rayner Unwin, of George Allen & Unwin (Publishers) Ltd., has kindly granted permission to publish the hitherto unpublished Ruskin letters in this book.

My special thanks are also due to: the Princeton University Library; the Cambridge University Library; the Bodleian Library, Oxford; the John Ruskin Museum, Coniston; the National Gallery of Art, Washington, D.C.; Mr. Michael Ameye; Mr. David F. Bizup; Dr. John L. Bradley, Mr. Ernest A. Braund; Mr. Herbert Cahoon; Mr. Laurence S. Galvin; Dr. O. Wendell Margrave; Miss Glenise Matheson; Don Otello Migliosi, Curia Vescovile of the diocese of Assisi; Dr. T. I. Rae; Mr. H. M. Simpson; Mr. Frank Taylor; Miss Marjorie Wynne; and my former teachers, Dr. Joseph P. Conerton, Dr. James Roy King, and the late Dr. Lionel Stevenson.

To my wife, Jeanne, who has worked on the typing and proofreading of my manuscript, and who has suffered through the thousand yearly trials this work has produced, I can only say that this book, like its editor, is for her.

College Park, Maryland   G.A.C.

CONTENTS

SHORT FORMS

Bembridge: The John Howard Whitehouse Collection, The Ruskin Galleries, Bembridge School, Bembridge, Isle of Wight.

Burd, *Winnington*: Van Akin Burd, ed., *The Winnington Letters of John Ruskin* (1969).

Carlyle's *Works*: Thomas Carlyle, *Works*, Centenary Edition, 30 vols. (1896–99).

Collingwood, I and II: W. G. Collingwood, *The Life and Work of John Ruskin*, 2 vols. (1893).

Collingwood (rev.): W. G. Collingwood, *The Life of John Ruskin* (1900). (A one-volume revised edition of the above.)

Cook, I and II: Sir Edward T. Cook, *Life of John Ruskin*, 2 vols. (1911).

Froude, I and II: James Anthony Froude, *Thomas Carlyle: A History of the First Forty Years of His Life, 1795–1835*, 2 vols. (1882).

Froude, III and IV: James Anthony Froude, *Thomas Carlyle: A History of His Life in London, 1834–1881*, 2 vols. (1884).

NLS: The National Library of Scotland.

Northampton: The Collection of the Marquess of Northampton.

Ruskin, *Diaries*: Joan Evans and John Howard Whitehouse, eds., *The Diaries of John Ruskin*, 3 vols. (Oxford, 1956–59).

Ruskin's *Works*: John Ruskin, *Works*, Library Edition, Sir Edward T. Cook and Alexander Wedderburn, eds., 39 vols. (1903–12).

Rylands: The John Rylands Library, University of Manchester.

Sanders: Charles Richard Sanders, "Carlyle's Letters to Ruskin: A Finding List with Some Unpublished Letters and Comments," *Bulletin of the John Rylands Library*, XLI (September 1958), 208–38.

Wilenski: Reginald H. Wilenski, *John Ruskin: An Introduction to Further Study of His Life and Works* (1933).

Wilson: David Alec Wilson, *Carlyle*, 6 vols. (1923–34).

THE CORRESPONDENCE OF
THOMAS CARLYLE AND JOHN RUSKIN

INTRODUCTION

The letters collected here span a period of almost thirty years and show the growth of a friendship that was one of the strongest and most fruitful in English literature. Through this friendship Thomas Carlyle was to exert a deep influence upon John Ruskin—an influence that provoked great changes in Ruskin's heart and mind, and produced unexpected but markedly great works of social comment that have kept their value to the present day. These letters show Carlyle's influence growing in successive stages. There is first the early acquaintanceship, which is largely that of a mildly flattered writer with his admiring reader. By the late 1850's, however, the relationship becomes that of a grateful master and his devoted disciple, and by the middle of the 1860's it has become, first a bond of mutual admiration and consolation, then a very close—even, eventually, a filial—intimacy between a lonely old man and a tortured younger one. One may also add a final, and not very important, last phase, in which the distance between Carlyle and Ruskin seems to widen as Carlyle passes the age of eighty and Ruskin passes the boundaries of sanity.

The date of the first meeting of Ruskin and Carlyle has never been determined precisely. The earliest letter from one to the other seems to be that of March 9, 1851, but this letter clearly indicates that their friendship had already begun. E. T. Cook, a leading biographer of Ruskin and one of the editors of the magnificent Library Edition of Ruskin's works, places the beginning of the intimacy between the two in the winter of 1849–50, but admits that he has "never been able to ascertain" the precise way in which Ruskin first met Carlyle.[1] Carlyle himself, in a letter to his brother John on December 18, 1850, speaks of a recent visit by "Ruskin and Wife, of the Seven Lamps of Architec-

[1] Cook, I, 283. The question is also left unanswered in the six-volume standard biography of Carlyle, by D. A. Wilson.

ture, a small but rather dainty dilettante soul, of the Scotch-Cockney breed"²—a reference which seems to indicate that Carlyle had not known Ruskin very long. An entry in the journal of John Welsh, a cousin of Mrs. Carlyle, records a visit made by Ruskin and his wife to Carlyle's house a day or two before July 6, 1850.³ This seems to be the earliest proven date of their meeting,⁴ but it is possible to compile at least a general history of Ruskin's early acquaintance with Carlyle, and to determine some of the dates by approximation. Carlyle came to Ruskin's attention in the spring of 1841. In a letter to W. H. Harrison, dated June 6, 1841, Ruskin wrote from Geneva: "What are these Carlyle lectures [i.e., *Heroes and Hero-Worship*]? People are making a fuss about them, and from what I see in the reviews, they seem absolute bombast—taking bombast, I suppose, making everybody think himself a hero, and deserving of 'your wash-up,' at least, from the reverential Mr. Carlyle."⁵ Later in the same day, however, Ruskin appears to have read the lectures, for an entry in his diary says: "Read some of Carlyle's lectures. Bombast, I think; altogether approves of Mahomet, and talks like a girl of his 'black eyes.'"⁶ We also know that Ruskin's friend George Richmond introduced him to Carlyle's *Past and Present* after the book was published in 1843, and Ruskin this time was favorably impressed.⁷

---

²MS: NLS, 513.65. See also C. R. Sanders, "Carlyle's Letters to Ruskin: A Finding List with Some Unpublished Letters and Comments," *Bulletin of the John Rylands Library*, XLI (September 1958), 209.

³See Leonard Huxley, "A Sheaf of Letters from Jane Welsh Carlyle," *Cornhill Magazine*, n.s. LXI (November 1926), 629.

⁴There are some indications from other sources that the two men may have become acquainted, or at least exchanged letters, as early as 1846. Mrs. Anne Thackeray Ritchie, in her *Records of Tennyson, Ruskin, and Browning* (1892), p. 103, remarks that Ruskin "came under Carlyle's influence" somewhere "between the publication of the first and second volumes of *Modern Painters*"—that is, between 1843 and 1846. Mrs. Ritchie's remarks, of course, might refer only to the influence of Carlyle's books upon Ruskin; but a letter from Carlyle to his sister on June 30, 1847, raises the possibility of a personal meeting between the two during the period Mrs. Ritchie describes. In this letter, Carlyle tells of a visit paid him by the young Duke of Saxe-Weimar, and he says that he showed the duke a portrait of Frederick the Wise. A note by the editor of the letter, Alexander Carlyle, says that this portrait was "an engraving by Albrecht Dürer, presented to Carlyle by John Ruskin" (*New Letters of Thomas Carlyle* [1904], II, 37). Charles H. Kegel, taking note of this portrait, has assumed that "Ruskin would not present a gift to Carlyle before he had met him personally," and he therefore states that the most likely date of the meeting would fall between September 1846 and June 1847 ("An Uncertain Biographical Fact," *Victorian Newsletter*, no. 10, Autumn 1956, p. 19).

⁵*Works*, XXXVI, 25.

⁶Ruskin, *Diaries*, I, 199.

⁷See Derrick Leon, *Ruskin: The Great Victorian* (1949), p. 239; and Ruskin's *Works*, XXXVII, 361. Ruskin's personal copy of *Past and Present*, now in the possession of the British Museum, is the second edition, published in 1845, and recommended by Ruskin in *Fors Clavigera*, letter 10.

Once Ruskin's interest was generated, it would have been an easy step for him to meet Carlyle. This was especially true during the winter of 1849–50, when Ruskin had recently married and returned from his wedding trip abroad to settle in London, and had begun escorting his wife to a number of prominent places and homes. In view of the evidence, it is perhaps best to say that Ruskin first read Carlyle in 1841, first became interested in him between 1843 and 1847, and first met him sometime between 1847 and 1850.

The question of when Carlyle and Ruskin met is not so interesting however, as the question of *why* they met. When one looks at both men as they were at the time the correspondence begins, it is amazing that such antipodal personalities ever bothered with each other at all. Carlyle had come from poor Scottish peasant stock, and throughout his fifty-six years had worked very hard to make his way in the world. He began as a student in Edinburgh, then struggled successively as schoolmaster, hack writer and translator, and essayist before achieving success as a historian with his *French Revolution* in 1837. After that time, however, he had to work just as hard to preserve his income, and throughout the 1840's he had produced a series of public lectures (*Heroes and Hero-Worship*), an extended book of social criticism (*Past and Present*), a biographical edition of Cromwell's letters and speeches (1845), and a series of essays on the "condition of England" entitled *Latter-Day Pamphlets* (1850). Ruskin, in contrast, was the only child of a wealthy, though self-made, Scottish wine merchant, and had been raised in a fashionable middle-class suburb of London. He was early encouraged in the development of his rich talents, and was supplied with full leisure, money, and constant opportunities to travel widely in England and Europe. He was sent to Oxford, where he received his B.A. in 1842. Relieved of the need to earn his living, he wrote only for his own pleasure, and by 1851 had gained fame as a brilliant critic of art and architecture through the publication of *Modern Painters* (volume I, 1843; volume II, 1846) and *The Seven Lamps of Architecture* (1849–50).

The two men differed even more in personality and behavior. Carlyle's personality was decidedly masculine and tough-minded—even awesome and intimidating—at first sight. The young James Anthony Froude, meeting Carlyle for the first time in 1849, has described his first impressions, which Ruskin may also have had in the same year:

He was then fifty-four-years old; tall (about five feet eleven), thin, . . . upright. His body was angular, his face beardless. . . . His head was extremely long with the chin thrust forward; the neck was thin; the mouth firmly closed, the under lip slightly projecting; the hair grizzled and thick and bushy. His eyes

Thomas Carlyle in the 1860's. Courtesy of the Library of Congress, Washington, D.C.

. . . were then of deep violet, with fire burning at the bottom of them, which flashed out at the least excitement. . . . he treated me—I cannot say unkindly, but shortly and sternly. . . . no one need look for conventional politeness from Carlyle—he would hear the exact truth from him, and nothing else.[8]

Carlyle was also known as an imposing and fascinating conversationalist. Ralph Waldo Emerson, having visited Carlyle a year before Froude, wrote that Carlyle was "an immense talker, as extraordinary in his conversation as in his writing—I think even more so." Emerson added that Carlyle's talk often reminded him of what was said of Samuel Johnson: "'If his pistol missed fire, he would knock you down with the butt-end.'"[9] But the shrewd Emerson also noted what many visitors and readers failed to note—that there was "nothing deeper in his constitution than his humor, than the considerate, condescending good nature with which he looks at every object in existence, as a man might look at a mouse."[1] Carlyle loved to argue, to prod, and to dominate a conversation in the manner of Johnson: he offered his opinions, which were many, strong, and emphatically phrased, not for consideration but for acceptance. He was, furthermore, an indignant opponent of all mercantile pretensions, and was equally scornful of the "Idle Rich," the excessively self-conscious artists and poets, and the "Dandies" and "Dilettantes" who spoke with false wisdom about unimportant topics. By the late 1840's, as Emerson tells us, he had come to "think it the only question for wise men, instead of art and fine fancies and poetry and such things, to address themselves to the problem of society."[2] Highly unorthodox in his religious views, he was yet indifferent to earthly pleasures, had a strong moral sense, and preached his famous doctrine of Work. His mind above all rejected theory and insisted upon "facts," practicality, and the orderly movement of mind and body toward feasible goals that could be attained here on earth. By 1851, his commitment to "the problem of society" was total. Primarily concerned with the state of mankind's soul, he saw few others sharing his concern, and in desperate indignation he denounced an English society that could allow the evils he saw. He was, in fact, a prophet who called everyone to bring himself into harmony with the inviolable moral laws of human nature and the universe itself.

The John Ruskin of 1851 would seem to be at the farthest remove from this craggy personality. He, too, was renowned for his conversa-

[8] Froude, III, 391.
[9] E. W. Emerson, ed., *The Complete Works of Ralph Waldo Emerson* (Boston and New York, 1904), X, 489, 493–94.
[1] *Ibid.*, X, 495.
[2] *Ibid.*, X, 497.

tional prowess, but he spoke in an entirely different manner, and about entirely different subjects. Very slender, with a thin angular face and deep-set, expressive eyes, he was a graceful and meticulous dresser, and was much loved for his thoughtfulness, his ability to make and keep friends, his generosity, and his warm *politesse*. When we remember Froude's description of his first meeting with Carlyle in 1849, it is enlightening to read F. J. Furnivall's description of his first meeting with Ruskin in 1848: "I never met any man whose charm of manner at all approached Ruskin's. Partly feminine it was, no doubt; but the delicacy, the sympathy, the gentleness and affectionateness of his way, the fresh and penetrating things he said, the boyish fun, the earnestness, the interest he showed in all deep matters, combined to make a whole which I have never seen equalled."[3] Such a man was well versed in social graces, and it is no surprise to find that, far more than Carlyle, Ruskin actively sought "cultural" acquaintances. He was frequently with aristocrats and famous men. He was known among the highest artistic circles, where he was admired as a critic and writer. His own interests were exclusively what Carlyle would have called "dilettantish"—he collected, and wrote about, geological specimens and fine pictures; he spent many hours each day drawing pictures of natural scenes for his own pleasure; and he had written two volumes of highly self-conscious nature poetry. Here, surely, was a dilettante to fit all Carlylean patterns, and it is not surprising to find Carlyle calling him just that in the letter quoted above.

Carlyle must have noted other important contrasts between himself and Ruskin. Ruskin, for instance, was highly animated and voluble, flashing from periods of great energy to periods of indolence and self-indulgence. His books written before 1851—*Modern Painters* I and II and *The Seven Lamps of Architecture*—dealt exclusively with artistic and aesthetic theories, and were little concerned with social problems or facts. Furthermore, at the time Ruskin met Carlyle he still seemed to be a strict Evangelical sectarian—apparently as insular and narrow in his religious views as Carlyle was liberal and broad. In short, where Carlyle was concerned with the problems of humanity and justice, Ruskin was concerned with the problems of art and beauty, and seemed little interested in philosophy or the state of mankind's soul. In his own way he, too, was a prophet, but a prophet of art, calling everyone to "regard the apprehension of beauty as a means of justifying the ways of God to man."[4]

[3]Cook, I, 231.
[4]Graham Hough, *The Last Romantics* (1961), p. 30.

John Ruskin in 1867. Courtesy of the Ruskin Galleries, Bembridge School, Isle of Wight.

Beneath these contradictory elements of character and social position, however, lay certain deep similarities between Carlyle and Ruskin. Both men were raised in puritanical households by Scottish parents who expected reverence, obedience, and abstention from "frivolities." A comparison of Carlyle's *Reminiscences* and Ruskin's *Praeterita* will show how similar Carlyle's parents were to Ruskin's, and Mrs. Helen G. Viljoen's *Ruskin's Scottish Heritage*[5] presents a vivid picture of the humble origins of Margaret and John James Ruskin and the severe life they led in the years before their son's birth. The force of parental influence seems to have been equally strong on both men, leading to the development of similar psychological traits in later life. Both Ruskin and Carlyle, for instance, suffered lifelong fits of depression and anxiety, which are amply described in their letters and even in their works, such as *Sartor Resartus* and *Fors Clavigera*; and they both developed ailments that were psychosomatic in origin. Carlyle's perpetual "dyspepsia" (which we might today call an ulcer) is the most obvious of these ailments, but there were others as well, such as insomnia, aversion to noise, frequent chills and colds, and recurrent irritability. Ruskin suffered from even greater hypochondria. His diaries and letters have many references to illnesses, real or imaginary, which recurred until he finally succumbed to the dreadful manic-depressive psychosis that deprived him of his powers in the last twelve years of his life. In sexual matters, too, both men seem to have suffered deficiencies that can only be guessed, but that sprang from strong repressive instincts instilled in them early in life.[6]

These parental and psychic similarities produced a still more important similarity of temperament in both men, in that they were both essentially dogmatic and prophetic. Both Carlyle and Ruskin were raised with a deep knowledge of the Bible. They both were originally trained by their parents in the hope that they would become clergymen. These facts, coupled with the strong repressions that resulted from such zealous religiosity, led to the development of an overpowering preoccupation with morality and a strongly emphatic and dogmatic manner of thinking, as well as an adroit ability to write and

[5]New York, 1957.

[6]Ruskin's marriage was annulled in 1854 because, as he himself admitted, it had never been consummated. He later denied charges that he was impotent, however, and the question has never been completely settled. The question of Carlyle's sexual impotency was unfortunately raised during the storm of controversy over Froude's biography of him, and is far more nebulous and inconclusive. The "literature" on the subject is admirably summarized and judged by Waldo H. Dunn in his *Froude and Carlyle* (1930), pp. 204–17, but even Dunn's conclusions must be regarded as tenuous.

speak in the most sweeping homilies. Both Carlyle and Ruskin were good examples of the personality described by Erich Fromm as the "authoritarian character,"—one who fears and represses his own baser instincts and therefore "equates the self-assertion of the masses with the assertion of his own instinctual drives,"[7] leading him to believe in strict control of the people by an authoritarian leader, and further leading him into a messianic conception of himself as the possible savior of man's soul. Certainly Carlyle, who was a moral prophet of biblical stature and poured forth fierce jeremiads on England's head for many years, fits that description. Ruskin's attempts to show people the error of their ways in not seeing the power of God behind the beauty of the universe—attempts made with fierce confidence in the first two volumes of *Modern Painters* and *The Seven Lamps of Architecture*—fit it equally well. Indeed, though Ruskin in 1850 was a prophet of art and Carlyle was a prophet of morality, they were not so disparate as one would suppose, for they were both essentially preaching the salvation of humanity.

It was in their mutual sympathy for humanity that Carlyle and Ruskin came closest to one another. Whatever their differences might have been, it was, as Derrick Leon has said, their "essential similarity of attitude"[8] that drew them together. Beneath Carlyle's invectives against society and beneath Ruskin's exhortations upon art lay a mutual desire to better mankind's condition—to bring about the fullest possible development of the spiritual and intellectual potentialities of every man, and to destroy all barriers, both social and personal, to that development. Carlyle, despite his nervous irritability and the "daily secretion of curses which he had to vent on somebody or something,"[9] possessed an acute sympathy for those who suffered—a sympathy that, in Harriet Martineau's words, constituted the "master-pain of his life."[1] Both Froude's and Wilson's biographies of Carlyle have many examples of Carlyle's warmhearted (and unpublicized) charity.[2] Such sympathy for individuals was, after all, but evidence of a larger concern for society in general—a firm social conscience and a belief that, though conditions in England were bad, society could be saved through the self-generated salvation of each individual in it.

This belief in the social value of each person's conscience and char-

[7] As cited in Gaylord C. LeRoy's excellent study, *Perplexed Prophets* (Philadelphia, 1953), p. 30.
[8] Leon, p. 240.
[9] Herbert Spencer, quoted in LeRoy, p. 27.
[1] See her *Autobiography*, ed. M. W. Chapman (Boston, 1877), I, 288.
[2] For an additional example see Letters 8, 9, and 10.

acter was the heart of Carlyle's social doctrine, and had wide influence. Springing as it did from Calvinistic emphasis on the individual
conscience and from the strong humanitarianism that pervaded the
Romantic period in the early nineteenth century, Carlyle's teaching
merged these forces to produce what Emery Neff calls "the turning of
English Romanticism from the problems of the individual to the problems of society."[3] Carlyle's salutary warning to "close thy Byron; open
thy Goethe,"[4] to turn from morbid self-analysis to the development of
the self through disciplined and useful work, came to have great meaning for the younger generation of listeners in the late 1840's and
1850's.

Ruskin, as we have seen, was one of these listeners, and by 1851 his
social conscience was awakened. As intelligent and innately sympathetic to the sufferings of society as Carlyle, and sharing the older
man's Calvinistic and Romantic heritage, he had gradually begun to
experience a great period of inner crisis that was to change his views.
During the writing of his first two books, he had lived in luxury, obliv-
ious to other lives around him. But he began to be plagued with a
sense of guilt about his life. As early as 1845, he had written a letter to
his parents from Champagnole describing his feelings after a sumptuous supper: "As I came back to my soufflee [sic] and Sillery, I felt sad
at thinking how few were capable of having such enjoyment, and very
doubtful whether it were at all proper for me to have it all to myself."[5]
This small thought was to grow rapidly in the next few years, for it
was this side of Ruskin that was "the real Ruskin with 'the ray of
Heaven' that Carlyle saw in him."[6] By the end of 1846, his concern for
society began to show in his works and brought about a change in the
tenor of them all—especially *Modern Painters*. John D. Rosenberg has
pointed out that "during the decade separating the second volume
(1846) from the third volume (1856) [of *Modern Painters*], Ruskin became less moved by the beauty of art and nature than by the waste,
mystery, and terror of life. The tone of the first two volumes is pious
and lyrical; that of the later volumes is humanistic and tragic."[7] Ruskin's reading of Carlyle during the 1840's was not the sole reason for
this change, of course, but it may have had much to do with it.[8] And

---

[3] *Carlyle* (New York, 1932), p. 209.
[4] In "The Everlasting Yea" chapter of *Sartor Resartus* (*Works*, I, 153).
[5] Cook, I, 175.
[6] See Wilenski, p. 28.
[7] *The Darkening Glass: A Portrait of Ruskin's Genius* (1961), p. 22.
[8] Harold I. Shapiro, in his edition of Ruskin's 1845 letters to his parents, has remarked that one can see in the Ruskin of that time "the beginnings of his later social

the awakening of Ruskin's social conscience was but one of the many changes in personality and attitude that were affecting him at the time and were especially conducive to the development of a friendship with Carlyle. Ruskin went to Italy alone in 1845—a small but significant gesture of defiance towards his parents. Now twenty-six years old, he was beginning to sense his mental and spiritual alienation from them, and was fighting to overcome it. In Italy, also, he first saw the beauty of the early Italian painters. He "spent six months in Italian churches, looked for the first time at Roman Catholic religious painting, and fell in love with the dancing angels in the pictures by Fra Angelico. . . ."[9] His Evangelical faith could not account for his strong response to this "superstitious" art, nor could his father share his new joy, and Ruskin was left to make some new adjustments in his art criticism alone. From this period on there began to appear some cracks in his filial and religious devotion, and they continued to widen for the rest of his life, though not yet openly. After the second volume of *Modern Painters* (1846), Ruskin became still more disturbed. He suffered long fits of deep depression throughout the first few months of 1847, and began to have alarming symptoms, described in a letter to his father on June 27, 1847: "my failing sight plagues me. I cannot look at anything as I used to do, and the evening sky is covered with swimming strings and eels."[1] He was sent to Leamington for a month's "cure," and while he was there he not only failed to shake off his depression, but had, according to E. T. Cook, "inner questionings on the foundations of a religious faith now first being shaken."[2] In this state he went to visit a friend at Crossmount soon afterwards, and there he had his first clear thoughts on social questions—thoughts that he later remembered as being "scattered afterwards up and down in *Fors* and *Munera Pulveris.*"[3]

As 1848 approached, he began to recover from his depression, but the uneasiness between himself and his parents, his religion, and even his love of nature continued. The revolutions of 1848 increased his confusion. He was much alarmed by the fearsome wave of republican fervor that seemed to be flooding Europe and England, and his sympathies were aroused, as well as his sense of guilt:

---

criticism." See H. I. Shapiro, *Ruskin in Italy: Letters to His Parents, 1845* (Oxford, 1972), pp. xviii–xix. Both E. T. Cook and Joan Evans have endorsed the belief that Ruskin was inspired to the production of *Modern Painters* by his reading of Carlyle's *Heroes and Hero-Worship* and *Past and Present.* See Joan Evans, *John Ruskin* (1954), p. 83; and Cook's article on Ruskin in the *Dictionary of National Biography.*

[9] Wilenski, p. 330.

[1] Cook, I, 211.

[2] Cook, I, 212.

[3] *Ibid.,* 215.

I begin to feel all the work I have been doing, and all the loves I have been
cherishing, are ineffective and frivolous—that these are not times for watching clouds or dreaming over quiet waters, that more serious work is to be
done. . . .

tell me whether it is of any use to write or think about painting any more,
now. . . . I feel very doubtful whether I am not wasting my life, and very sad
about all.[4]

A few months after his marriage on April 10, 1848 (the day of
the great Chartist demonstration in London), Ruskin went to France,
and saw at first hand the startling revolutionary events taking place
there—Louis Philippe driven out, a republic proclaimed, bloody and
violent riots in Paris, and other forces leading to the election of Louis
Napoleon as president. He was thoroughly shaken by the great "mental and moral degradation" and the "hopeless suffering" everywhere.
Like Wordsworth on an earlier trip to France, he had to face the problem of man's sin and brutality, and this provoked a similar crisis of
belief. Eventually he wrote that it all made him think about

God's government of this world, and many other difficulties which stand in
the way of one's faith. . . . And I tell you also frankly that the more I investigate and reason over the Bible as I should over any other history or statement,
the more difficulties I find, and the less ground of belief. . . .[5]

Ruskin was able to hide most of these doubts during the next few
years, but he could not destroy them, and his guilt grew. He was experiencing a change of attitude that made him especially susceptible to
Carlyle's urgent messages and personal power over people. Just as he
was to do at the end of every decade of his life after 1839, Ruskin
paused to see how far he had come in life—a fascinating habit of self-
review, which usually ended in a desire to do something useful with his
life. In view of Ruskin's behavior, after all, Carlyle would seem to be
the only man in England who could have met his personal needs at the
time.

And Carlyle did not fail him. *The Seven Lamps of Architecture* contains many hints of social concern, including the idea that national art
reflects national character and the idea that the basic question to be
asked of all ornament is "was the carver happy while he was about it?"
One sentence in particular shows both Ruskin's expanding sympathies
and the influence of Carlyle's *Past and Present*: "It is not enough to
find men absolute subsistence; we should think of the manner of life

[4]Ruskin to Mary Russell Mitford, April 21, 1848; and Ruskin to George Richmond,
May 1, 1848. Both quoted in Cook, I, 221–22.
[5]Ruskin to his father, August 24, 1848. In Cook, I, 227.

which our demands necessitate; and endeavor, as far as may be, to make all our needs such as may, in the supply of them, raise, as well as feed, the poor."⁶ The earliest record of Ruskin's meeting with Carlyle, too, shows him continuing to ponder religious problems, and is thus significant. John Welsh, in his journal of July 6, 1850, speaks of a visit made to Carlyle in which

Mr. Ruskin drew out Mr. Carlyle's religious opinions and by judicious questioning hemmed him into expressing his whole *confession*. He denies the personal existence of a devil—he says that he feels a devil within him but denies that any power can clip the wings of that devil but his own. Christianity seems to be with him out of date and something else must supply its place although what it is he gives no utterance. He evidently does not see the length towards Deism that he has gone. . . .⁷

Carlyle was not a Deist, of course, but in his desire to break through the barriers of fundamentalist mythology that had been erected around the essential feelings of the Christian religion and in his broad attitudes toward the erasure of narrow sectarianism and unnecessary dogma, he had made his "exodus from Houndsditch," left the "Hebrew old clothes" of Old Testament myths behind him, and urged a return to the basic truths of humanity found in all religions. Ruskin, searching and doubting, did not reject Carlyle's theories, but went to the older man, as John Welsh's report shows, for help and advice. He, too, was beginning to shed his narrow views and Hebrew old clothes, and while his works at this time give little evidence of this, his private actions and writings prove it.⁸ Not long after his conversation with Carlyle, he published a pamphlet on Protestant church unity, which is mentioned in the first letter of this collection—a pamphlet that, while still highly devout, was broader in its approach to religion than any of Ruskin's previous writings, and surely owed something to Carlyle's influence. Ruskin had, as we have seen, been conducting his own study of the Bible for years, and it was in 1851 that he wrote to a friend:

You speak of the flimsiness of your own faith. Mine, which was never strong, is being beaten into mere gold leaf, and flutters in weak rags from the letter of

⁶ *Works*, VIII, 264.
⁷ Quoted in Huxley, p. 629.
⁸ Frederic Harrison, in his *John Ruskin* (New York, 1906), p. 72, says that Ruskin "undertook to found a comprehensive scheme of the imaginative faculties on a creed which he had imbibed as a child and held with childlike fervour, without any solid study of its philosophy, or its history, or its social fruits. When all this was forced on him by the prophetic homilies of Thomas Carlyle, and by the facts of society and art he witnessed in Catholic countries, and which he learned about in Catholic ages, his rapid imagination and his sympathetic nature took fire and tore off, as did Sartor himself, 'the rags of Houndsditch,' as Carlyle called the Biblical orthodoxy of his youth."

its old forms; but the only letters it can hold at all are the old Evangelical formulae. If only the Geologists would let me alone, I could do very well, but those dreadful Hammers! I hear the clink of them at the end of every cadence of the Bible verses—[9]

Though Ruskin continued to write about art and architecture in the 1850's, his interest was flagging, and by 1853 his faith in the Bible as the word of God had greatly diminished. Beneath the surface of his Evangelical religion, his insularity, and his devotion to art, a new Ruskin was emerging—a Ruskin closer to the Carlylean mold and farther removed from the faith of his fathers.

Carlyle's initial attitude toward Ruskin during the early years of their association was ambiguous. He was never able to overcome his innate aversion to Ruskin's preoccupation with the fine arts, nor could he entirely tolerate Ruskin's effervescent personality. His description of Ruskin as a "dainty dilettante soul" is hardly flattering when one considers all of the damnable elements Carlyle included in his definition of the word "dilettante," and Ruskin's attempts to elicit Carlyle's religious views at the time could not have created a friendly feeling in one who was always reluctant to reveal his opinions on such matters.[1] Yet Carlyle saw much to admire in Ruskin. He read Ruskin's works often in the 1850's, and offered frequent encouragement for the continued growth of the younger man's social writings and social conscience.

There is no doubt that such encouragement was welcomed by Ruskin at this crucial time of his life. Carlyle, after all, had read *The Stones of Venice* and especially praised it for its *social* message at a time when Ruskin's father was displeased with his son's social writings. Carlyle was quick to sense the presence of Ruskin's growing social conscience, and equally quick to sense that Ruskin was sincere. Strongly interested in—even obsessed with—the deplorable state of society in his time, his strong mind could exert an immense influence upon the receptive mind of Ruskin, and yet perceive that he had in Ruskin an independently great ally in the war against the shams and amorality of industrialism.

Ruskin's letter of January 23, 1855, confesses the influence of Carlyle's "stronger mind" upon him, while at the same time confessing

[9] *Works*, XXXVI, 115.
[1] See Letter 150. C. R. Sanders, in a note on the subject, cites a remark made by W. H. Wylie: "To a friend of ours who happened once to say that he held the same religious views as himself, Carlyle with some heat retorted, 'my religious views! And who told you *what* my religious views are?'" ("Carlyle's Letters to Ruskin," *Bulletin of the John Rylands Library*, XLI [September 1958], 234.)

that over three years had gone by since the two men had last met in 1851.

After Ruskin's wife left him and sued for annulment in 1854, however, Ruskin began to visit the Carlyle house in Chelsea more frequently, and his letters show the slow development of closer bonds between the two men. The rapprochement was gradual, however, for there was still much to be overcome. The reaction of *both* Carlyles to Ruskin's marital difficulties, for instance, was mixed. Mrs. Carlyle, not yet warmed to the charms of Ruskin's generous nature, wrote to her brother-in-law, Dr. John Carlyle, on May 9, 1854, that:

> There is a great deal of talking about the Ruskin's here at present. . . . There is even a rumour that *Mrs.* Ruskin is to sue for a divorce. I know nothing about it, except that I have always pitied Mrs. Ruskin, while people generally blame her,—for love of dress and company and flirtation. She was too young and too pretty to be left on her own devices as she was by her Husband, who seemed to wish nothing more of her but the credit of having a pretty, well-dressed Wife.[2]

Later, however, she developed more sympathy for Ruskin. In 1856 she attended a soiree at Lady Ashburton's in Bath, and her report of what happened reveals much about her feelings:

> We took with us to that party, at Lady A's request, Mr. Ruskin! And considering how people have *stared* at that man—ever since he had the happiness to be divorced by his wife, I displayed, I think, a *certain* force of mind in taking his arm to go in, instead of Mr. Carlyle's, and getting myself announced "Mrs. Carlyle and Mr. Ruskin"! How horribly ill bred people are,—as a general rule![3]

Though he was known to have strong views on the indissolubility of marriage, and though many critics have agreed with Joan Evans that he blamed Effie Ruskin for not accepting her lot,[4] Carlyle seems to have been tight-lipped about Ruskin's marriage. In a letter to his brother John on November 27, 1855, he even spoke of the matter with some lighthearted distractedness: "His [Ruskin's] wife, I hear, with her new Husband, is or was at Wm. Stirling's enjoying the hospitalities of Keir,—more power to them. Ruskin is as cheerful as if there had been no marriage invented among mankind."[5]

The same letter contains still another pen-portrait of Ruskin, which shows Carlyle's mixed views of him. "Ruskin," Carlyle says, is "a bot-

---

[2] Alexander Carlyle, ed., *New Letters and Memorials of Jane Welsh Carlyle* (1903), II, 77.
[3] Jane Carlyle to Kate Sterling, May 14, 1856. MS: Carlyle House, Chelsea.
[4] See Evans, p. 206.
[5] MS: NLS, 516.20. Pbd: Sanders, p. 213.

Jane Welsh Carlyle in 1857. Photograph by Robert Tait.

tle of beautiful *soda-water* . . . only with an intellect of tenfold vivacity. He is very pleasant company now and then—a singular element—very curious to look upon—in the present muddle of the intellectual artistic so-called 'world' in these parts at this date." The image of the bottle of soda water is repeated a year later, and is combined with another image that intensifies Carlyle's opinions and reservations. On May 16, 1856, he wrote to Lady Ashburton:

Ruskin I have found in all things to mean well, and aim high with the very highest; but he strikes me always as infinitely too hopeful of men and things, in fact as having soared aloft out of all contact with the rugged *facts*; which class of objects he contemplates, as with outspread level wings, very much at his ease, far up in the azure aether.— It is certain, however, he does teach various working young men to *draw*, and has a boundless zeal to continue teaching more and more. . . . The man himself I find exceedingly amiable, in spite of all that is said. But he flies out like a soda-water bottle; gets into the *eyes* of various people (being incautiously *drawn*) and these of course complain dreadfully![6]

Ruskin's mercurial mind seems to have been of great concern to Carlyle, and he did what he could to control it. There is a tone of genuine interest, mixed with faint condescension, in these efforts. "Be patient, quiet," he advises Ruskin in 1855—"you go too fast"; and he then suggests the remedy of "*doing nothing*."[7] Later, he perceives that a speech by Lord Stanhope has set "the high moral small-beer of Ruskin all into a froth,"[8] and he takes steps to prevent Ruskin from "pitching into poor Stanhope." Even as late as 1865, he urges the forty-six-year-old Ruskin to "be a good boy."

Carlyle's interest in Ruskin strongly increased during the late 1850's despite his impatience at Ruskin's instability. He perceived, at length, that Ruskin was a "sincere human soul" whose thoughts were wholly in accord with his own, and he constantly encouraged Ruskin to "go on and prosper" in his attacks on English "blockheadism." At his urging Ruskin visited Cheyne Row more often, and he began to read Ruskin's works with waxing interest.

Ruskin, in the meantime, came to rely on Carlyle's encouragement all the more as he went through his transition. By the time he had finished the fourth volume of *Modern Painters* in 1856, he had lost most of his interest in art criticism, and it was only because of the

[6] MS: Northampton.
[7] Sanders, p. 211, comments that this is "a favourite doctrine with Carlyle, to be considered along with his dynamic doctrine of work. He gave John Sterling the same advice in the years before his death."
[8] From a letter to Lady Ashburton in March 1856. MS: Northampton. See Letter 12.

wishes of his father that he wrote the fifth and last volume at all. In December 1857 he delivered his first public statements on the condition of English society when he lectured on "The Political Economy of Art." Under Carlyle's guidance, he was reaching the momentous period in which he would finally reject both his mother's Evangelical beliefs and his father's mercantile principles. In 1858 his long debate with evangelical religion ended in a Waldensian chapel in Turin, where, as is well known, he heard a "little squeaking idiot" preaching Calvinistic damnation, and left "a conclusively unconverted man."[9] His increased alienation from his parents, and his growing dedication to the relief of human misery, rendered him depressed and paralyzed in will. He felt himself alienated from all he knew, and was overcome with a sense of uselessness. In March 1859 he wrote to Carlyle of his entirely "dim notions of what ought to be done," and in November of the same year, after he had reluctantly begun the last volume of *Modern Painters*, he wrote of his feeling that he should "have to give up painting—writing—. . . everything but reading" (Letter 20). He added also that he had been reading "little now but Mr. Carlyle," and in the spring of 1860 he wrote to Mrs. Browning that he had

fallen into the lassitude of surrendered effort and the disappointment of discovered uselessness, having come to see the great fact that great Art is of no real use to anybody but the next great artist; that it is wholly invisible to the people in general—for the present—and that to get anybody to see it, one must begin at the other end, with moral education of the people, and physical, and so I've to turn myself quite upside down, and I'm half broken-backed and can't manage it.[1]

In the midst of this dark period of self-review, Carlyle again encouraged Ruskin, and wrote to him that "circling among the eddies" was but a natural part of his "wide voyage" (Letter 19). The effects were decisive. After reading "little but Mr. Carlyle" and vowing to make Christmas and New Year's presents of Carlyle's *Past and Present*, Ruskin went off to Chamounix in May 1860. By July, the first of the essays that were collectively called *Unto This Last* appeared in *The Cornhill Magazine* under Thackeray's editorship.

Unto This Last, with its subtle style, sharp analysis, and specific identification of issues, was Ruskin's own book. Although Ruskin told a friend that Carlyle had "led the way" for the insights in the book, the work clearly developed out of the studies that Ruskin had been

[9] *Works*, XXIX, 89.
[1] *Works*, XXXVI, 348.

pursuing "on independent principles" since 1855.[2] Significantly, Carlyle is nowhere mentioned in the work. Ruskin, it would seem, still thought of himself as an independent thinker, not as a spokesman for Carlyle. Rather, he seems to have thought of himself as the spokesman for the common experience of everyman, which exposed the false view of man propounded by the political economists of the day. It is on this ground—his own—that he chose to stand or fall in public view.

The book electrified the public. Although Ruskin had been dealing with social questions for many years, his first book of social criticism seemed to the public to be an abrupt shift of interest. Unfortunately, to many it also seemed to be silly and wrongheaded, and it was denounced and ridiculed so violently that Thackeray had to stop publishing the essays after the October issue of the magazine. Ruskin was dismayed. He fell into a still deeper period of depression, more prolonged than any he had known before. His parents, now grown old, had reacted to his new ideas with understandable alarm, and this further alienated them from their son. Driven by the feeling that he was being rejected by both England and his parents, Ruskin went on a self-imposed exile to Switzerland in the years 1861 to 1863, and even thought of making his permanent home in Mornex. His feelings of uselessness and religious doubt returned threefold, and so did his numerous psychosomatic ailments. He complained of headaches, dyspepsia, and coughs, and he even felt that he was dying. In August 1861 he wrote to Carlyle that "the great questions about Nature and God" had so overwhelmed him that both his thoughts and his health were "overturned." And on November 15, 1861, he wrote to his father that he intended to leave the subject of Political Economy: "I cannot write when I have no audience. Those papers on Political Economy fairly tried 80,000 British public with my best work; they couldn't taste it; and I can give them no more."[3] To Ruskin, the prediction, once made by his father, that his writings on social questions would be but "slum buildings," susceptible to ruin by the tides of criticism, must have appeared to have come true.

At this critical time in Ruskin's career, Carlyle came forward with help and encouragement. *Unto This Last* seemed to him to be the fulfillment of all his hopes for Ruskin, and he responded with enthusiasm. While others carped and jeered, he sent off a warm letter of praise for the book. If Ruskin had been afraid, or wondering what to do, here

[2] See his letter to Dr. John Brown, November 11, 1860. In *Works*, XXXVI, 349.
[3] Cook, II, 42.

was his answer, aimed judiciously to appeal to his natural impulse to teach, and more or less making the younger man the acknowledged aide of Carlyle in the great and lonely battle against the vast host of "Dismal-Science people." "More power to y^r elbow," Carlyle wrote (Letter 27), and added: "If you chose to stand to that kind of work for the next 7 years, and work out there a result like what you have done in painting: yes, there were a 'something to do,'—not easily measurable in importance to these sunk ages. Meantime my joy is great to find myself henceforth in a minority of *two* at any rate!"

Further to bolster Ruskin's sagging spirits, he made the first of many personal visits to Ruskin and his parents in 1860 and 1861,[4] and he seems to have tried very hard to mend the growing break between parents and son. When, for instance, John James Ruskin expressed his fears about the unpopularity and incoherence of one of his son's lectures, Carlyle hastened to assure him that the lecture suffered only from excess of greatness and was "quite the reverse of 'failure'" (Letter 31).

Of even greater significance is Carlyle's quiet effort to keep Ruskin writing. When, in 1861, Ruskin decided to be done with political economy, Carlyle quickly wrote a letter to his friend James Anthony Froude, then editor of *Fraser's Magazine.* Froude, in turn, wrote a letter to Ruskin[5] in which he offered to publish any new comments Ruskin cared to make on the subject of political economy. It was enough to galvanize Ruskin into renewed effort. The result was a series of "Essays on Political Economy," which appeared in *Fraser's* during 1862, and which was published in book form ten years later as *Munera Pulveris,* with a dedication by Ruskin to "the man who has urged me to all chief labour—Thomas Carlyle."

When public disapproval caused Froude to stop publishing the essays, however, Ruskin again despaired of continuing. But by this time Carlyle was too much in favor of Ruskin's writings to allow them to

---

[4] A letter from Ruskin's father to W. H. Harrison on January 28, 1861, describes one of these early visits and their effect: "Thomas Carlyle rode over yesterday for a call but remained till after seven talking as only he can talk in a most marvelous manner. When a boy of 15 I drank Tea with his namesake Dr. Carlyle called by Walter Scott Jupiter Carlyle whose auto biography is now going through the reviews. A man also never to be forgotten but the Chelsea one is the Jupiter—he has a Horse allowing for the difference betwixt Man & Beast, as extraordinary as himself—I was pleased to hear it knows this House and when at the Top of Tulse Hill it pricked up its ear, set off at a rapid pace & stopped at the gate. As Mr. Carlyle is always on Horseback for a distant call he is only seen by my son John or by chance by me about 3 or 4 o'clock. It was a great catch to get him yesterday to stay to Dinner." (MS: Carlyle House, Chelsea.)

[5] See Letter 32.

stop. He described Ruskin's articles as "valiant,"[6] and in early August 1862 he proclaimed to a friend: "I have read nothing that pleased me better for many a year than these new Ruskiniana."[7] To Ruskin he wrote that he found the essays "definite, clear; rising into the sphere *of Plato*" (Letter 39). A letter from Froude to Ruskin describes still another effort by Carlyle to soothe the apprehensive John James Ruskin. "I was at Carlyle's last night," Froude writes:

He said that in writing to your father as to the subject of the "Essays in Political Economy," he had told him that when Solomon's temple was building it was credibly reported that at least 10,000 sparrows sitting in the trees round declared that it was entirely wrong, quite contrary to received opinion, hopelessly condemned by public opinion, etc. Nevertheless it got finished, and the sparrows flew away and began to chirp in the same note about something else.[8]

When Ruskin began again to fear that he was dying, Carlyle told him that "moulting" would be a better word,[9] and again wrote a letter of praise urging him to continue (Letter 42). By the middle of 1864, Ruskin began to feel better, and plunged with zest into new work.

It is interesting to note that this work, like many of Ruskin's works from 1862 on, frequently has direct quotations from Carlyle, and proclaims Ruskin's intellectual obligation to Carlyle in many ways. If we remember Ruskin's earlier assertion of independence, it would now seem that he had come to think of himself as an actual follower of Carlyle's doctrines, and therefore felt that he should give public reverence to his "master"—a decision that seems to have been deliberate. Ruskin's motivations remain difficult to ascertain at this point. Having been so recently attacked for his own work, he obviously felt the need of Carlyle in many ways. Faced with further tasks of social criticism, and having grown much closer to Carlyle in the 1860's, Ruskin found it intellectually necessary to be influenced by Carlyle, psychologically comforting to be intimate with him, and professionally necessary to be deferential to him.

Ruskin gratefully returned the encouragement and affection that Carlyle provided in these years, and the friendship flowered. Their letters show that many visits passed between the two men, and Ruskin's fondness for both the Carlyles was reflected in his generosity. He continually sent gifts of eggs, strawberries, brandy, cigars, pictures, and

[6] In a letter to Lord Ashburton, August 31, 1862. MS: Northampton.
[7] See his letter to Thomas Erskine, in Froude, IV, 252–53.
[8] October 24, 1863. In Cook, II, 57.
[9] See Ruskin's letter to F. J. Furnivall, September 26, 1863, quoted in Wilenski, p. 68.

books for the Carlyles' enjoyment. When he left home, he left word for Carlyle to make use of the fine horses and garden at Denmark Hill,[1] and his letters were filled with warm, thoughtful inquiries about Mrs. Carlyle's health and Carlyle's progress in the laborious writing of *Frederick the Great*. Carlyle, after all, often experienced his own fits of depression while working on his long history of Frederick, and as he aged he developed a sense of being "written out" and nearing death in utter solitude himself. His opinion that he and Ruskin formed a "minority of two" gives some indication of his feelings at this time, for he seems to have thought that his writings had made little difference in the world, and that he was a lonely prophet crying to morally deaf worshippers of Mammon. Ruskin, knowing Carlyle's thoughts, offered reciprocal encouragement, and even offered to take the Carlyles to Switzerland to "finish Fredrick" (Letter 36). His many remarks on the superior value of Carlyle's works (as in Letter 40) are, at least in part, made to reassure Carlyle of his seminal power for other minds.

During this period, too, Ruskin tried to bring his parents into more sympathetic contact with Carlyle, and the number of letters from Carlyle to Ruskin's father indicates that he succeeded. He had to overcome their fears about Carlyle's influence over his mind, for they had correctly judged its extent. In 1861 he wrote to his father that "Mamma has a horror of these people—Carlyle, etc.—because she thinks they 'pervert' me," and then added, "but I never understand them until I find the thing out for myself."[2] Two years later, he was more explicit in his efforts to present Carlyle in a better light:

It is really very hard upon you that my courses of thought have now led me out of the way of fame—and into that of suffering—for it is a dark world enough towards the close of life, with my creed. One thing, however, I wish you could

---

[1] After only a few visits Ruskin diplomatically kept Carlyle out of his garden. In an unpublished note to *Praeterita*, he explains why: "But there was one insuperable obstacle: the smoking. For *his* sake, I would have borne with the forms of American frankincense obtained by the combination of tobacco with lilac blossoms or laburnum; but I could not stand the spitting. The entire service of the garden, to me, depended on the perfect cleanliness of its ground, so that I could always lie down either on the gravel walks, the lawns, or the dry flower-beds, with no more harm than some dust on my coat. . . .

"It was as much as I could bear patiently to attend Carlyle, while he wished to talk to me, where I was leading what streamlet of fresh water I could bring from the Thames, to ripple over the golden gravel, . . . and I was never happy in listening to Carlyle, but when the end of his pipe was up his own chimney."

(From the second galley proofs of Ruskin's *Praeterita*, in the H. G. Viljoen bequest of MSS and papers at the J. Pierpont Morgan Library.)

[2] *Works*, XXXVI, 396.

put out of your mind—that either Carlyle, Colenso, or Froude, much less any one less than they, have had the smallest share in this change. . . .[3]

Largely through these efforts of Ruskin, his parents put aside their fears, and Carlyle was able to pay several pleasant calls at Denmark Hill. Ruskin himself continued to visit Carlyle at Chelsea, and his kindness and thoughtfulness brought him closer to Carlyle than ever before. "No one managed Carlyle so well as Ruskin," said Mrs. Carlyle of his visits during this period, "it was quite beautiful to see him. Carlyle would say outrageous things, running counter to all Ruskin valued and cared for. Ruskin would treat Mr. Carlyle like a naughty child, lay his arms around him, and say, 'Now, this is too bad!'"[4] The two men had, indeed, reached a plane of friendship that rose above their knowledge of each other's weaknesses. That knowledge, as the letters reveal, always remained behind all their dealings with each other, but it never destroyed the bond of sympathy and affection that grew in these years.

In the years 1864 to 1867, several events occurred that were to strengthen the friendship even more, and other events were to give proof of its depth. In March 1864, Ruskin's father died. He had been both good and bad for Ruskin—"a father," as Ruskin described him on the eve of his funeral, "who would have sacrificed his life for his son, and yet forced his son to sacrifice his life to him, and sacrifice it in vain."[5] The alienation of mind that had grown between father and son in the previous decade was complicated by Ruskin's inability to free himself from parental control, and Ruskin had developed an ambivalence toward his parents that was to persist throughout his life. The history of this ambivalence cannot be dealt with here, but there seems to be little doubt that Ruskin felt a new sense of freedom after the death of the man who, as recently as September 1863, had suppressed the publication of his essay "Gold." A new feeling of ambivalence arose, however, when Ruskin's sense of freedom conflicted with his sense of duty toward his mother, who was now in her eighties and was alone but for him. He vowed immediately that he would provide her with years of "peaceful and hopeful happiness," and Carlyle, paying a visit to Denmark Hill a few days after the funeral, remarked that Ruskin's mother "seemed to be a *new* interest for him."[6] Yet Ruskin wished to be free from the fetters of Denmark Hill, and he in-

---

[3] *Ibid.*, 460.   [4] Cook, II, 561.   [5] *Works*, XXXVI, 471.
[6] See his letter to Jane Carlyle, in Trudy Bliss, ed., *Carlyle: Letters to His Wife* (New York, 1953), p. 361.

stalled his cousin, Joan Agnew, in the house to be his mother's companion. Still unable to break away, he became frustrated and resentful, and Carlyle, after spending an unpleasant evening at Denmark Hill in August, noted that Ruskin had "no real regard for one. His eye is hard, rayless, in comparison; his face lean."[7] Carlyle tried to help in whatever way he could, and gradually Ruskin heeded his advice. Years later, in *Praeterita*, Ruskin spoke gratefully of Carlyle in "those spring days, when he used to take pleasure in the quiet of the Denmark Hill garden, and to use all his influence with me to make me contented in my duty to my mother."[8]

Soon Ruskin plunged into new writings and activities. From July 1864 to December 1865, he sent a flurry of letters to the newspapers on various economic and political questions, some of which Carlyle is known to have read and liked.[9] He began to spend much of his time at a girls' school called Winnington Hall,[1] and in December 1865 he published a book that grew out of his experiences there—*Ethics of the Dust*—which Carlyle praised as a "most shining Performance" (Letter 55) after he had paid a visit to Denmark Hill to hear Ruskin talk about geology.

Although Carlyle's praise for this book has been decried because it may have encouraged Ruskin to turn back toward childhood in his mind,[2] it seems likely that his words did much more good than harm. Carlyle, after all, praised the poetry of the book and the evidence it gave of Ruskin's renewed interest in social questions. Furthermore, it is certain that a harsh word from Carlyle at this time might have hastened the appearance of the first warning symptoms of mental trouble Ruskin experienced in 1867.

Carlyle, meanwhile, had at last finished his *History of Frederick the Great* in 1865, and had become an old man in the course of the hard thirteen years' work on it.[3] He now walked with a stoop, and began to have trouble using his right hand. Though he felt worn out and very old, and feared that death was near, he had reached the height of his fame and influence, and at the end of 1865 he was elected rector of

[7] *Ibid.*, p. 370.

[8] *Works*, XXXV, 540–41.

[9] See Wilenski, p. 80. On November 17, 1864, Carlyle wrote to his brother John that Ruskin's "Daily Telegraph Fract^ns . . . may amuse for half an hour!" (MS: NLS, 526.19).

[1] See Letter 20, n. 1.

[2] See Evans, pp. 285–86.

[3] On August 15, 1865, Ruskin wrote to Charles Eliot Norton, "Carlyle has got through the first calamity of rest after Frederick, among his Scotch hills, and I hope will give us something worthier of him before he dies" (C. E. Norton, ed. *The Letters of John Ruskin to Charles Eliot Norton* [Boston and New York, 1905], I, 150).

Edinburgh University. Whatever relief such honors brought him did not last long, however, for in April 1866, just after he had delivered his famous inaugural address at Edinburgh, Jane Welsh Carlyle died suddenly of heart failure. Carlyle was desolate, and was to remain so for many years. Ruskin, as fate would have it, had come to pay a visit to Mrs. Carlyle just a few hours after she died, and so found out the news directly. Although he occasionally resented Mrs. Carlyle's quick and ready wit, there is no doubt that he thought highly of her in all other respects. His kindnesses, as well as his letters to her, were frequent, and their last letters to each other are both warmly informal and delightful. The letter that he wrote to Carlyle in consolation has not been preserved, but Carlyle's response to it leaves no doubt about Ruskin's sympathy, and in June 1866 Ruskin wrote to a friend that the deaths of Mrs. Carlyle and Lady Trevelyan had taken from him his "two best women friends of older power: and [he was] not zealous about anything."[4]

While the death of his wife made Carlyle feel even more solitary and desolate, it also brought him closer to Ruskin. "Come *oftener* and see me, and speak *more* frankly to me (for I am very true to your highest interests and you)" he wrote (Letter 61), and Ruskin's diary records many visits made to Chelsea during the remainder of 1866. Carlyle was grateful, and seems to have held Ruskin in higher esteem than ever before. To a friend who had criticized Ruskin, he wrote that he was in agreement to some extent, "except when you seem to question not his [Ruskin's] *strength* alone, but his *sincerity* a little too; whh latter I can testify to be *complete*, and even vehement and painful to him. If he live, there will be mission enough for him in the next twenty years."[5] In August 1866, he tried to start a magazine with Ruskin and Froude as coeditors, but could not succeed in making Ruskin "bite very ardently."[6] And a few months later, Carlyle joined Ruskin's Oxford friends in trying to get Ruskin an appointment as professor of poetry at Oxford.

Ruskin's joy over Carlyle's increased regard for him was great, and when Carlyle became chairman of a committee formed to defend Governor Eyre of Jamaica, Ruskin came to help him with an active, if not totally willing, hand. Constantly busying himself with interviews and paperwork, he labored hard for the committee in order to relieve the

---

[4] *Works*, XXXVI, 509.
[5] Carlyle to C. A. Ward, June 16, 1866. MS: Carlyle House, Chelsea.
[6] Carlyle to J. A. Froude, August 2, 1866. In Waldo H. Dunn, "Carlyle's Last Letters to Froude," *Twentieth Century*, CLIX (January 1956), 47.

sorrowing Carlyle of the burden, but his defense of Eyre surprised many of those who knew him, and even cost him several Liberal friends who had formerly looked upon him as an ally.[7] Amabel Williams-Ellis has called this incident the "most inappropriate" one of Ruskin's life,[8] but all of Ruskin's actions at the time reveal that he not only sympathized with Eyre's cause, but did constructive work for the committee. Certainly Carlyle thought so, for in September 1866 he wrote that Ruskin's speech in Eyre's defense was a "right gallant thrust," and added that "while all the world stands tremulous, shilly-shallying from the gutter, impetuous Ruskin plunges his rapier up to the very hilt in the abominable belly of the vast blockheadism, and leaves it staring very considerably."[9]

During the winter of 1866–67, Ruskin continued to help Carlyle in many ways. Knowing that Carlyle now felt lonely and useless, he suggested topics for Carlyle to write about, and even offered to serve as Carlyle's amanuensis. When Carlyle went on a vacation to Mentone (now called Menton), he tried to help again by suggesting places for Carlyle to visit, and he himself made visits to Carlyle's relatives with great pleasure. By April 1867, when Ruskin had begun his "Letters to a Working Man" (later published in book form as *Time and Tide by Weare and Tyne*), Carlyle had returned from Mentone and asked Ruskin to come and see him. He also expressed his private opinion that the *Time and Tide* letters were "pungent" and "well worth reading . . . among the deluge of stuff that requires to be read."[1]

In the same letters, Ruskin referred to Carlyle with special warmth and significance: "Carlyle and I (mind, I only speak of myself together with him as a son might speak of his father and himself). . . . The best friend I have in the world, next to Carlyle, is . . . Charles Eliot Norton. . . . Next to Carlyle, for my own immediate help and teaching, I always look to Emerson."[2] If any time were to be cited as that in which Carlyle and Ruskin reached their highest point of mutual affection, perhaps this period, the winter of 1866–67, should be it. Afterwards, Ruskin's growing mental troubles and Carlyle's advancing old age were to cause a gradual lessening of sympathies, but at this time both men were working together with full resources, and their friendship had grown so strong as to be like the love between father and son.

---

[7] "It was startling to some persons to find the author of *Unto This Last*, this 'merciful, just, and godly' person, on the side of lawless oppression of the weak" (Frederic Harrison, *John Ruskin* [New York, 1906], pp. 119–20).

[8] *The Tragedy of John Ruskin* (1928), p. 269.

[9] Carlyle to Miss Davenport Bromley, September 15, 1866. In Froude, IV, 330.

[1] Carlyle to Lady Ashburton, April 20, 1867. MS: Northampton.

[2] *Works*, XVII, 476–77.

It is fortunate that such a deep friendship did exist at this time, for events were soon to put it to a severe test, and no lesser devotion could have survived.

On May 7, 1867, one of Ruskin's *Time and Tide* letters appeared in the *Manchester Examiner and Times*. It contained Ruskin's report of a conversation with Carlyle on Thursday, April 25, 1867. According to Ruskin, Carlyle had said that

in the streets of Chelsea, and of the whole district of London round it, from the Park to the outer country (some twelve or fifteen miles of disorganized, foul, sinful, and most wretched life), he now cannot walk without being insulted, chiefly because he is a grey, old man; and also because he is cleanly dressed—these two conditions of him being wholly hostile, as the mob of the street feel, to their own instincts, and, so far as they appear to claim some kind of reverence and recognition of betterness, to be instantly crushed and jeered out of their way.[3]

After this passage had "made the rounds" of the papers, a "working man from Rochdale" wrote to Carlyle to inquire if it were true,[4] and Carlyle sent a reply to him on May 22, 1867: "The thing now 'going the rounds' is untrue, diverges from the fact throughout, and in essentials is curiously the reverse of the fact; an 'incredible' (and at once forgettable) 'thing.' That is the solution of your difficulty."[5] A few days later, on May 27, Ruskin wrote to William Michael Rossetti that "Carlyle was furious at what I said of *him*, but I didn't care. That also goes in the reprint."[6] He was referring, of course, to the reprint of the letters that was to appear in book form as *Time and Tide*, but he must have failed to convey his intentions to Carlyle. On May 28, Carlyle repeated his disavowal in a letter "to the editor of the Pall Mall Gazette" printed the following day:

Sir,— In reference to a newspaper paragraph now idly circulating, with my name in it as connected with "insults in the streets" and other such matter,— permit me to say that it is an untrue paragraph, disagrees with the fact throughout, and in essentials is curiously the reverse of the fact; a paragraph altogether erroneous, misfounded, superfluous, and even absurd.[7]

Ruskin, reading this letter in the papers, noted in his diary for May 29: "At Carlyle's. Foolish letter of C[arlyle's] in papers."[8] He then

---

[3] *Works*, XVII, 480–81.
[4] *The Express*, May 29, 1867, p. 1. The author was probably Thomas Dixon, a cork cutter who was prominent in Ruskin's *Time and Tide* letters.
[5] *Ibid.*   [6] *Works*, XVII, 478.
[7] MS: Dr. Frederick W. Hilles. Pbd: R. H. Shepherd, *Memoirs of the Life and Writings of Thomas Carlyle* (1881), II, 250; and, of course, *The Pall Mall Gazette*, May 29, 1867, p. 4.
[8] See Ruskin, *Diaries*, II, 619.

wrote a fairly mild letter to Carlyle (Letter 72) asking for a "succinct statement" of what Carlyle remembered to have said so that Ruskin might "substitute" it in the "edition of collected letters." Carlyle answered in a letter that Ruskin later burned, and on June 1 Ruskin wrote a bitter letter in which he bemoaned the fact that Carlyle had "given the lie publicly" to the man who "of all men living, most honoured" him (Letter 73).

Apparently, Carlyle thought that his letter to the papers had ended the matter, for on June 1 he wrote to his brother John that, while Ruskin was in "great agony about the beggarly *Pall-Mall* 'paragraph' Affair," he had "at least ended it, and the dirty rumour of impertinent nothingness about it." Ruskin, he continued, "feels, or will feel, that the head long folly he fell into *was* absurd."[9] Still in a conciliatory attitude after receiving Ruskin's letter of June 1, Carlyle sent off a semi-retraction to the editor of the *Times* on June 7, four days after the *Times* had made the quarrel the subject of a leading article. The letter, which was published on June 8, is too long to quote in full here, but it made two points in particular that should be mentioned—first, that Carlyle did not join in "heavily blaming Mr. Ruskin" except for the "practical blunder" of printing Carlyle's name, and then of "carelessly hurling topsy-turvy into wild incredibility" all Ruskin had to report of him, which "struck with amazement" Carlyle and all of his "vast multitude of harmless neighbors" in London. His second point, however, was that "in regard to the populace or *canaille* of London . . . distinguishable by behaviour as our non-human, or half-human neighbors," he was willing to "substantially agree with all that Mr. Ruskin has said of it."[1]

While he was still in a comparatively amenable mood, Carlyle wrote to Ruskin on June 8 to inform him of this letter, and to urge him to be silent on the matter for four or five weeks until he "arrived at complete contrit[n] . . . and mathematical clearness on both sides" (Letter 75). Possibly remembering Ruskin's phrases in *Time and Tide*, he tactfully reminded Ruskin that the younger man's "state of provocat[n]" had in it "something generous and *filial*; like the poignant sorrow of a very good, but far too headlong *son*, getting his rebuke from *papa*. . . ." Ruskin's answers on June 10 and 12 (Letters 76 and 77) found him

[9] MS: NLS, 526.61. Pbd in Sanders, p. 227, n. 1. Dr. John Carlyle responded thus on June 2, 1867: "I see by Ruskin's letter that he is in great embarrassment. Perhaps the best way for him would be to leave out the inconvenient passage altogether in the collected letters. I thought there was exaggeration only and much imprudence in what he reported." (MS: NLS, 518.37.)

[1] See Shepherd, II, 251–52, or Letter 75 for full text.

unready to be placated, and Carlyle's next letter, written on June 13 (Letter 78), repeats the injunction to observe the question from all sides until it became clear. This letter seemed to have soothed Ruskin's "wildly exaggerative mind," for Ruskin's next letter, on June 25, has him requesting a conciliatory meeting with Carlyle, and Ruskin's diary records that on June 26 he was "at Carlyle's in evening with Scotch provost," [2] and after that the friendship between them was resumed as before. That Ruskin finally came to some kind of "resolution" about the matter is revealed in a letter written by Carlyle's niece, Mary Aitken, to Lady Ashburton soon afterwards. "I think it was very generous of Ruskin to come back to Carlyle and never allude to any misunderstanding at all," she wrote. "My uncle seems to like him far better now than he did before." [3] Though there are no letters extant from either Carlyle or Ruskin for the year 1868, Ruskin's diary records many visits paid to Cheyne Row, and all seems to have subsided into customary affection.

Though the quarrel in itself proved to be of little importance, it is especially interesting as an opportunity to study the behavior of both men. Carlyle, of course, had every right to be upset over Ruskin's unauthorized use of his name in print, but his reaction was too extreme, and even unfair to Ruskin. Charles Eliot Norton, writing of the subject in 1869, was of the opinion that:

> It was a direct issue, and there is not the least question that Carlyle was wrong. He *did* say, so I heard from a person who was present when he said it, what Ruskin reported; but he said it in one of his wild moods of half-cynical, half-humorous exaggeration, very likely forgot his words as soon as uttered, and at least had no intention that they should be taken *au pied de la lettre*, or that he should be held responsible for them. [4]

Carlyle's excessive concern over his popularity with the working classes is somewhat atypical, and may have arisen because he felt the need to defend himself after having championed Governor Eyre against the Liberals. There may be some connection, too, with the agitation that was gripping England over the Reform Bill of 1867. Carlyle was to publish his violently antidemocratic essay "Shooting Niagara: and After?" in August, and he may have felt the need to reassure the people that he had their best interests at heart and was not against democracy because he was contemptuous of the middle class. Whatever

[2] See Ruskin, *Diaries*, II, 621.
[3] Mary Aitken to Lady Ashburton, undated. MS: Northampton.
[4] Norton to G. W. Curtis, July 22, 1869. In S. Norton and M. A. DeW. Howe, eds., *The Letters of Charles Eliot Norton* (Boston and New York, 1913), I, 362.

the reason for his anger, it is an excellent example of the irascibility for which he was notorious. His later efforts to smooth the matter over when Ruskin reacted with such shrill indignation, however, reveal a hidden side of his character—a side which often urged calmness and tact, and tried to be reasonable in the face of emotional situations. His two letters to Ruskin in June are masterpieces of patience and understanding and deserve to be noticed more often for the thoughtfulness they reveal.

Ruskin's behavior is even more interesting. Though he had good reason to be angry over Carlyle's public refutation of him, there is a note of violent irrationality in his letters, and his strong, obstinate rejections of Carlyle's peace overtures seem unreasonable to the last degree. Carlyle must have been exasperated, and we marvel at his patience. A passage in his letter of June 13, however, explains the reason for it, and further reveals the real reason for the whole ugly episode. "If I *had* in any degree injured a *cert^n interest* (of which I was not thinking at all), that w^d indeed have been a cruel and most forbidding circumstance," he writes with some traces of restrained exasperation. He then touches the heart of the matter when he says, "nor do I now believe (what^r your wildly exaggerative mind may do) that it will have the weight of a fly's wing in the beautiful resolute and candid soul on whose vote you alone depend. . . ." The truth was that Ruskin had already begun to suffer the pains prelusive to his eventual mental breakdown and had for some months been experiencing morbid fits of despondency, sleeplessness, nervous prostration, floating sparks before his eyes, and a long series of dreams and nightmares. His condition, which gave ominous warnings for the future, was the result not only of his lifelong tendencies in that direction, but also of his obsessive devotion to a young girl from Ireland, Rose La Touche.[5]

Ruskin had first met Rose in 1858, when she became, at the age of ten, one of his art pupils. He was soon enraptured with her, and proposed marriage in 1866, when Rose was eighteen. But she was young, and (ironically) a devoted Evangelical, and both she and her parents looked upon the forty-seven-year-old Ruskin with a mixture of admiration and suspicion. His fame as a writer was well known to them, but so were his liberal religious views, and so too was the fact that Ruskin had been married once before. When Ruskin proposed to Rose, Mrs. La Touche exacted a promise from him that he would not

[5]For the best and fullest insight into this pathetic episode in Ruskin's life, see J. L. Bradley, ed., *The Letters of John Ruskin to Lord and Lady Mount-Temple* (Columbus, Ohio, 1964).

publicly reveal his religious views for ten years, but Rose was still not sure of herself or Ruskin, and postponed her decision for three years, until she reached the age of twenty-one. Ruskin became more and more obsessed with her, and all the more apprehensive about his courtship as his "waiting period" wore on. By May 1867, halfway through the period of probation, she was in his mind constantly, and he was in a state of great turmoil. Thus when, at the end of May, Carlyle published his letter about "insults in the streets," Ruskin's extreme reaction to it sprang from his desire to avoid appearing as a subject of public controversy, lest he injure his cause by placing himself in a still worse light in the eyes of the increasingly hostile La Touche family. His tortured state of mind probably made him fail to perceive the "half-humour" in Carlyle's talk as well, and it was not until Carlyle himself saw how the incident was connected with Rose that he was at last able to bring Ruskin back to a sense of perspective.

As it turned out, Rose's family had already decided to have nothing to do with him, and Ruskin had to correspond with his loved one secretly thereafter. His courtship was never to succeed. When Rose came of age in 1869, she again postponed her decision for another three years, and then her health, both mental and physical, declined. She died in 1875, wasted away in mind and body, leaving Ruskin desolate from years of frantic anxiety. In reading Ruskin's letters from 1867 on, one must never forget the terrible effect his love for Rose La Touche had on his personality. The whole affair precipitated his advancing manic-depressive psychosis, and all of his work and behavior patterns reflect his increasing instability of temperament.

In the years 1868 to 1877, the relationship between Ruskin and Carlyle became a filial bond between a lonely, sad old man and a tortured and unstable younger one. In 1867, Ruskin had already remarked that "Carlyle is old and weary, and feels that he has done his work,"[6] and his observation was justified by Carlyle's later actions. Made comparatively inert and gloomily apathetic by the loss of his wife and the advance of old age, Carlyle spent the last dozen years of his life in virtual silence, producing only some topical essays for the newspapers and the inconsequential studies of early kings of Norway and portraits of John Knox. His last writings of real value were the series of *Reminiscences* written after his wife's death and finished by 1868, though published posthumously. Ruskin, faithful as ever, continued to urge Carlyle to write spontaneously on such topics as history

[6] *Works*, XVII, 478.

or religion, but to no avail. And so, aflame with the impulse to preach and fully realizing that he was now the only active member of the "minority of two," Ruskin resolved to carry on Carlyle's work himself—attempting "the fulfilment, [*sic*] so far as in me is, of what you have taught me" (Letter 109). Throughout the decade of the 1870's he relied heavily on Carlyle for comfort and advice. He even sent Carlyle all of his writing to examine before publication, just as he used to send his writings to his father before 1864. It was during this decade that he began to call Carlyle his "master," indicating not only his adoption of Carlyle's friendship, but also the depth of a devoted discipleship that had begun, as we have seen, as early as 1855.

Although nearly half the letters in the Ruskin-Carlyle correspondence were written between 1869 and 1879, they are less significant than the earlier letters. They show clearly, of course, the strength of Ruskin's devotion to Carlyle, and they show Ruskin launching a Carlylean course of wider usefulness, but they add few new revelations of any important developments in the course of the friendship, and they bear mainly upon Ruskin's multifarious activities and writings, both of which were motivated by ideas he had already expressed in the 1860's.

In the spring of 1869, after Rose had again postponed her decision to marry him, Ruskin had another of his periodic fits of despondency. This was the most serious since 1861, and seems to have made him resolve to change the course of his life and writings from that point on. Overwhelmed by a sense of futility and fading powers, he became obsessed with both the social evils he saw around him and the private anguish he felt within. His *Queen of the Air*, written in 1869, reveals an alarming obsession with "storm Clouds," which he began to see everywhere, and reveals his unstable and incoherent state. As early as May 1868, he had resolved to "use his social influence to the utmost,"[7] and for over a year he had toyed with the idea of founding a society that would be devoted to his principles for the reform of England. He now vowed to stop thinking and writing about social and economic questions and spring to action "in hope of wider usefulness."[8] With this motivation, he once again read Carlyle's works, just as he had done in 1859, when he was also preparing for a major program of change. In 1869, after rereading *Sartor Resartus*, he wrote to Carlyle that he had "nearly all my clothes to make, fresh—but more shroud-shape than any other" (Letter 82). During a summer "full of

[7] Wilenski, p. 92.
[8] *Ibid.*, p. 100.

sadness" in Italy, he formed a strange, hyperconfident scheme to curb the torrents of the Alps with dams and reservoirs to "make the lost valleys of the Alps one Paradise of safe plenty,"[9] and when he returned to London in September he brought with him fresh plans to found the "St. George's Guild"—a communal group of his followers, who were to live a rustic life according to his economic and moral principles. To further this cause, he also began the long and wandering series of public letters, addressed to present and future members of this group, which appeared sporadically after 1870 under the title of *Fors Clavigera*. When news came that he had been elected Slade Professor of Art at Oxford in 1869, he gladly accepted that post with the knowledge that he could do much good for society by influencing the upper classes at Oxford. For this reason, among others, he filled his lectures on art with digressive tilts at social conditions and orthodox religion, to the wonder and delight of his audience. He was now launched upon the final, most active phase of his career, in many ways as pathetic as it was influential, for it was to end in the attacks of insanity that began to engulf him after 1878.

When Ruskin came to Carlyle in September 1869 to talk about his new plans, Carlyle listened with interest, but he sensed that all was not well. He still, however, had great faith in Ruskin's abilities. Charles Eliot Norton, who visited Carlyle in the summer of 1869, reported that "Emerson and Ruskin are the only distinguished living men of whom Carlyle spoke . . . with something like real tenderness."[1] Carlyle himself wrote, after Ruskin's September visit, that Ruskin was full of projects that seemed "chimerical," but quickly added that there was "a ray of real Heaven in poor Ruskin;—passages of that last book (Queen of the Air) went into my heart like arrows."[2] His encouragement continued for many years in his letters to Ruskin, but privately he began to have doubts about Ruskin's stability, and he frequently became irritated by Ruskin's increasingly nervous and erratic behavior.

These doubts, too, must be kept in mind as the reader looks through the many passages of praise and compassion found in Carlyle's letters of these years. When, on December 27, 1870, Ruskin sought Carlyle's counsel about the opening letter of *Fors Clavigera*, Carlyle's response must have been mild enough, for there is no record of any attempt by Carlyle to dissuade Ruskin. Indeed, Carlyle's enthusiastic response to the fifth *Fors* letter (Letter 108) gives evidence to the contrary, and

[9] *Ibid.*, p. 98.
[1] C. E. Norton to Miss E. C. Cleveland, June 7, 1869, In Norton, I, 333.
[2] Carlyle to J. A. Froude, September 14, 1869. In Cook, II, 164–65.

shows him warmly in favor of some of Ruskin's efforts. But one must also remember that Carlyle's doubts had been expressed elsewhere. Four days after Ruskin's letter of December 27, 1870, Carlyle sent his brother John the first of the *Fors* letters, and referred to it thus: "There is further waiting for you an astonishing Paper by Ruskin. . . . I think you never read a madder looking thing. I still hope (though with little confidence) that he will bethink him and drop the matter in time: . . . though alas, I fear he will plunge into it all the same."[3]

Carlyle's hopes were not to be realized, and gradually he came to worry more and more about the growing evidence of Ruskin's disquietude, though he still applauded Ruskin's efforts, and followed them with interest. Two letters written in 1872 reveal this ambivalent view starkly:

I am reading Ruskin's books in these evenings. . . . I find a spiritual comfort in the noble fire, wrath, and inexorability with which he smites upon all base things and wide-spread public delusions; and insists relentlessly in having the ideal aimed at everywhere; for the rest I do not find him wise—headlong rather, and I might even say weak.[4]

There is nothing going on among us as notable to me as those fierce lightning-bolts Ruskin is copiously and desperately pouring into the black world of Anarchy all around him. No other man in England that I meet has in him the divine rage against baseness that Ruskin has, and that every man ought to have. Unhappily he is not a strong man; one might say a weak man rather; and has not the least prudence of management, though if he can hold out for another fifteen years he may produce, even in this way, a great effect. God grant it, say I.[5]

Unfortunately, Ruskin was not able to "hold out" for fifteen more years. As the letters show, Carlyle had seen little of Ruskin in 1871 and 1872, and thus could not know the depth of mental anguish to which new events had driven him. In December 1871, Ruskin's mother died, and a few months later his old nurse went to her grave. Rose La Touche finally refused to allow Ruskin to see her in 1871, and in the summer of that year he had a severe attack of illness at Matlock that almost killed him. Then, early in 1872, Rose at last decided to refuse his hand. The result of all this was frequently alternating periods of manic confidence and depressed anxiety—and a desperate effort to fight even harder against what he considered to be overwhelming personal and public forces. By late 1872, Carlyle noted that

[3] MS: NLS, 527.37.
[4] Carlyle to his brother John, February 24, 1872. MS: NLS, 527.61.
[5] Carlyle to Ralph Waldo Emerson, April 2, 1872. In Joseph Slater, ed., *The Correspondence of Emerson and Carlyle* (New York and London, 1964), p. 589.

Ruskin was "very good and affectionate, but I got little light out of him, except that he was fallen into thick quiet despair again on the personal question; and meant all the more to go ahead with fire and sword upon the universal one."[6]

It was in these months, too, that Ruskin began to suffer from an increasing number of delusions and obsessions, which were to last throughout the decade. R. W. Wilenski, in his study of Ruskin, lists the major ones:

The first was a notion that a new kind of Storm Cloud and Plague Wind had come to destroy the beauty and pleasantness of the physical world; the second was the notion that he was a lonely and pathetic orphan; the third was a series of images connected with Rose La Touche; and the fourth an obsessional fear connected with fireflies and fireworks.[7]

During this period there also came upon Ruskin a strong swell of religious fear that had been developing since 1867—fears that the Devil was chasing him and sending the "plague wind," and that evil was lurking everywhere in nature. In his distress, he resumed his former habit of reading the Bible at random every day, and his letters have increasing numbers of references to biblical passages as the years pass.

His strong sense of solitude in a futile fight against evil and ignorance continued, and he became still more unsettled. In October 1873 he wrote to Carlyle that he had "not the least pleasure" in his work anymore, "except because you and Froude and one or two other friends still care for it" (Letter 123), and he added, significantly, "the loss of my mother and my old nurse leaves me without any root, or, in the depth of the word any home. . . ." A few days later Carlyle wrote that Ruskin was "treading the winepress alone; and sometimes feels his labours very heavy."[8] Two months later he said that Ruskin "looks lean but ardent, vehement; and is very talkative and speculative"[9]—and that Ruskin is "full to overflowing with far glancing projects and speculations."[1] Much as he continued to encourage Ruskin, he now became more fearful for him, and sensed that his disciple's new behavior was loosening the bond between them.

Carlyle's growing fears, and Ruskin's growing instability of character, must be kept in mind as one reads the letters written by Ruskin to

[6]Carlyle to John Forster, December 20, 1872. MS: Victoria and Albert Museum, 48E.18.

[7]Wilenski, p. 124.

[8]Carlyle to C. E. Norton, November 3, 1873. MS: Houghton Library, Harvard University.

[9]Carlyle to his brother John, December 20, 1873. MS: NLS, 527.104.

[1]Carlyle to his brother John, January 8, 1874. MS: NLS, 528.3.

Carlyle throughout 1874. In December 1873, Ruskin stopped referring to himself as Carlyle's disciple and began calling himself Carlyle's
"son" (Letter 128), and by April 1874 he began to address Carlyle as
"papa." We must remember, however, that in October 1873 Ruskin
had already mentioned his feeling that he was an orphan, and in early
April 1874, in *Fors Clavigera* (Letter 41), Ruskin said, "Now father
and mother and nurse all dead, and the roses of spring, prime or
late—what are they to me?"[2] The sense of being a homeless orphan, as
much as love for Carlyle himself, seems to have caused his adoption of
Carlyle as a substitute father, and goes far in explaining his decision in
the summer of 1874 to write to Carlyle every day, as he used to write
to his own father. Ruskin was later to call his friend Rawdon Brown
"papa" as well,[3] so that his attachment to Carlyle must be viewed with
some reservation.

The letters of 1874, then, though they are more numerous, merely
reveal the continued growth of Ruskin's mental imbalance. In them
one can see vivid demonstrations of the delusions and obsessions already mentioned—the sense of orphanhood, the feelings of solitude
and ennui, the obsessions with rose imagery and representations of
saintly young women (like St. Ursula or Ilaria del Carretto) who reminded him of Rose La Touche, and the deep religious disturbances
that, as a result of his trip to Italy in 1874, were eventually to lead him
to desperate flirtations with both Catholicism and spiritualism. For it
was during this summer, while he was staying in Assisi, that he first
began to think of himself as a brother of the Third Order of St. Francis, and his friend Mrs. Cowper-Temple had already introduced him to
several spiritualistic seances.[4]

When Ruskin returned from Italy in the fall of 1874, the knowledge
of Rose's impending death began to press upon him as well, and while
he tried, as always, to cover his unrest with feigned cheerfulness, his
behavior belied his efforts. He continued to visit Carlyle regularly
while he lectured at Oxford, and Carlyle's few letters show a decent
appreciation of his intentions and his work. Carlyle was then working
on his essays on the early kings of Norway and the portraits of John
Knox, and when the book was published in 1875 it bore a hopeful
dedication to "dear ethereal Ruskin, whom God preserve."

[2] *Works*, XXVIII, 79.
[3] See Ruskin's *Works*, XXXVII, 222.
[4] J. L. Bradley, in his edition of *The Letters of John Ruskin to Lord and Lady Mount-
Temple* (Columbus, Ohio, 1964), p. 9, states that Ruskin had attended seances as early
as 1863, and had developed an even greater interest in spiritualism in the 1870's.

But Ruskin's personality was slipping beyond the grasp of Carlyle's intimate friendship, and from 1874 on Carlyle's comments on Ruskin are increasingly apprehensive, irritated, and critical. "I do not get much good of him," he wrote on November 6, 1874, "so high-flown is his strain of flattery, springing doubtless from the nervous nature of his being which is never to be got rid of in dialogue with him and spoils all practical communication."[5] And again, on November 17, he writes:

I have seen Ruskin, these three Saturdays in punctual sequence at two P.M. . . . . I get but little real insight out of him, though he is full of friendliness and is aiming as if at the very stars; but his sensitive, flighty nature disqualifies him for earnest conversation and frank communication of his secret thoughts.[6]

Ruskin's works at this time, which were mostly publications of his Oxford lectures, were more concerned with artistic problems than they had been, though they contained many digressions on society and economics; and Carlyle reacted with some disappointment. On January 1, 1875, he wrote that he had received "a whole half-dozen or more" of Ruskin's latest books, and had begun to read them "with real interest."[7] But by September 9, 1875, he remarked sourly, "Ruskin's books, when he launches out upon high Art, are very hard reading, abstruse and fine-spun, yielding me next to no spiritual nourishment when I sum them up."[8]

Fors Clavigera, though it was not about "high Art," also continued to disappoint and alarm Carlyle. If the *Fors* letter of January 1, 1875, was "good for little,"[9] the October 1 issue was even more startling. "Ruskin's last Fors," he wrote,

awoke in us here the dreadful idea that he was losing his wits but in a day's time this horrid idea dissipated itself again and I could only perceive still with real regret what a mad and ruinous career he was running and like to run, with such a splendid outfit of faculty and opportunity, one would have said, as few of his generation had been gifted with.[1]

The *Fors* letters were never to allay Carlyle's fears, for only a few months before this, in May 1875, Rose La Touche had died, and Ruskin reverted to reminiscences of his younger, happier days when he chose new material for his monthly publications. In a further effort to escape his grief, he increased his activities involving the St. George's

---

[5] Carlyle to his brother John. MS: NLS, 528.19.
[6] Carlyle to his brother John. MS: NLS, 528.20.
[7] Carlyle to his brother John. In A. Carlyle, *New Letters of Thomas Carlyle*, II, 310.
[8] Carlyle to his brother John. MS: NLS, 528.25.
[9] See Carlyle's letter to his brother John, November 17, 1874. MS: NLS, 528.20.
[1] Carlyle to his brother John, October 26, 1875. MS: NLS, 528.41.

Guild, and he became a more frequent visitor to the seances held at Mrs. Cowper-Temple's home at Broadlands. On one occasion, he even thought that he saw the ghost of the departed Rose, and this experience served only to increase the weakening of his spirit. As the years passed, also, he contemplated the problems of life and death more and more, and once again drew close to Christianity.

The letters to Carlyle written during this period give some indication of the drift of his mind, but they do not fully reveal how much he had come to believe in the possibility of life after death, and in the Franciscan doctrines of love and simplicity of habits. Knowing how much Carlyle disliked Catholicism and spiritualism,[2] Ruskin seldom mentioned these subjects in his letters, and in fact he seems to have been afraid to share some of his views with Carlyle. As his mental troubles increased, so did his obsession with childhood memories, Catholicism, and spiritualism, and his letters to Carlyle decreased correspondingly in length and frequency, while his visits to Cheyne Row became more infrequent. Carlyle, now in his eighties, sensed Ruskin's growing alienation from him, and lamented it. "We lately had a short letter from Ruskin," he wrote to his brother John on October 14, 1877, "he seems to grow more and more distracted, making some people guess that he will possibly turn to papistry at last and become a monk of Assisi. I hope better things, though thus I speak."[3]

Ruskin, by this time, had fallen into an alarming mental condition. In the spring of 1877 he found himself unable to concentrate on anything for more than a few minutes, and he became listless and apathetic for long periods of time. By the summer he had become abusive, and he even wrote an irritated letter to Carlyle (Letter 187) in which he complained of Carlyle's lack of interest in *Fors Clavigera*. The *Fors* letters themselves were vituperative and rambling during that summer (it was in July that Ruskin wrote a wild paragraph attacking the painter J. A. M. Whistler, which eventually led to a lawsuit), and by early 1878 they were deeply agitated and given to frequent bursts of anger. Finally, in late February 1878, Ruskin had his first attack of delirium. "I went mad because nothing came of my work," he later said, but the reasons were many and complex, as we have seen. For months he was in a state of anguished delusion. He imagined that he was being plagued by devils, and on separate occasions he believed Satan himself was present in the shape of a peacock under his window or a cat next

[2] See Ruskin, *Diaries*, III, 843: "I saying that I felt greatly minded sometimes to join the Catholics . . . Carlyle said 'he would desire in such case rather to have me assassinated.'"

[3] MS: NLS, 528.78.

to his bed. Once, too, he watched the firelight flickering on his bedpost and came to see a cackling witch in its place. All the years of tormented thoughts and suppressed emotions had finally taken their toll. From this time forward, Ruskin was to lose his fight against insanity, though he still had before him another ten years of scattered and distracted activity before he was to succumb.

By June 1878, Ruskin had sufficiently recovered from his attack to write about it to Carlyle with some humor. "It was utterly wonderful to me to find that I could go so heartily & headily mad," he wrote (Letter 194), and added that he was "not in bad *spirits*," but "on the condition . . . that I think of nothing that would vex me." Carlyle, though the letters provide little evidence, seems to have treated Ruskin with utmost kindness, and did not give up hope in him. The poet William Allingham, in his diary entry on March 11, 1878, records a conversation in which Carlyle began by disparaging the St. George's Guild, which he called "utterly absurd" and thought "a joke at first," but then added that Ruskin had "a celestial brightness in him," and that his morality was "the highest and purest."[4] An account told by Mrs. Anne Thackeray Ritchie of a visit that occurred soon after Ruskin's attack of delirium is especially revealing. "I heard," Mrs. Ritchie writes,

a pretty account once from Mr. Alfred Lyttelton of a visit paid by Ruskin to Carlyle in the familiar room in Cheyne Walk. . . . Mr. Ruskin had been ill not long before, and as he talked on of something he cared about, Mr. Lyttelton said his eyes lighted up, and he seemed agitated and moved. Carlyle stopped him short, saying the subject was too interesting. "You must take care," he said, with that infinite kindness which Carlyle could show; "You will be making yourself ill once more." And Ruskin, quite simply, like a child, stopped short. "You are right," he said, calling Carlyle 'master,' and then went on to talk of something else. . . .[5]

When one remembers Mrs. Carlyle's description of Ruskin's treating Carlyle like "a naughty child" in the early 1860's, one can see that the wheel had made a full, ironic turn. Like Carlyle's treatment of Ruskin during their quarrel of 1867, it is a side of him that is seldom noticed, and it further serves to emphasize the fact that the friendship between the two men always remained strong despite their mutual recognition of each other's failings.

Not long after the visit described by Alfred Lyttelton, Carlyle made another visit to Ruskin's home, despite the fact that he felt Ruskin to be "threatened with softening of the brain, at lowest with much spir-

[4] William Allingham, *A Diary* (1907), p. 203.
[5] *Records of Tennyson, Ruskin, and Browning*, pp. 103–4.

itualism, which to friends of his looks rather ominous of that."[6] But Ruskin was not at home, and did not see Carlyle for many months thereafter. Sensing the reason for Ruskin's absence, Carlyle wrote to his brother John in February of 1879:

I have heard nothing whatever from Ruskin . . . but the other night I received from him under the title of Proserpina no. V one of the prettiest pieces of writing I have seen for many years. . . . I have understood that he is quite gone over to what they call Spiritualism and my conjecture is that he, who knows how much I detest and despise that horrible absurdity, avoids writing to me on that account though he loves me as well as ever poor soul and can write upon other subjects so beautifully, as I say.[7]

Two weeks later, on March 1, he again wrote to his brother about Ruskin's hopes for "a millennium to be provided by the St. George's Guild," and went on to say that, while Ruskin was "perfectly sane" concerning "all that," he had "other very distracted notions about spiritualism so-called, a branch of matters which he keeps quite secret from me, knowing that I despise and even abhor it. He keeps quite hid from me."[8]

There may be, however, too much exaggeration in Carlyle's views of the matter, for Ruskin's involvement with spiritualism was not so extensive as Carlyle feared, and his absence from the Carlyle household seems to have sprung from his desire to avoid being ill-mannered by spreading gloom about the rooms at Cheyne Row. He was, after all, still recovering from his attack throughout 1879, and since he could not be as cheerful as his personal rules of courtesy demanded, he chose to avoid any contact with those most dear to him. That his love for Carlyle did not diminish greatly is evident in his letter of March 28, 1879 (Letter 196). "I dare not come up to London," he writes, though "it grieves me never to see you. . . ." A few days later, at the end of March, he finally visited Carlyle, and the visit was witnessed by the ubiquitous Allingham, who noted in his diary that:

[Carlyle and Ruskin] greeted each other affectionately, and Ruskin knelt on the floor, leaning over Carlyle as they talked. Carlyle began to speak of Irish saints, and referred to me for some account of Saint Bridget and her shrine at Kildare, to which I added that Bridewell . . . had come to mean a prison.
    This seemed to interest Ruskin particularly, and he remarked, "We make prisons of the holiest and most beautiful things."
    He then took leave, very affectionately kissing Carlyle's hands. . . .[9]

[6] Carlyle to his brother John, October 11, 1878. MS: NLS, 528.88.
[7] Letter of February 15, 1879. MS: NLS, 528.102.
[8] MS: NLS, 528.104.
[9] Allingham, p. 275.

This is the last description that can be found of the two men together, but it is sufficient to show that their friendship had not dimmed appreciably in its thirty-year course, despite the vicissitudes of their lives and the many contrasts in their personalities.

The last letter in this collection was written in December 1879, and even it gives evidence of a continuing friendship. Although there is no indication of any further correspondence between the two men during the remaining thirteen months of Carlyle's life, there is much evidence that Ruskin was just as devoted as ever. In a letter of August 1880, Ruskin said of Carlyle that "we feel so much alike, that you may often mistake one for the other now";[1] and in October 1880 he wrote to the students of the Liberal Club of Glasgow University, saying, "I hate all Liberalism as I do Beelzebub, and . . . with Carlyle, I stand, we two alone now in England, for God and the Queen."[2] He preserved the sense of unity with Carlyle to the very day when the "minority of two" was dissolved by Carlyle's death on February 5, 1881. Prematurely aged now, and still in precarious mental health, Ruskin reacted to the news of Carlyle's death with typical stoicism and some equally typical feelings of guilt, which were akin to the feelings he must have had after his own father's death.[3] On February 15, 1881, he wrote to Mary Gladstone:

The death of Carlyle is no sorrow to me. It is, I believe, not an end—but a beginning of his real life. Nay, perhaps also of mine. My remorse, every day he lived, for having not enough loved him in the days gone by, is not greater now, but less, in the hope that he knows what I am feeling about him at this—and all other—moments.[4]

Despite his protestations, however, the sorrow he felt over Carlyle's death was deep, and did much to precipitate his second attack of insanity, which came just one week after his letter of February 15. This attack, which he later described as "terrific delirium," lasted about a month and was, according to Ruskin himself, "partly brought on by the sense of loneliness—and greater responsibility brought upon me by Carlyle's death."[5] After his recovery, he vowed to throw himself "into the mere fulfilment [*sic*] of Carlyle's work," and, in what was almost an exact repetition of the decision he made in 1870, he began

---

[1] Ruskin to Susan Beever. In *Works*, XXXVII, 320.

[2] Ruskin's *Works*, XXXIV, 548–49.

[3] In his diary, he seems to have commemorated Carlyle's death by simply marking a cross next to the date. For a discussion of this see Helen Gill Viljoen, ed., *The Brantwood Diary of John Ruskin* (New Haven and London, 1971), p. 265.

[4] Ruskin's *Works*, XXXVII, 341.

[5] Ruskin to George Richmond, May 20, 1881. In *Works*, XXXVII, 361.

once again to send out his monthly *Fors Clavigera* letters. In 1883 he resumed his Oxford lectures despite his weakened mental condition, and certainly his resolution to continue "Carlyle's work" must have had much to do with this unfortunate decision. Although he had recurring attacks of insanity until his final lapse into permanent madness in 1889, his devotion to Carlyle never wavered, and the social conscience that his "master" and "papa" had nurtured remained in full force until that sad time.

Because Ruskin was so devoted to Carlyle, and knew him so well, his connection with the infamous controversy that arose between James Anthony Froude and Carlyle's descendants after Carlyle's death is well worth noting.

On March 5, 1881, James Anthony Froude published his edition of the *Reminiscences* that Carlyle had written years before his death. Carlyle had given the manuscripts of these memorial sketches, and most of his other unpublished private papers, to Froude during the years following 1871. Froude thus became Carlyle's "official" biographer and editor.[6] With Carlyle's knowledge, he began editing the papers and writing the biography in the 1870's, and thus was able to publish the *Reminiscences* only one month after Carlyle's death. The book, unfortunately, dismayed many of its readers and brought abuse upon both Carlyle and Froude. One of Carlyle's most personal works, it contained frank and vivid sketches of people he had known well, all drawn with his inimitable sharpness of perception and honesty of vision. The book began with lengthy memorials of Carlyle's father, Edward Irving, and Lord Jeffrey, then moved toward a close with a remorseful tribute to Jane Welsh Carlyle, written by Carlyle during the months immediately following her death.[7] Froude also added an appendix containing Carlyle's early and equally vivid sketches of Southey and Wordsworth. Acting, as he said in his preface, "with Carlyle's consent but without his supervision," he decided to make whatever omissions were necessary in order to avoid offending any living persons mentioned in the book. But he also decided that it would be foolish to remove Carlyle's general observations and opinions, for these were the heart of the book, the things that let Carlyle be "his own biographer" and "paint . . . his own portrait."[8]

[6] Carlyle's letter to Ruskin on July 30, 1874 (Letter 154), alludes to the subject.

[7] A moving glimpse of Carlyle's remorse can be seen in his letter of May 10, 1866 (Letter 61), in which he speaks of his wife's "epic greatness" known only to God and himself.

[8] Thomas Carlyle, *Reminiscences*, ed. J. A. Froude (New York, 1881), p. vii. Hereafter referred to as "*Reminiscences* (Froude)."

Unhappily, the Victorian reading public was not ready for such fidelity to fact. Their tendency to idolize great authors as great moral leaders was aggravated by contemporary editorial practices, which demanded that anything not "suitable" to the honor of an author's name be expunged from posthumous editions or biographies. The public was thus shocked to discover that its idol, Carlyle, was human after all. Ignoring Carlyle's generosity, sympathy, and honesty, it chose to remember only his vivid but negative remarks about both himself and other authors—especially Wordsworth, Southey, Lamb, and Montagu. It therefore deemed him to be excessively harsh, censorious, and even duplicitous in his remarks about his friends and acquaintances, and it found him to be unexpectedly morose in his views of life and himself. The result was inevitable damage to Carlyle's reputation, and severe criticism of Froude for allowing such "injudicious smudges" to come to light.

Mary Aitken Carlyle, whose name and letters appear near the end of the present volume of correspondence, was outraged. On March 26, 1881, she wrote to Charles Eliot Norton:

It was very painful to me to read the *Reminiscences* which Froude has printed. My uncle often said his memory wd be safe in Froude's hands, for whether he wrote a good book or a bad one he would always be so gentlemanly and reticent. These *Reminiscences* are no more a picture of him than the hideous black patches of *silhouettes* are likenesses of his Father and Mother.[9]

On May 4, 1881, she published a letter in the *Times* in which she accused Froude of publishing the *Reminiscences* (especially the memorial to Jane Welsh Carlyle) against the expressed wishes of Carlyle himself. Thus the long and complicated "Carlyle-Froude War" began.[1] When Froude publicly answered Mrs. Carlyle's letter, she tried to prevent him from writing his biography of Carlyle. On May 7, she sent another letter to the *Times*, claiming that she, not Froude, was the owner of the private papers of her uncle, and that Froude should give them to her at once. Froude replied that Carlyle himself had told him to return them to her as soon as he was finished with them, and proceeded to write the first part of his biography of Carlyle. Entitled *Thomas Carlyle: A History of the First Forty Years of his Life, 1795–1835*, it was published in two volumes on March 30, 1882. Again re-

[9] Quoted in Hyder E. Rollins, "Charles Eliot Norton and Froude," *Journal of English and Germanic Philology*, LVII (October 1958), 651.

[1] The long history of this ignominious war has been thoroughly examined by Waldo H. Dunn in his *Froude and Carlyle: A Study of the Froude-Carlyle Controversy* (1930). I am indebted to this valuable work, and to the article by Rollins, for much of my information about this controversial subject. See also volume II of Dunn's *James Anthony Froude: A Biography* (Oxford, 1963), in which the subject is reviewed.

fusing to apply the usual canonizing scissors, Froude explained his artistic principles in his preface to the work. It would have been easy, he asserted, to "recast" the wealth of material he was working with and exhibit "the fair and beautiful side of the story only," thus drawing "a picture of a faultless character":

> But it would have been a portrait without individuality—an ideal, or, . . . an "idol" to be worshipped one day and thrown away the next. Least of all men could such idealising be ventured with Carlyle, to whom untruth of any kind was abominable. If he was to be known at all, he chose to be known as he was. . . . He has himself laid down the conditions under which a biographer must do his work if he would do it honestly, without the fear of man before him; and in dealing with Carlyle's own memory I have felt myself bound to conform to his own rule.[2]

Previously, in a letter to his friend John Skelton on February 17, 1882, he had expressed confidence that this method of writing a biography would be best for Carlyle, for it would make him seem more human to the readers, and the result would be "that Carlyle will stand higher than ever, and will be loved more than ever."[3]

Mary Aitken Carlyle did not agree. To her, Froude's un-Victorian attitude seemed to be a treacherous profanation of her uncle's memory, and a violation of his trust. She was especially concerned about Froude's presentation of the relationship between Carlyle and his wife, for she felt (with justification, as events later proved) that many readers would sympathize with Mrs. Carlyle because so much emphasis was put upon Carlyle's eccentricities and occasional grumpiness. On August 9, 1882, she wrote to Charles Eliot Norton that Froude, in his treatment of Carlyle's courtship and the early years of his marriage, made it appear that Jane Welsh "left wealth and fortune to ally herself with poverty and squalor." She also said that Froude was perverse in seeming to blame Carlyle "for selfishness in making his wife live in solitude at Craigenputtock"[4] during the first few years of marriage, and she railed in general at the parts of Froude's biography that seemed to prove that Carlyle, both as husband and as companion, was "ill to live with." For whatever motives—family pride, lack of literary sophistication, desire for profit, personal dislike of either Froude or Mrs. Carlyle, prudery, or even fierce but misguided love for her uncle—she kept up her personal and public attack upon Froude for many years thereafter, and enlisted the aid of others more famous than she, thus drawing

---

[2] From the preface to Froude's *Carlyle*, I, vi–vii, quoted in Dunn, pp. 44–45.
[3] Quoted in Dunn, p. 47.
[4] Rollins, p. 652.

more attention to her uncle's "faults"—and more distorted interpretations of them—than Froude alone could ever have done.

The most famous and effective of Mary Carlyle's allies was Charles Eliot Norton, the gentlemanly American scholar who had been an admiring acquaintance of Carlyle since 1869, and who was one of Ruskin's close friends. Norton sympathized with Mary after the publication of the *Reminiscences*, and he hastened his editing of the Carlyle-Emerson correspondence in the hope that his edition could serve to correct the picture of Carlyle that Froude had revealed. The first half of Froude's biography appeared, however, before Norton's work was finished, and the American was so shocked that he doubled his efforts. He thought Froude "artfully malignant," and said that Froude had "committed treachery to the memory of one who had put faith in him."[5]

As early as 1881, Norton had made his opinions known to Ruskin, who was both startled and perplexed over the whole situation. Finding himself squarely in the middle of a bitter quarrel between two of his best friends over his revered "master" and "papa," Ruskin at first tried to be diplomatic toward both Froude and Norton, though he left no doubt that he favored Froude. As early as 1874, while he was lecturing at Oxford, he had, after all, written to Froude: "I am not the institutor, still less the guide . . . but I am the Exponent of the Reaction for Veracity in Art which corresponds partly to Carlyle's and your work in History, and partly to Linnaeus's in natural science. You put the real men before us instead of the ideal ones."[6] It is thus easy to understand why Ruskin, seven years later, wrote to Froude and told him he was "ABSOLUTELY right to publish the Reminiscences, and Miss Aitken was a mere selfish and proud and cowardly Scotch Molly Foulservice."[7] A few days later he wrote to his friend George Richmond that the British public was merely a group of "ugly, puffy, perturbed polycroaks" to find in the *Reminiscences* "nothing but the bits of brick that hurt their own puffy personages, and see and feel nothing of its mighty interests—its measureless pathos."[8] Ruskin did not write to Norton for a full year after August 1881, and when he did write again, after hearing about Norton's proposed edition of the Carlyle-Emerson letters, he was gracious but firm. "I have not been so glad of anything for many a day as about more Emerson letters," he said. "Nevertheless, one of my reasons (for causes) of silence this long time

---

[5] *Ibid.*, loc. cit.　　　　　[6] See Ruskin's *Works*, XXXVII, 83.
[7] Quoted in Dunn, p. 210.
[8] See Ruskin's letter of May 20, 1881. In *Works*, XXXVII, 361.

has been my differing with you (we do differ sometimes) in a chasmy manner about Froude's beginning of his work. . . ."⁹ "I am very fond of Froude, and am with him in all that he has done and said, about C, if it had to be said or done, at all, and I never saw any one more deeply earnest and affectionate in trying to do right."¹ To another friend, he wrote in January 1883 that the whole affair was merely "useless gossip and mischievous curiosity," and he said bluntly that "nobody has any business with Carlyle's ways to his wife—or hers to him;—but you may depend on it—whatever Froude says or does, about him will be right. . . ."² When Norton's edition of the Emerson-Carlyle letters was finally published in February 1883, Ruskin told Norton that the letters were "infinitely sweet and wise," but again added that he was not with Norton "in thinking Froude wrong about the Reminiscences," which were to him "full of his [Carlyle's] strong insight, and in their distress far more pathetic than these bawlings of his earlier life about Cromwell and others of his quite best works; but I am vexed for want of a proper epilogue of your own. . . ."³ Norton replied gingerly, "Even you, I sometimes fancy, underrate the worth of the man, and let the trivial and external traits of his unique individuality go for too much in your estimate of him."⁴ Such a remark must have been infuriating to Ruskin, who honored Carlyle above all men and knew both Froude and Carlyle far better than Norton did. Furthermore, Norton's implication that Carlyle's "unique" personal traits should be subordinated in any attempt to estimate his worth must have seemed ridiculous to Ruskin, whose principles of art so closely resembled Froude's in their insistence upon truth and actuality. Norton's remarks may well have precipitated Ruskin's later decision to write his own biography of Carlyle, for, while he believed in Froude's approach to biography, he did not entirely agree with Froude's estimate of Carlyle, and felt that his own judgment of his "master" was more valuable than Froude's or Norton's.

In an attempt to mitigate the animosity between the two men, Rus-

---

⁹Ruskin to Norton, August 30, 1882. In Norton, II, 175–76.
¹Ruskin to Norton, August 30, 1882. MS: Houghton Library, Harvard University. The passage is omitted by Norton in his edition, but is published in Rollins, p. 653.
²Ruskin to Miss Jessie Leete, January 31, 1883. In *Works*, XXXVII, 435–36.
³Ruskin to Norton, March 10, 1883. In Norton, II, 189–90.
⁴Norton to Ruskin, April 3, 1883. In Norton and Howe, II, 147. Norton here adds an "epilogue" for Ruskin's benefit. Carlyle's "essential nature," he says, "was solitary in its strength, its sincerity, its tenderness, its nobility. He was nearer Dante than any other man. Like Dante his face was black with the smoke of Hell, and the street boys called him names and threw mud at him. His stomach sometimes got the better of his head, but that it did not master his heart or break his will is a marvel."

kin continued to offer his impartial opinions of both Froude and Norton between 1883 and 1886. It became increasingly difficult to do so, however, because of Norton's implacability and Ruskin's own emotional disturbances. When Froude brought out Carlyle's annotated edition of the *Letters and Memorials of Jane Welsh Carlyle* on April 2, 1883 (just two months after Norton's publication of the Emerson-Carlyle letters), both Norton and Mary Aitken Carlyle were again incensed. The letters and memorials, with their sharp comments on life in the Carlyle household, once again aroused negative opinions of Carlyle in the minds of many readers, and greatly lessened the effect of Norton's efforts. Carlyle's own comments against himself in the volume, made in the midst of his period of shocked sorrow and self-criticism in the years immediately following Jane's death, created an even more negative impression, for the public failed to recognize either the exaggerated self-depreciation Carlyle displayed "in remorse for real or imagined faults of his own"[5] at the time, or the nobility of his wish to "set things right" by publishing a true account of his wife's greatness and heroism. When Froude published the last two volumes of his biography on October 6, 1884, with its depiction of Jane's supposed jealousy of Carlyle's friendship with Lady Ashburton and its realistic portrayals of Carlyle's gruff and gloomy moments, the wave of sympathy for Mrs. Carlyle swelled. Mary Aitken Carlyle immediately gave Carlyle's private papers (which Froude had conscientiously returned to her after he had finished with them) to Norton, hoping that he could "correct" Froude's misdoings and do honor to Carlyle after all. Norton went to work with renewed vigor.

Ruskin, though alarmed at the turn of events, was at first rational and candid in his criticism of both men, and tried to dull the edges of the sharp quarrel, though he did not hide his own sympathies. A visitor to Ruskin in December 1884 heard him say that Carlyle "was not really as unhappy as the life by Froude made him out to be; that he [Carlyle] had a wretched digestion and a way of talking about his miseries, but that his life was not really as unhappy as Turner's."[6] Ruskin also conveyed this opinion to Norton, but he added his own views of both Mrs. Carlyle and Norton as well. "I am so very glad you have got those letters to edit," he wrote to Norton in 1885. "Carlyle is entirely himself when he stops talking of himself, but I totally disagree with you about the wife letters being sacred. . . . I used to see the two con-

⁵Dunn, p. 306.
⁶Edith Mary Fawkes, "Mr. Ruskin at Farnley," *Nineteenth Century*, XLVII (April 1900), 621–23; quoted in Ruskin's *Works*, XXXIV, 671.

stantly together—and there was never the slightest look of right affection. She always called him Carlyle, never Tom—and he—rarely attended to a word she said."[7] Ruskin then added a frank and perceptive
observation about the relative merits of Froude and Norton as judges
of the Carlyles. "I am every hour more at one with Froude in his estimate of both. Your entirely happy and unselfish life puts you out of
court in judging of these mixed characters—C[arlyle], or E[merson],
or me!"[8] Norton, however, did not take the hint. In 1886 he published
his judiciously edited *Early Letters of Thomas Carlyle*, designed to
show more sides of the young Carlyle than Froude or Mrs. Carlyle's
Letters had shown. Ruskin, in turn, began to think more and more
about publishing something of his own on both Carlyles. In April
1886 he wrote to Norton:

> I'm not so anxious about your having your ideal Carlyle, as getting my own
> extremely familiar view of him—and his Miss Welsh—put into such pho-
> tography as I can. . . .
>   You see—you don't agree with Carlyle to begin with—and don't enjoy his
> Billingsgate as I do.[9]

In June of the same year he again wrote Norton, saying that he had
received Froude's permission to "take out" Carlyle's descriptions of
people and edit them himself.[1] Ruskin, however, had already had a severe "brain attack" (his fourth) in July 1885, and his mental abilities
failed him before he could write.

Ruskin's increasing attacks of insanity may have had much to do
with the hostile shift in the tone of his criticism of Norton, though
Norton's stubborn animosity toward Froude did not help matters. In
July 1886, Norton published an article called "Recollections of Carlyle" in the *New Princeton Review*. In the article he severely criticized
Froude's sloppy editing of Carlyle's *Reminiscences*, and he even went
so far as to question Froude's motives. When he wrote a letter to com-

[7] Ruskin to Norton, October 20, 1885. In Norton, II, 209–10.
[8] Ruskin to Norton, October 20, 1885. MS: Houghton Library, Harvard University.
Norton omitted these passages from his edition. During the same year, Ruskin also
spoke slightingly of Mrs. Carlyle in his *Praeterita* (see *Works*, XXXV, 166), and re-
served all his pity for Carlyle. His own temperament, of course, distorted his judgment
of relations between the sexes. L. Allen Harker, a visitor to Ruskin in the late 1880's,
reported that he disliked people who spoke of Mrs. Carlyle as a "martyr" to Carlyle's
bad temper: "He admitted that Carlyle was grumpy and habitually melancholy—'but so
am I'—and he was easily irritated. 'That clever shrew,' his wife, well knew this, and by
the very tones of her voice as she 'rasped out his name' could set his nerves on edge in a
paroxysm of febrile irritation." (L. Allen Harker, "Ruskin and Girlhood: Some Happy
Reminiscences," *Scribner's Magazine*, XL [November 1906], 568.)
[9] Quoted in Rollins, p. 658.
[1] Ruskin's *Works*, XXXVII, 568.

miserate with Ruskin after another of his recent mental attacks, Ruskin fired back a crisp reply:

> How many wiser folk than I go mad for good and all, or bad and all, like poor Turner at the last, Blake always, Scott in his pride, Irving in his faith, and Carlyle because of the poultry next door.
>
> You had better, by the way, have gone crazy yourself than written that niggling and naggling article on Froude's misprints.[2]

In a last effort to make Norton understand Froude's motives, Ruskin then sent Norton part of a sad letter of complaint he had received from Froude—a letter in which Froude mildly wished that Norton would stop his wrongheaded attack because he "does not know what he is doing."[3] When Norton ignored this and instead published his own edition of Carlyle's *Reminiscences* in 1887, with a preface that was derogatory to Froude, Ruskin apparently flew into a fury, which never abated. So violent were his letters written after 1887 that Norton destroyed most of them. Some of the letters that have survived, however, may give an idea of the nature of the whole of them, and show why Norton decided not to print any of them in his own edition of the Ruskin-Norton correspondence. The letters written by Ruskin to Norton during June 1889, for instance, have been found among the unpublished proofs of Ruskin's *Dilecta*. In the first one, dated June 11, Ruskin began by half-jokingly saying he wanted to give Norton, "editor of Carlyle's Early Letters," as "thorough a literary dressing, pickling, and conserving, as ever one living scribe got from another." He then chided Norton for various misprints he had found in the Carlyle letters, being deliberately as "niggling" and "naggling" as Norton had been to Froude. Two days later, he wrote another, more violent letter in which he asked four nasty questions of Norton. The third question—"What ever put it into your head that *you* could understand Carlyle better than Froude or I could?"—is blunt enough, but the last one is a volley of uninhibited rancor:

> What demon of insolence, and cowardice, provoked you, (the era of duelling past) to write of one of the most deliberate, learned, and religious, of European historians, in terms which, when the era of duelling was *not* past, you could not have used to the poorest parliamentary hanger-on to his party's petticoats, without being thrashed, or shot, on the following morning?[4]

[2] Ruskin to Norton, August 29, 1886. In Ruskin's *Works*, XXXVII, 569. The letter is also published in Norton, II, 216, with a note added by Norton to remind the reader that Ruskin had lately come "very much under the influence" of Froude.

[3] Rollins, p. 661.

[4] From the proofs of Ruskin's *Dilecta*, IV, quoted with the permission of Dr. Samuel E. Brown of the University of Maryland, who has kindly allowed me to consult his cop-

Finally, towards the end of June, Ruskin fired off four more questions, deeply sarcastic and personally insulting to a man of Norton's sensitivity. When did Norton become "converted" to Carlyle, and how many of Carlyle's works did he know? was the first question. "On what subjects do you recommend the teaching of Carlyle to your young Americans? On Slavery? Kinghood, Stump Oratory, or Hudson's Statuary?" was the second. Third, Ruskin maliciously wanted to know what "advantage of personal intercourse" Norton had with Carlyle after becoming Carlyle's disciple, and his last question must have been the most shocking of all to Norton: "As a man of extreme refinement . . . how came you to indulge Mrs. Alexander Carlyle in her singular wish to illustrate the sanctities of private life by supplementing Mr. Froude's account of her uncle's literary consumption of the oil of midnight with his own of the sanitary effects of the castor oil of morning?"[5] Small wonder that Norton (*and* Cook and Wedderburn) omitted these letters from their editions! They are among Ruskin's last written words, for after 1889 he fell into the sad silence of his last decade. Some evidence shows that as late as 1889 he again proposed writing a book on Carlyle that would both vindicate and supplement Froude,[6] but by then all was too late, and what might have been one of his most interesting books was never written.

We can only imagine what the book would have been like, and how valuable it would have been to those trying to understand Carlyle. While Ruskin would probably have interpreted Carlyle in terms of his own abnormalities and blind spots, his knowledge was nevertheless based on close and intelligent personal experience, and his devotion to the principles of "Veracity in Art" would probably have made his book as vivid and arresting as Froude's. His views would also have been more realistic than those of Norton, who was forced to judge from afar. The pleasant thoughts about Carlyle that Ruskin recorded in his *Praeterita* in 1885[7] show us something of the warm friendliness he would have revealed in Carlyle's nature. His remarks about Mrs. Carlyle indicate that, having been through the same storm of gossip and controversy himself, he probably would have omitted, or carefully dismissed, any references to Carlyle's alleged sexual problems.[8] He

---

ies of them. See also Helen Gill Viljoen, ed., *The Froude-Ruskin Friendship: As Represented Through Letters* (New York, 1966), pp. 139–46, where these letters are published.

[5] *Ibid.*

[6] See Ruskin's *Works*, XXXV, xxiv–xxv.

[7] See *ibid.*, pp. 539–41.

[8] Dunn, II, 209 and 210, claims that Ruskin corroborated Geraldine Jewsbury's statement that the Carlyles' marriage had never been consummated. Ruskin, Dunn says, ob-

would, however, have inserted many of the famous Carlylean pen portraits of people that he admired so much and, even more than Froude, he would have refrained from using editorial scissors. In 1885 he berated England for receiving "for thirty years, with rage and hissing, the words of the one man, now at rest among his native hills, who told her that her merchants should be honest and her statesmen sincere."[9] From this and other evidence we can guess that Ruskin would have emphasized strongly the solitary valor and superiority of Carlyle's character.

His book would not, however, have been an uncritical panegyric. Ruskin knew Carlyle's faults as well as his virtues, and he would undoubtedly have made some negative, though honest, statements about his revered master. What he chiefly deplored was Carlyle's excessively abstract and gloomy attitude toward the beauty of concrete natural surroundings. In 1883, and again in 1885, Ruskin clarified these opinions and applied them to the young Carlyle in Scotland:

What in my own personal way I chiefly regret and wonder at in him is, the perception in all of nature of nothing between the stars and his stomach,—his going, for instance, into the "north watch" for two months, and noting absolutely no Cambrian thing or event but only increase of Carlylean bile.[1]

The ocean coast and mountain border of lower Scotland were salutary to Scott—withdrawing him from the morbid German fancies which proved so fatal to Carlyle. Scott's was a joyful admiration of the past and the scenery which he loved with "all the sensibility of his soul;" Carlyle's mind, fixed anxiously on the future and besides embarrassed by the practical pinching, as well as the unconfessed shame, of poverty, saw and felt from his earliest childhood nothing but the faultfulness and gloom of the Present.[2]

Ruskin also admitted that Carlyle was often melancholy and irritable and, while he did not dislike Carlyle for this, he did find that all the more personal works of Carlyle published after 1881 had "vexed" and "partly angered" him with their "'me miserum'—never seeming to feel the extreme ill manners of his perpetual whine."[3]

What may be especially and ultimately valuable to us, however, is Ruskin's acute recognition of the complicated psychology behind Carlyle's expressions of anger and pessimism. According to Ruskin, Car-

---

tained the information from his cousin, Dr. W. J. Richardson, who had examined Mrs. Carlyle during one of her illnesses. Unfortunately, Dunn does not refer to the specific source of his own information, and the matter is still unresolved. Ruskin's own sexual troubles complicate the objectivity of his evidence.

[9] Letter to the *Pall Mall Gazette*, February 24, 1885; quoted in *Works*, XXXIV, 579.
[1] Ruskin to Norton, March 10, 1883. In Norton, II, 189–90.
[2] From *Praeterita*, in *Works*, XXXV, 545–46.
[3] Ruskin to Norton, March 10, 1883. In Norton, II, 189–90.

lyle's "way of talking about his miseries"[4] made him seem more unhappy than he actually was, and in fact was a form of pleasure to both himself and his audience. Holbrook Jackson, in a more recent study of Carlyle, warns us how important and misleading this "way of talking" can be. "Carlyle's letters and pamphlets, carelessly read, give an impression of invincible gloom and bad temper," Jackson says,[5] because of Carlyle's deliberate use of exaggeration. But we must remember that Carlyle "enjoys overstatement as much as he enjoys grumbling. Exaggeration is also one of his ways of being humorous." Thus many of Carlyle's irritable and provocative phrases are at the same time "among the little jokes which Carlyle explodes like Chinese crackers for amusement as well as the good of his friends and readers."[6] This "habit of vituperation," or "intellectual brawling," seems to be part of Carlyle's Scottish heritage, and Ruskin, with his own Scottish background, may have been in a better position to understand it than either the Englishman Froude or the American Norton. Oliver Elton has offered his opinion that Froude, in writing of Carlyle, made too much of Carlyle's "acrimonies and self-reproaches" because Carlyle himself made too much of them:

He [Carlyle] was more genial and less selfish than he makes himself out to be. The bitter sallies, when spoken, were frequently explained away by the accompanying guffaw, and by the vernacular Scots habit of using outrageous language which is understood all round, in Scotland, to be half-jocose. Any one who has known Scots of the primitive type will recognize the trait. It may not be endearing, but it is certainly misleading.[7]

Ruskin seems to have recognized and enjoyed this paradoxically humorous side of Carlyle as much as he recognized Carlyle's intense and sincerely solemn side. Thus he could at once criticize Froude for overestimating Carlyle's unhappiness and Norton for being unable to judge such a "mixed" character as Carlyle or to enjoy Carlyle's "Billingsgate" as it should be enjoyed. Though Ruskin was never able to write about this aspect of Carlyle's personality, we may well heed his hints and understand more truly the Carlyle who appears in the letters before us. Certainly many passages in these letters can be read as evidence of such semihumorous use of exaggerated phrasing and tone, and even Ruskin himself may be found to use it on occasion. The

[4] See Edith Mary Fawkes, "Mr. Ruskin at Farnley," *Nineteenth Century*, XLVII (April 1900), 622.
[5] *Dreamers of Dreams: The Rise and Fall of Nineteenth Century Idealism* (New York, n.d.), p. 62.
[6] *Ibid.*, p. 58.
[7] *A Survey of English Literature, 1830–1880* (1932), I, 8.

seemingly violent description of the English constitution in Ruskin's letter of November 27, 1875,[8] for instance, may change its tone for us once we realize that the phrasing was designed to amuse, as well as to shock, Ruskin's reader. For us, after all, even more than for Norton, it is indeed hard to judge such "mixed characters," and Ruskin himself can give us one perspective from which to view the psychic landscapes that surround us as we read.

The total effect of Carlyle's influence upon Ruskin is difficult to summarize. As we have seen, the similarities between the two men in doctrine and attitude are great, but there are also important differences, as their letters show. Although Ruskin absorbed much of Carlyle, much of himself remained, and he never became a mere echo of his master's voice. Carlyle realized this even in the 1860's, when he praised Ruskin's "lynx-eyed logic," saying with clever humor that Mill himself "keeps not closer to his dialectics."[9] The formal, logical method of argument was foreign to Carlyle's mind and style, but was more congenial to Ruskin's. It has often been pointed out that Ruskin's style became less ornate and more conversational after he came under Carlyle's influence, but we must remember that Ruskin never extensively used the stylistic devices for which Carlyle is famous. Carlyle's thundering repetitions, his emotionalized thought, which convinced more through intuition than through logic, his epic breadth and tempo, his habit of dramatizing argument through the use of fictitious characters, and his ability to synthesize thought, feeling, and structure by using symbols and metaphors[1]—all these devices, and more, find smaller representation in Ruskin's works. As his earlier writings show, Ruskin was fond of impressing conscious and logical— even, at times, superficial—patterns of organization upon his works, and then enlarging or refining his arguments and distinctions to fit the preestablished patterns.[2] After 1855, he no longer felt at ease in working with these abstract schemata, but his habits of thought made it difficult for him to develop a better method of organization. There is in

[8]See Letter 175.
[9]See Letter 27.
[1]These stylistic devices and others are brilliantly discussed in John Holloway's *The Victorian Sage* (1953), pp. 26–57.
[2]In the first two volumes of *Modern Painters*, for instance, Ruskin's argument is predetermined by his need to stay within the fine categorical distinctions established through the use of such terms as "Ideas of Power," "Ideas of Truth," "Ideas of Beauty," "Ideas of Imitation," and "Ideas of Relation." The same deductive approach controls *The Seven Lamps of Architecture* and *The Stones of Venice*. The mechanical unity of these works is, of course, alien to the method of organic unity employed by Carlyle.

Ruskin no equivalent to such lengthy, organically unified works as *The French Revolution* or *Sartor Resartus*, and if the style is the man we must cite this fact as evidence of a lack of organic unity in Ruskin himself. It is here, in fact, that we may well find the deepest differences between Carlyle and Ruskin.

The Ruskin who appears in these letters is a man in constant debate with himself, searching for self-integrity and truth until the search itself wears him down. Constantly trying to form both doctrines and self, he ultimately forms neither, yet at all times he is brilliantly aware of his changing and often contradictory course. Much of the power of Ruskin's letters lies in the intensity with which he makes this awareness evident. There is at times a tragic nobility in his acute moments of self-recognition, and an awesome integrity in the intellectual honesty he exhibits as he constantly sees his inconsistencies and feels the need for revisions and improvement. One wishes, in fact, that one could see more of this in Carlyle—at least the Carlyle who appears in these letters. By 1850, Carlyle's doctrines had all been formed, and thereafter he carried them into his old age with no change in their substance, although there was change in their emphases.[3]

Carlyle's letters show clearly enough that, as he grew older, he grew more severe and patriarchal in his manner of thought, and less given to reexamining his beliefs. Like an Old Testament prophet, he emphasizes the "laws of God" for the good of man, and grows more and more intense in his dark jeremiads. The universal laws of righteousness and justice are his first concern, and second is his concern for the relation of man to these laws. Thus duty, work, power, and obedience become excessively important to him, and lead him to places where Ruskin cannot always follow. For Ruskin, although he is also a prophet, is one imbued with the spirit of the New Testament. As Carlyle saw, it was *philanthropos*, not Rhadamanthus, that governed Ruskin. We need only cite the titles *Unto This Last* and *Latter-Day Pamphlets* to see the implied differences in attitude. As much as Ruskin may have agreed with Carlyle's views of universal justice and the relation of man to God, he nevertheless emphasizes compassion and mercy, urging men to love one another. And where Carlyle preaches the doctrine of work, Ruskin qualifies it by insisting on *happy* work. Happiness, in fact, seems to have been much more important to him than to Car-

---

[3] It is interesting to note that in 1854 John Stuart Mill wrote that Carlyle had "written himself out, and become a mere commentator on himself." He added his opinion that only Comte and Ruskin, of all contemporary writers, seemed to draw what they said "from a source within themselves," although he had "the greatest objections" to their doctrines (Mill, *Diary*, ed. Hugh S. P. Elliot [1910], II, 361).

lyle.[4] Ironically, however, it is Carlyle who seems to have gained greater happiness at the last.

The reason for this may lie in the quality of self-harmony: the comparative ability of both men to reconcile thought, emotion, and action within themselves. From the first of his letters to the last, Carlyle shows that his strength is derived from the universality of his vision. His belief that the divine idea of justice runs through all things has permanent roots within him, and gives him greater psychic stability. Thus he can look sourly at democracy and industrialism in his first letter to Ruskin, but predict that they will be the agents of a "new Renaissance" that will come in time. And near the end of his life he can still illustrate his faith by pointing to a passage in *Past and Present* which proclaims that justice and reverence are the "everlasting central law of the universe." The extreme scarcity of dogma in Carlyle, and his indifference to theology, were the products of an intense belief in the religious instinct itself, and gave him a rewarding perspective from which to believe in both himself and the world around him.[5]

Ruskin, however, never seems to have attained this illuminating perspective. He accepted most of Carlyle's negative ideas about society, and many of Carlyle's positive ideas as well, but he absorbed imperfectly (if at all) the philosophical—and even mystical—faith upon which Carlyle based his own thinking. Most of all, he seems to have been emotionally unconvinced that the great soul of the world was just. His letters of the 1870's, in fact, show that he came to feel that evil ran through all things—evil in the form of a personal devil that Carlyle had long ago cast off with the rest of his Hebrew old clothes. Without Carlyle's metaphysical sophistication or his ability to *feel* the grand truth of a thought, Ruskin found his wider range of interests and his keener faculty of analysis to be more a curse than a blessing. The internal war between his intellect and his emotions never stopped. Instead, it left the battlefield too scarred for further fighting.

Ruskin's later letters shed light on his tragic ambivalence, and his

[4] See Benjamin E. Lippincott, *Victorian Critics of Democracy* (Minneapolis, Minn., 1938), p. 67: "Righteousness was not for [Ruskin] the aim of man, as it was for Carlyle. Ruskin believed in right conduct, but also in happiness; in fact, he held that happiness was the ideal at which man should aim."

[5] "You have perfectly shown the value of sincerity in *any* faith moderately concurrent with the laws of nature and humanity," Ruskin wrote to Carlyle on June 27, 1874 (Letter 143). But Oliver Elton remarks that, though both Ruskin and Carlyle had the same "mixture of intense conservatism with extreme paucity of dogma," and though they compensated for it through the "intensity with which they held to their primary tenets," Ruskin seems not to have shared Carlyle's faith "in the ultimate might of goodness" (Elton, *Survey of English Literature, 1830–1880*, I, 230–31).

incomplete absorption of Carlyle. Much as he was influenced by Carlyle's historical works, for instance, he does not seem to have grasped the metaphysical views that lay behind Carlyle's idea of history. His letter of March 31, 1867 (Letter 70), shows him asking Carlyle to write him a guide through history and to explain what makes "the Spaniard of today" what he is. Even later, after he has read *The French Revolution* and proclaimed Chelsea to be his "theatre of History—& Humanity," [6] he cannot understand why Carlyle should favor the Germans in the Franco-Prussian War; nor can he really share Carlyle's belief in anything German—including even Goethe, who was such a tremendous shaping force in Carlyle's life. His own convictions about history are simpler and more moralistic than Carlyle's. With no commitment to ideas about the progress of justice and civilizations, he uses a historical approach closer to that found in the Old Testament: he is greatly concerned with the elements of "national character," and with the rise and fall of individual nations. He equates piety with strength, and because he cannot envision the changes of centuries he sees moral decay as a much more urgent and alarming phenomenon than did Carlyle. He thus becomes much more intense and impatient than Carlyle, places greater faith in systems and institutions, and tries to instigate the mechanics of change at a rate that leaves Carlyle shaking his head in disbelief. Furthermore, while he shares Carlyle's aristocratic views and insists upon the need for great men, he makes no mention of any heroes of his own, and (with some justification) he has reservations about several of Carlyle's—especially Frederick the Great.[7] Although he has a natural tendency to revere kings and great men, he has just as natural a tendency to see them as men rather than as embodiments of greatness. John Hobson, noting this fact, has cited it as an example of the conflict between Ruskin's "analytic faculty" and his "emotional faculty." Ruskin believed in heroes, Hobson points out, but he had "an uncommonly shrewd eye for their defects." [8] He thus continued to stress the virtues of authoritarianism, but could find no single hero to show his readers as a model of authority.

Most revealing of all is Ruskin's persistent request to Carlyle for positive religious ideas during the late 1860's and the 1870's. That Ruskin could say, on May 1, 1869, that *Sartor Resartus* was the book that belonged to him more than any other of Carlyle's works, and then exclaim that he had "nearly all my clothes to make," is an irony of

[6] See Letter 97.
[7] See Letters 120 and 187.
[8] *John Ruskin: Social Reformer* (1898), p. 188.

most unfortunate dimensions. Coming so late in his life, it shows the desperate futility of his position, arising in large part from his inadequate absorption of Carlyle's faith. The irony is intensified in 1874, when Ruskin tells Carlyle, "I don't know what your own inner thoughts are of the faith," then complains that Carlyle does not "say what a Master ought now to teach his pupils to believe . . . ," and finally says "I can't get my foundation on *any* faith." [9] The very fact that he had to ask Carlyle for positive religious ideas, after supposedly making *Sartor* a part of him, shows that he did not understand Carlyle's concepts because he did not *experience* them. To put it in terms that *Sartor* itself defines, one might say that Ruskin lost his Wordsworthian sense of communion with benevolent Nature and entered the pit of the "Everlasting Nay" early in life, but that he never learned to see both himself and the world as Carlyle learned to see them during the experiences he presents in his great spiritual autobiography. The 1850's and 1860's may well have been Ruskin's "Center of Indifference," but the pattern of conversion seems to have stopped at that stage for him, even though he tried to commit himself to the doctrine of action in his later years. When Diogenes Teufelsdröckh abandons his excessive concern for himself and goes off (presumably) to dedicate his life to action, he does so because he has reached a state of inner harmony that makes his deeds the natural extension of his faith and being. But when Ruskin, in the 1870's, went off to build roads, drain marshes, preach to the aristocracy, and found revolutionary agricultural communities, he did so because he hoped that action and deeds would produce faith and inner harmony. The result was predictably ineffectual. His deeds were numerous but incomplete, and they lacked coherent direction. They were accompanied by a tense search for faith and a final need to accept the universe on some spiritual principle. Thus we can see him in his last years, turning first to spiritualism and then to a kind of medieval, simplistic interpretation of Franciscan Catholicism, while the religious experience of *Sartor* fades farther away from him and Carlyle watches in helpless silence, until he finally sees the inner reality of Nature as evil.

Somehow, Carlyle had learned to synthesize reason and emotion in a complex but rewarding process of belief. The polarity of his thought left room for paradox and doubt, and the breadth of his experience could reconcile many opposites. But Ruskin could not enjoy this hard-won and precarious peace. The gulf between his rational and his emotional approaches to the world widened, rather than narrowed, in the

---

[9] See Letters 141, 143, and 159.

course of his life. It is, of course, another great irony that he never achieved the harmony of being that he so devotedly preached, while Carlyle, who so often seemed enraged and discordant, managed to retain some portion of inner resolution to his dying day. Whether Ruskin or Carlyle is to be more admired is a question that the individual reader must answer for himself.

Ultimately, the evaluation of Carlyle's influence on Ruskin must also be made by each reader. Lord Clark of Saltwood, a recent anthologist of Ruskin, has evaluated Carlyle's influence negatively:

His [Carlyle's] influence on Ruskin's style . . . seems to me to have been salutary. But I cannot say the same for his influence on Ruskin's thought. Carlyle's mind was tough and could accommodate the toughness, not to say the brutality, of heroes. Ruskin's mind was tender, and the ruthlessness of leadership did not really suit him.[1]

There is much justice in this view, although its emphasis on Carlyle's authoritarianism is misleading, as is its implication that Carlyle was in some way the cause of Ruskin's final illness. Ruskin, as we have seen, had an innate tendency to be Carlylean before he ever met Carlyle, and much of his development was both self-instigated and inevitable. It is true that Carlyle enlarged and intensified tendencies that Ruskin already had, but it is equally true that he gave Ruskin at least a temporary sense of direction by contributing encouragement and specific ideas that helped to organize Ruskin's thought and develop his social conscience toward the usefulness that Ruskin wanted so much. If it can be argued that Carlyle thereby helped tear down the foundations of Ruskin's sanity, it can also be argued that Carlyle helped postpone Ruskin's insanity. He gave Ruskin a focused sense of social mission to replace his frustration at being a "mere" prophet of art. If Ruskin had been even more heavily influenced by Carlyle, perhaps his insanity might have been postponed even further. We shall never know. The correspondence between the two men shows that Ruskin was more a disciple of Carlyle than many people have believed, but less a disciple of Carlyle than Ruskin himself believed. He remained himself through it all. His unique qualities may have brought him to self-destruction, but they also took him to greatness, and carried his voice to places that Carlyle himself could not have foreseen.

[1] Kenneth Clark, *Ruskin Today* (New York, 1965), pp. 268–69.

I

A SINGULAR SIGN OF
THE TIMES

"The spirit and purport of these Critical Studies of yours are a
singular sign of the times to me, and a very gratifying one."
Carlyle to Ruskin, March 9, 1851
Letter 1

❧

LETTERS 1-26

March 9, 1851, through March 15, 1860

Ruskin publishes *Stones of Venice*. He resumes London life after the
annulment of his marriage. Publication of *Modern Painters*, volumes
III, IV, and V. His preparations for his new role as social critic.
Carlyle works on *Frederick the Great*.

1. Carlyle to Ruskin

Chelsea, 9 March, 1851

Dear Ruskin,—

I did not know yesterday till your servant was gone that there was any note in the parcel; nor at all what a feat you had done! A loan of the gallant young man's memoirs[1] was what I expected; and here, in the most chivalrous style, comes a gift of them. This, I think, must be in the style *prior* to the Renaissance! What can I do but accept your kindness with pleasure and gratitude, though it is far beyond my deserts? Perhaps the next man I meet will use me as much below them; and so bring matters straight again! Truly I am much obliged, and return you many hearty thanks.

I was already deep in the "Stones;"[2] and clearly purpose to hold on there. A strange, unexpected, and, I believe, most true and excellent *Sermon* in Stones—as well as the best piece of School-mastering in Architectonics; from which I hope to learn in a great many ways. The spirit and purport of these Critical Studies of yours are a singular sign of the times to me, and a very gratifying one. Right good speed to you, and victorious arrival on the farther shore!— It is a quite new "renaissance" I believe, we are getting into just now: either towards new, *wider* manhood, *high* again as the eternal stars; or else into final death, and the murk of Gehenna[3] for evermore! A dreadful process, but a

---

Letter 1. Approximately half of the MS, from "The spirit and purport of these Critical Studies . . ." to "Adieu: here is an interruption," is in the possession of the estate of Mrs. Helen Gill Viljoen. Pbd complete in Collingwood, I, 175–76.

[1] Probably a reference to Sir Herbert Edwardes (1819–68), who, as a young lieutenant, had bravely led English troops to victory at Kinyeri, India, in 1848. Edwardes (now a major) was in England in 1850–51, and in the winter of 1850 had published an account of his campaign, entitled *A Year on the Punjab Frontier: 1848–1849.* He had also married Emma Sidney, the stepdaughter of John James Ruskin's physician, Dr. Grant, and had thus gained the friendship of the whole Ruskin family. John Ruskin later edited Edwardes' journals of the 1848 campaign and published them under the title *A Knight's Faith* as part IV of *Bibliotheca Pastorum* (1885). Carlyle, in a letter to Charles Kingsley on March 21, 1851 (MS: NLS, 3823.243), mentions having just read Edwardes and calls him "a gallant brisk young fellow."

[2] Ruskin's *The Stones of Venice,* volume I, published in March 1851. For "Sermon in Stones," see Shakespeare's *As You Like It,* II.i.17: "Sermons in stones and good in everything."

[3] Gehenna, one of Carlyle's favorite words, refers to the valley of Hinnom, near Jerusalem. It was a place of abomination where fires were continually kept burning to destroy the city's refuse, and it thus became a synonym for Hell in the New Testament. Carlyle's handwriting here makes my use of the word "murk" disputable. Collingwood

needful and inevitable one; nor do I doubt at all which way the issue will be, though which of the extant nations are to get included in it, and which to be trampled out and abolished in the process, may be very doubtful. God is great:—and sure enough, the changes in the Construction of Sheepfolds,[4] as well as in other things, will require to be very considerable!—

We are still laboring under the foul kind of influenza here, I not far from emancipated, my poor wife still deep in the business, though I hope past the deepest. Am I to understand that you, too, are seized? In a day or two I hope to ascertain that you are well again.—Adieu: here is an interruption, here also is the end of the paper.

With many thanks and regards.
[signature cut away]

2. *Ruskin to Carlyle*

Denmark Hill, Camberwell
Monday, 23rd January [1855]

Dear Mr. Carlyle

I am some thoughts of making a true *foray* upon you this evening— having been rendered desperate by Woolner's[1] telling me that it was *three years* since I had seen you.— but this morning it looks so much as if—could I once get to Chelsea—you might have some difficulty in getting quit of me again till a thaw came—that I will not venture—. Only I warn you that I really must come & see you one of these days, if you won't come & see *us*.

People are continually accusing me of borrowing other men's thoughts, & not confessing the obligation. I don't think there is anything of which I am more utterly incapable than of this meanness—but it is very difficult always to know how much one is indebted to other people—and it is always most difficult to explain to others the degree in which a stronger mind may guide you—without your having at least

---

(I, 175) has "mask," which may be right; and Peter Quennell, *John Ruskin: The Portrait of a Prophet* (1949, p. 74), has "marsh," which seems incongruous. Another possible reading is "mark."

[4]A reference to Ruskin's "Notes on the Construction of Sheepfolds," an essay on Protestant church unity that was appended to volume I of *The Stones of Venice*. Carlyle here uses the phrase in the same symbolic manner Ruskin used it, with reference to the Biblical "and there shall be one fold, and one shepherd" (John 10:16).

Letter 2. MS: NLS, 555.1. Pbd: Ruskin's *Works*, XXXVI, 183–84; and in Cook, I, 476–77.

[1]Thomas Woolner (1825–92), English sculptor and poet.

intentionally, borrowed this or the other definite thought.[2] The fact is, it is very possible for two people to hit *sometimes* on the same thought —and I have over and over again been somewhat vexed as well as surprised at finding that what I really *had* and *knew* I had, worked out for myself, corresponded very closely to things that you had said much better. I entreat you not to think when (if you have ever patience to do so) you glance at anything I write, and when you come as you must sometimes, on bits that look like bits of yourself spoiled,—to think that I have been mean enough to borrow from you knowingly, & without acknowledgment. How much your general influence has told upon me, I know not—but I always confess it—or rather boast of it, in conversation about you and you will see what—considering the way malicious people *catch* at such confessions, is certainly a very frank one— at the close of the lecture of which I send you a Builder containing a report.[3] I have marked the passage, p. 639.

—with sincere regards to Mrs. Carlyle, believe me, my dear Sir,

Most faithfully Yours,

J Ruskin

3. *Carlyle to Ruskin*

Chelsea, 23 Jan^y, 1855

Dear Ruskin,

It has been a thousand times a sorrow in my thought that I have not seen you all this time; and the worse as I partly had to give myself the blame of it. I got your sumptuous and excellent gift (Stones of Venice II and III to add to Vol. I); and never had the grace to utter one word of acknowledgement (I do suspect and believe) manifold thoughts and emotions to that effect as I necessarily had! Sinner that I am,—heavy-laden bewildered sinner; not willing one, no;—whom, in your goodness, and candor of merciful judgement, you cannot but forgive!—

The truth is, I have been eclipsed into nearly utter darkness this long while, by Prussian dust[1] and other sore sufferings hard and tender; and

---

[2] Ruskin had been accused, for instance, of borrowing from Pugin, in an anonymous review of *The Stones of Venice* in *The Ecclesiologist*, XI (August 1851), 276. These accusations gave rise to Ruskin's essay on "Plagiarism," which he appended to volume III of *Modern Painters* in 1856 (*Works*, V, 427–30), and which includes a further discussion of the nature of Carlyle's influence.

[3] A report of Ruskin's lectures on "Decorative Colour." For this and the "passage," see *Works*, XII, 507 and n.

Letter 3. MS: Rylands, English MS 1191/1. Pbd: Sanders, pp. 210–11.

[1] Carlyle had been working hard since 1852 on his *History of Frederick the Great*.

Carlyle's house in Cheyne Row, Chelsea, in the 1870's. Photograph by J. Patrick. Courtesy of the Edinburgh University Library.

have *done* very little except diligently hold my peace, in hope of better days,—wh^h on some occasions takes a good deal of doing.

If you will really come and see me any evening or day (especially after half-past 3,—or otherwise giving *warning* before), it will be a chosen mercy to me, I can answer you. The view of a sincere human soul, even *without* thought in it, is like music to me; how much more if there is an opulence of human thoughts and cheery ingenuities and socialities in it!

We have tea every ev^g (hardly ever out) about half past 7. If I had a horse,—nay if I had *not* a lame foot at present (thanks to the genus *Sutor citra crepidam*,[2] with quack *Sutor* powerless to make a *real* shoe!) I w^d come to Denmark Hill myself, in a hurry, and seek you out.— Manage to come, speedily, if you will do me a most welcome kindness.

Yours truly
T. Carlyle

4. *Carlyle to Ruskin*

Chelsea, 23 May, 1855

Dear Ruskin,

There is clearly nothing to be made of that *Grampus* Wake.[1] The leather jerkin of George Fox has buttoned him up from the sight of the Sun and Moon. We (that is, you) fairly offered him human help, if he would have had it.

I am very sorry to hear of your coughing and continued sickliness.

[2] Carlyle underlines the word "*citra*" twice, and the phrase is thus roughly translated as "shoemaker *without* a shoe." It is a play upon a familiar Latin proverb—"Ne sutor supra crepidam"—that nineteenth-century schoolboys found in Pliny the Elder's *Natural History* and translated as "let the cobbler stick to his last." Its more literal translation, with the addition of Pliny's verb *judicaret*, means "let the shoemaker not judge beyond shoes," and Carlyle's phrasing thus describes a cobbler who could not even judge shoes, or had never made a good shoe to "stick to." When Ruskin published his *Unto This Last* in 1860, an anonymous critic in *Fraser's Magazine* (November 1860, p. 659) suggested changing the title to "Beyond the *Last*." "We never knew a more signal violation of the good old rule, '*Ne sutor ultra crepidam*,'" he grumbled.

Letter 4. MS: Rylands, English MS 1191/2. Pbd: Sanders, pp. 211–12.

[1] Unidentified. Sanders (p. 211) believes this may be Henry T. Wake, an engraver whom both Carlyle and Ruskin knew. He adds, however, that he has found "no hint of his being a Quaker or of any difficulty which would have caused Carlyle to call him a Grampus (fish of the dolphin family)." The *Oxford English Dictionary* lists another meaning for "Grampus," which was in use by 1836—"a person who breathes loud." Wake may thus have "spouted off" and got into trouble somehow.

Carlyle praises George Fox's "perennial suit of leather" as a symbol of testimony against "Mammon-worship" in *Sartor Resartus*, book III, chapter I. Its use in this letter, however, seems to imply excessively impractical testimony on Wake's part.

Be patient, quiet;—this is a monition to you to take more time.! My impression generally is that you go too fast; in many senses, this;—and that you will have to learn the other side of the business too,—what infinite profit there occasionally is in sitting absolutely down (were it even in a desperate mood, on hest of inexorable necessity), and *doing nothing*. This is very true; and I hope you will learn to believe it:—at all events, act upon it at present, on trust; and be *loyal* to the idle Summer Air, till that has set you on your feet again.

Some afternoon, were you once home, you must come out hither, and take me to your place; I will wander about with you till night; and not fail to make my way *back* on my own resources. That, I suppose, might answer? To myself it would be a pleasant half holiday; a pause in the sandy wilderness on reaching some convenient stopping-place. Keep it in your eye.

My Prussian affairs are as bad almost as *Balaklava*,[2] and indeed resemble that notable Enterprise of the Turk War in several respects,—in this especially, that *I* had no business at all to concern myself in such an adventure, with such associates; and that a *good* result to it does not seem (for most part) so much as possible! "The longer you look at it," as Sir John Burgoyne[3] says, "the less you see your way through it." Really my own experience ought to teach me pity and some touches of forgiveness towards the poor Noodles who are professing to lead armies out there, and publishing the shame of England, at home and abroad, in too sad a manner! They too are willing to *die* mutely in the mud, and so expiate their Noodlism in some small degree. A thing worth being laid to heart, by certain others of us!—

Don't quarrel with Tunbridge![4] I remember it as a place of airy expanses and respectable chalk-hills; where at least the winds blow free about one. Take thankfully what it offers; and let us see you home again, soon, and in sound worthy condition.

Yours ever truly,

T. Carlyle

[2] Scene of the infamous "Charge of the Light Brigade," which took place on October 25, 1854, during the Crimean War.

[3] Sir John Fox Burgoyne (1782–1871). The quotation has not been identified. Carlyle may have seen it in a newspaper, or heard it from Burgoyne himself. Burgoyne, who was inspector-general of fortifications and was second in importance to Lord Raglan during the Crimean War, had been recalled to England in February 1855, and the British press had made him a scapegoat for advising the disastrous march to the southern side of Sebastopol in 1854.

[4] Ruskin was at Tunbridge Wells, being cured of an illness by his cousin, Dr. William Richardson. See *Praeterita*, part III, chapter 1, paragraph 11 (*Works*, XXXV, 484).

5. Carlyle to Ruskin

Chelsea, 29 June, 1855

Dear Ruskin,

The wife when consulted says Thursday or Wednesday; let it therefore be Wednesday or Thursday, at your discretion, next week.

Of the times etc. I say nothing; only put down, by way of guidepost, on my side of the border, the following facts:

1. Work ceases with me about 3½ in the afternoon, so that if left till towards that time, an adventure does not cost me anything,—tho' I am willing to spend, too, on a good adventure.

2. I taste no food between breakfast and dinner; dine, with convenience (provided it be with simplicity, on something like a mutton chop), at any hour between 5½ and 7½.

3. We should like to be home not later than 11; and are capable of shifting easily in that particular.

Arrange all these things as seems good on *your* side of the Border; and please send us a line to say how they are settled,—I mean what the hour of your appearance *here* is.

[signature cut away]

6. Ruskin to Carlyle

[ca. October 1855]

Not that I have not been busy—and very busy, too. I have written, since May, good six hundred pages,[1] had them rewritten, cut up, corrected, and got fairly ready for the press—and am going to press with the first of them on Gunpowder Plot day, with a great hope of disturbing the Public Peace in various directions. Also, I have prepared about thirty drawings for engravers this year, retouched the engravings (generally the worst part of the business), and etched some on steel myself. In the course of the six hundred pages I have had to make various remarks on German Metaphysics, on Poetry, Political Economy, Cookery, Music, Geology, Dress, Agriculture, Horticulture, and Navigation, all of which subjects I have had to "read up" accordingly, and this takes time. Moreover, I have had my class of workmen out sketch-

---

Letter 5. MS: Rylands, English MS 1191/3. Pbd: Sanders, p. 212.

Letter 6. MS not located. Pbd in above form in Collingwood (rev.), pp. 158–59.

[1] Volumes III and IV of *Modern Painters*, in which most of the subjects Ruskin mentions here are found.

ing every week in the fields during the summer;[2] and have been studying Spanish proverbs with my father's partner,[3] who came over from
Spain to see the Great Exhibition. I have also designed and drawn a
window for the Museum at Oxford; and have every now and then had
to look over a parcel of five or six new designs for fronts and backs to
the said Museum.

During my above-mentioned studies of horticulture, I became dis-
satisfied with the Linnaean, Jussieuan, and Everybody-elseian arrange-
ment of plants, and have accordingly arranged a system of my own;
and unbound my botanical book, and rebound it in brighter green,
with all the pages through-other, and backside foremost—so as to cut
off all the old paging numerals; and am now printing my new arrange-
ment in a legible manner, on interleaved foolscap. I consider this ar-
rangement one of my great achievements of the year. My studies of
political economy have induced me to think also that nobody knows
anything about that; and I am at present engaged in an investigation,
on independent principles, of the natures of money, rent, and taxes, in
an abstract form, which sometimes keeps me awake all night. My
studies of German metaphysics have also induced me to think that the
Germans don't know anything about *them*; and to engage in a serious
enquiry into the meaning of Bunsen's great sentence in the beginning
of the second volume of the "Hippolytus," about the Finite realization
of infinity;[4] which has given me some trouble.

The course of my studies of Navigation necessitated my going to
Deal to look at the Deal boats;[5] and those of geology to rearrange all
my minerals (and wash a good many, which, I am sorry to say, I found
wanted it). I have also several pupils, far and near, in the art of illumination; an American young lady to direct in the study of landscape
painting, and a Yorkshire young lady to direct in the purchase of Turners,—and various little bye things besides. But I am coming to see
you.

[2] Ruskin taught a landscape-drawing class at the Working Men's College from October 1854 to May 1858. He frequently had his class come with him to sketch in the country during the summer term.

[3] Pedro Domecq, one of John James Ruskin's partners in the wine trade, was Spanish
and owned vineyards at Xerez (now Jerez de la Frontera), though he lived in Paris.

[4] Christian, *Freiherr* Bunsen (1791–1860). The reference is to his *Hippolytus and His
Age*, 4 volumes (Longman, Brown, Green, and Longmans, 1852), II, 38. In appendix II
of volume III of *Modern Painters*, entitled "German Philosophy," Ruskin calls Bunsen's
phrase concerning "finite realization of the infinite" "a phrase considerably less rational
than 'a black realization of white.'" See *Works*, V, 424–25.

[5] Ruskin went to Deal to make studies of shipping for use in the preface to his book
on Turner's *Harbours of England*, published in 1856. See *Works*, XIII.

7. *Jane Carlyle to Ruskin*

Friday [July 1855]

Dear Kind Mr Ruskin,

If "virtue is ever its own reward," (which "may be *strongly* doubted," as we say in Edin^r) decidedly the same cannot be said of *discretion*! How long might I have been discreet, "silent", and all that sort of thing, without accomplishing any such good for myself, as in blurting out that foolish little thought; "I wish *this* had been the 14th" ^1 —

Oh yes! Won't we go with you again, and be glad *to*! M^r C says "Well, my Dear, I desire nothing better than to spend another afternoon with Ruskin out there", and with me, the only possible objection I could find, were I to assuage all tho' my female mind, is that I in a manner begged an invitation. But really, I had no such thought at the moment, and you are a man, are you not, who believes what one says, in as much as you mean what you say yourself.

Yours very sincerely
Jane W Carlyle

8. *Carlyle to Ruskin*

Chelsea, 3 dec^r, 1855 —

Dear Ruskin,

Among other things you gave me to think about, since you were here I have been twice or thrice reflecting upon your munificence to those old dames at Deptford.^1 Your Gift of £10, no doubt it was gratifying to your own pious feeling, — but would it not have been safer, in the given case, to have added it to our subscription? The old women have, to my own knowledge, had an amount of £130 (140 with yours) added, this year, to their usual income; and the question, what good it may have done them? appears to be a little uncertain!

Well, the £10 is gone; but the intended annuity of £5, it is upon this

Letter 7. MS: Duke University. Hitherto unpbd. The back page of the letter has "Mrs T. Carlyle / July 1855" in Jane Carlyle's hand.
^1 July 14 was Mrs. Carlyle's 54th birthday.
Letter 8. MS: Duke University. Hitherto unpbd.
^1 Carlyle and Ruskin, with several other notable literary men, were starting a fund to help the aged and indigent Misses Lowe, one of whom was the goddaughter of Samuel Johnson. A manuscript fragment by Carlyle, in Yale University's Beinecke Library, identifies the ladies as "Ann Elizabeth Lowe (born 29 Sept^r), the *God-daughter*" and "Frances Meliora Lucia Lowe (born 20 jan^y 1783)," daughters of the man mentioned in Johnson's will as "Mauritius Lowe, Painter." See Carlyle's "Statement and Appeal for a Certain Miss Lowe and Her Sister," *Times,* November 1, 1855.

that I will now obtrude upon you my surmise. If your purpose is quite *fixed* in regard to this new eminent piece of bounty, would it not suit as well if you join with us in regard to it;—namely threw in a sum at once which would purchase such an annuity, or enabled us in some authentic way to mark you as a Donor to that annual extent? I am very clear that, for the sake of the two old women themselves, the two adventures ought to be thoroughly *conscious* of one another, and to be virtually if not formally *one*. In fact, I think, unless you surrender your project altogether, it would be worth *your* while to consider this suggestion, which it is well worth *our* while to impress upon you!

The truth I have just retrieved from an interview with Forster[2] (who in the temporary absence of Dickens is my sole coadjutor in that matter of the "Miss Lowe Subscription"): Forster reports rather a beggarly amount of the last 18 days,—an increase of precisely £30 (£202..2 this w^k);—and in short a clear demonstration that the voluntary Principle has just about exhausted itself; and that in the way of "falling like dew", £202..2 is nearly what the British Nation can do in this matter. More could be raised, no doubt, by "aggressive methods" common in such cases, and probably a touch of that (applied at least to the 20 or 25 $gent^n$ that signed the Memorial) will be resorted to, as coming within the rule: but farther it will not be pleasant to go,—at least if one can help it at all.

It was in these circumstances that I mentioned your bounteous doings; and Forster, headlong mortal, urged me to apply to you as above; which in fact I did not till now see the very great impudence of doing! However, it is done; and I know also you will forgive me, and not call it quite so impudent as I assure you I do myself.

So let us *announce* your Donation, or in some way to join it with our (too limited) "fall of dew"? If you absolutely dislike it, say No, at once, and fear nothing. Yours ever truly,

T. Carlyle

9. *Ruskin to Carlyle*

4th December [1855]

Dear Mr. Carlyle

I *wish* everything to be arranged as you wish it—or rather as you think best—for as you wish in all respects I fear it can never be. I hope

---

[2] John Forster (1812–76), biographer of Dickens, Goldsmith, and Landor, was Carlyle's good friend and a member of the "Misses Lowe" committee.
Letter 9. MS: Victoria and Albert Museum, 65a. Hitherto unpbd.

however that the first £10 will not be lost as I gave it not to the old lady to buy horses with—or "let a coach be called"[1]—but to Miss Erdman[2]—on the understanding that there was a difficulty in the Washing department—pitiful to hear of in an old ladies house— which said sum might do away with—as I hope it has. For the rest— every autumn at fuel time—my 5 pounds shall be ready, and you shall dispose of them in whatever way you think best[3]—and may inform the public of the same in any manner most calculated to impress them with the propriety of Subscription— I had a happy too short evening the other day. Coming again, soon. Ever affectionately Your serv^t Carlyles

J. Ruskin

10. *Carlyle to Ruskin*

Chelsea, 6 dec^r, 1855

Dear Ruskin,

Many thanks. This is abundantly all that could be wished,—for certain, all that I ever did wish,—and I think it must satisfy Forster himself; to whom I now send your announcement,[1] with charge to make it known in the way most advantageous and least obtrusive. And may the Heavens reward you (as I have no doubt they will, in their own fashion) for your piety to the *Manes* ["spirit"] of Turner[2] and compassion for the straits of those old women.

For the rest you must undertake the bestowal of your Annual Bounty yourself: the sole reward I claim in reference to these poor Misses Lowe is that, after this unblessed bother is once all down, I

[1] Probably an echo of *Hamlet*, IV.v.72–73: "Come, my coach! Good night ladies, good night, sweet ladies. . . ."

[2] Miss Erdman was the custodian of the Misses Lowe Fund.

[3] A line inserted here, in Carlyle's handwriting, reads: "this I have quite declined. T. C."

Letter 10. MS: NLS, 1796.93. Pbd: Sanders, p. 213.

[1] On the same day, December 6, Carlyle wrote to John Forster: "Here is Ruskin's answer: he does not give us the money all at once, but makes the Annual £5 sure (during his life at least), and even permits us to announce it in good time: really that is about the same thing, and we ought to be content with it. I have told him *you* were to have charge of making it known to the Public in the way most advantageous and least obtrusive." (MS: NLS.)

[2] The painter J. M. W. Turner had died in 1851. Ruskin had, of course, praised and discussed Turner in every volume of *Modern Painters* to date, and had recently done work on the *Harbours of England*. In addition, he had been made one of the executors of Turner's will, and was awaiting cessation of litigation over it so that he could begin the exhausting job of cataloguing Turner's remaining drawings for the National Gallery.

may never in this world or the next hear more of them;—that is a reward I cannot dispense with, nor must you grudge it me! God knows I had no need of new weight thrown upon my poor back just at present; and I have often asked myself, why in devil's name I, of all mortals, got connected with such a thing? I will take better heed another time!

With regard to Miss Erdman, and the £10 towards washing purposes (for now I see it must have referred to that), there came to me a distracted scratch of writing from the elder Lowe some time since, very high and defiant of the said Erdman, but otherwise quite Sybilline and unintelligible,—for the rest, of no worth whatever:—I have looked for it this morning to read; but I suppose it is gone into the fire. Whither may all nonsense soon go. Amen, Amen!—

I am longing for your Book,[3] the feeling you have about matters is altogether my own; and you have not yet hacked your sword blunt in striking at the stony head of Human Stupidity, but rush upon it as if it were *cleavable* or conquerable,—more power to your elbow. It is and will be incumbent . . . our whole soul, till we die; . . .[4] that it cannot be cleft, but is unconquerable by the very gods (according to Schiller), and lasts till the Day of Judgement at soonest.

We go into Hampshire for a month (17th Dec[r], that is, Monday week), and return on the 17th Jan[y]; observe these dates and remember that you are due here,—payable the sooner the better.

I find a Misses-Lowe annuity of £25 will come rather cheaper than was expected; in spite of the weather symptoms, we can still hope to achieve some approximation to that. That, with your five pounds, solves the problem, therefore,—or at least *absolves* me from it.

[signature cut away]

11. *Carlyle to Ruskin*

Chelsea, 18 Jan[y], 1856

Dear Ruskin,

Last night your beautiful book was handed in to me; a very handsome welcome indeed on one's return home. I have already galloped extensively up and down over it; find that it will be excellent read-

---

[3] Volumes III and IV of *Modern Painters*, published in 1856.

[4] Part of letter cut away. The reference to Schiller is undoubtedly to the quotation cited by Joseph Slater in his edition of *The Correspondence of Emerson and Carlyle* (New York: Columbia University Press, 1964), p. 145. Slater cites Schiller's *Die Jungfrau von Orleans*, act III, scene vi, as the source of the quotation, translated by Carlyle in his *Life of Schiller* as "Stupidity can baffle the very gods" (Carlyle's *Works*, XXV, 164).

Letter 11. MS: Rylands, English MS 1191/4. Pbd: Sanders, p. 214.

ing for me in the coming nights. That is the real Sermon of the season
and Epoch; Sermon "meaning many things,"[1] by the most eloquent
Preacher I have heard these 20 years, and who does mean wholly what
he says. A beautiful enthusiasm is in him, a sharp flashing insight and
very potent melody of utterance; a noble audacity, and confidence in
Truth's gaining the victory,—much *sooner* than it will do! For the
odds are terrible against it, in these utterly decadent and indeed quite
rotten times. I wish you long life; and more and more power and opportunity of uttering forth, in tones of sphere-harmony mixed with
thunder, these salutary messages to your poor fellow creatures,—
whom (including us) may God pity. I also am, for my own particular
share of the booty, grateful, as I may well be,—beyond what shall be
written at present.

You will do us a real kindness any night you turn your steps hither,
the earlier the better, for all manner of reasons. Also, if you see the
good Mr. Furnivall,[2] say I had his letter, but cannot possibly undertake
to "talk," on any terms, to any class of creatures, my usual lodging
being about the Center of Chaos (not far from that, just now), which
is a very taciturn inarticulate locality.

We wish you heartily "many good New Years." There are few
whom they will suit better. I am always,

Yours with many thanks,

T. Carlyle

12. *Carlyle to Ruskin*

Chelsea, 5 March, 1856

Dear Ruskin,

It is certainly a sad "*land*-change"[1] these words of the Sea-Hero
have suffered in the House of Lords. "This bit of work done, or else
my life!" into, "That peacock's feather got, or else life lost!"— A most
sordid platitude; well worthy of being reprobated and rebuked.[2] If in-

---

[1] Volume III of *Modern Painters* was subtitled "Of Many Things."

[2] Frederick James Furnivall (1825–1910), English scholar of philology and literature,
who was at the time teaching, and helping to administer, at the Working Men's College.

Letter 12. MS: NLS, Acc. 3187. Hitherto unpbd.

[1] A pun on "sea-change." See Shakespeare's *The Tempest*, I.ii.399–401: "Nothing of
him that doth fade / But doth suffer a sea-change / Into something rich and strange."

[2] On March 4, 1856, a debate was held in Parliament on a motion, introduced by
Philip Henry Stanhope (the fifth Earl Stanhope) to create a British National Portrait Gallery. The motion was passed, and somewhere during the proceedings Stanhope delivered
the quotation from Lord Nelson that Carlyle refers to in this letter. Carlyle's letter to
Lady Ashburton in this same month tells us more of the incident: "Ruskin is in a great
passion with Lord Stanhope and the poor House of Lords for that Reading of Nelson's
last speech: 'A coronet or Westminster Abbey' said his poor Lordship, instead of 'Vic-

deed there *is* any public still left to whom you can appeal, on behalf of the Heroic, against platitudes done in high places and low? Which we are bound to believe there is; tho', for my share, I often think I do not know where it lives at present,—and in fact have taken shelter by withdrawing out of the dirty welter altogether for the time; and never by any chance look into a morning Newspaper; but keep well to windward rather, while these big Tumbrils of the Spiritual Night-soil are in passage, poisoning the blessed air of the Heaven-sent new Day of one's life! Do you, therefore, if you still have faith, pitch into that turpitude; and call a dull-nosed public to look at it: I can have no opportunity upon it. I should not have known what you meant, had not a man happened to call yesterday, with some rumour that there had been a Debate (bless the mark!) *about* having a National Picture Gallery, wh^h has long been an aspiration of mine. "A *Coronet* or Westminister Abbey": O Heavens, Oh Earth!—

You are a happy swift man; I here, slower than the snail or the boring worm and less human, am very unhappy; buried in endless Giant-Mountains of Prussian Pedantry, Prussian Stupidity and *In*fidelity; seeking a poor prize after all, even if I should attain it! However, I shall perhaps get *out* one day, and that will be blessedness enough: We must have faith.— Your Book[3] is scatering [*sic*] the astonished cohorts of chaos into strange agitated groups, I perceive. Which is the natural effect of it, and surely a salutary one by way of preliminary. Go on and prosper.

My wife here has caught cold a week ago, and sits prisoner; otherwise we are in the old way. Ought you not to come and see with your eyes now at last?

Yours ever truly,
T. Carlyle

13. *Carlyle to Ruskin*

Chelsea, 27 March, 1856

Dear Ruskin,

I learn for certain (tho' I have not Southey's Book by me) that the Stanhope phrase imputed to Nelson is *not* an error, but unfortunately

---

tory or West^r Abbey,' nobody correcting him; which sets the high moral small-beer of Ruskin all into a froth. Instead of 'this piece of work done, or else my life!' to make it 'that peacock's feather got, or death in seeking it!' What a platitude and turpitude, thinks Ruskin and decides to 'pitch into it' (as he says) asking me first to do so; who refuse utterly, tho' in a benevolent manner. *Ach Gott, ach Gott!*" (MS: Northampton.)

³ Volume III of *Modern Painters*.
Letter 13. MS: NLS, Acc. 3187. Hitherto unpbd.

as good as correct: "A peerage or West^r Abbey!" said the Admiral, in very deed, before the Battle of Aboukir went off,[1]—a saying proving the existence of not a little wind in the heroic Admiral!

Do not, therefore, pitch into poor Stanhope about it, at least not till you have ascertained!—

Every morning lately there are Denmark Hill Eggs here, rare in quality, and agreeable even to the human *mind*; which pleasantly recall the visit we had. Let there be another at *much* shorter interval, we pray you;—*quam primum* ["first thing"]: why not?

My wife is still weak; but gets out when the sun is shining or the wind in a safe quarter.— I am pretty nearly brokenhearted in these Prussian Dust-whirlpools; yet *shall* get out if I live.—

Yours ever truly
T. Carlyle

14. Carlyle to Ruskin

Chelsea, 2 May, 1856

Dear Ruskin,

We know not what night you are coming; but hope only it will be soon. I have got your Fourth Volume[1] (best thanks for such a gift), and have not yet time to read it except in snatches, but struggle forward towards a freer day before long. You have an enviable and admirable power of clearing off, in articulate swift piercing utterance, the divine indignation that may be lying in you against the genus charlatan; whereby you can then say *Exoneravi animum meum* ["I have disburdened my soul"], and proceed to new enterprises: it is very different, and I assure you a much worse case, when said indignation *cannot* be got cleared off, but lies sticking upon a man, like burning sulphur on the skin of him,—like to drive the poor soul mad till he somehow or other do get rid of it! *Euge*; ["well done"]—and be thankful to Heaven.

---

[1] The actual words of the great admiral were "Before this time to-morrow, I shall have gained a peerage or Westminster Abbey." See Robert Southey, *The Life of Nelson* (1890), p. 122. The occasion for the remark was the dinner that Nelson gave for his officers, his "band of brothers," just before entering Aboukir Bay in the late afternoon of August 1, 1798, where he would completely annihilate the French Mediterranean battle fleet in what later came to be called the Battle of the Nile. Nelson's expectations were quite correct. Having survived the engagement with but a superficial wound to the head, he was created Baron Nelson of the Nile and of Burnham Thorpe by letters patent as soon as news of the victory reached England.

Letter 14. MS: NLS, Acc. 3187. Hitherto unpbd.
[1] Of *Modern Painters*.

It seems the genus charlatan has broken out in strong counter-cry, in some of the Reviews, this month: that also is very well, and indicates to a man that the physic has begun griping, [*sic*]—more power to it. I can well understand how a comfortable R.A. reading these Books of yours, may be driven to exclaim, "I, stiff old stager, cannot *alter* according to this Ruskin's precepts: I must either blow my brains out, or convince myself that *he* is wrong!"——Nevertheless I bid you be gentle withal; consider that it is a stupid bedrid old world, *torpid* except at meal-time this long while; and never would, in Art or elsewhere, correspond anyway handsomely to the Ideal of its duties. Besides it makes a dreadful squealing, if you whip it too hard; and does you a mischief in the long run.— This is Pot speaking to Kettle, you will say,—and truly with too much reason. Pot has been longer on the fire (that is all), and regrets his extreme blackness, if he could have helped it by any method!

I have a message for you, or indeed two messages. The first is from Lady Ashburton,[2] a very high lady both extrinsically and intrinsically, who invites you hereby to her Party at Bath House for Wednesday Evg next: the place, as you perhaps know, is in Piccadilly (first gate, to left in Bolton Street there), the hour of rally is probably 10 or after, and the Party I suppose will consist of the usual elements in their highest figure of perfection. Perhaps you will consent to have a look at such a thing in its best perfection, for once? There are very fine Pictures in the House, and many of them, Durer's Murillos etc., etc: and I certify the Host & Hostess to be themselves highly worth knowing. If you thought of coming, it would be pleasantest if we all went together;— tho' that, for practical result, is not of the least moment:—we two (unfortunately, I may well call it) are to *dine* previously that night, somewhere in the Portman Square region, and wd need to be taken up there (with a good loss of distance to you) if you pleased to like that method of entrance. Either way will do, if indeed you decide to go at all; which I may privately hope or not, but have no business to advise or desire in an audible manner.

The second message is from Lord Ashburton: You made an Address at Manchester lately; which perhaps was printed, separately or at least in the Newspapers: his Lordship (an amiable, clear-minded, *high-minded* man,—uniformly high in volitions at least) desires to see a

---

[2] William Bingham Baring, second Lord Ashburton (1799–1864), and his wife Harriet Mary (1805–57), both mentioned in this letter, were old and dear friends of Carlyle. (See also Letter 40, n. 3.)

copy of this address; and bids me ask it of you.[3] Comply if you can; even take a little trouble to comply.

And this is all I had at present: sufficient for the day is the evil thereof![4] You will have to write your determination on those important points. We are out on Saturday Ev⁹, not otherwise, nor like to be, except as here indicated.

> Yours ever truly,
> T. Carlyle.

15. Carlyle to Ruskin

> Chelsea, 5 May, 1856

Dear Ruskin,

Our dining place on Wednesday (day after tomorrow) is "71 Gloucester Place, Portman Square" (Mr. Rennie's);[1] and it is now proposed that you should call for us there at 10½,—half past 10;—we will of course come down to you directly, and that will bring us to Bath House in excell^t time. To get out of it again, with a carriage—*ille labor hoc opus*[2] (like the route to a certain other place);—but we can advise about that too, if such is your resolution.

I have little doubt the *Oxford* Address is what Lord Ashburton meant, but I could not find him yesterday, on trial;—and it was agreed I should take you to him in person Wednesday evening, and let him tell his own story. Take no trouble therefore about the Address till then,—unless by accident you hear again tomorrow, wh^h is not likely.

Mr. Rennie, 71 Gloucester Place, Portman Square; at ½ past 10 Wed^y Ev⁹: that is the essential point;—and I will hope a pleasant meeting.

> Yours always truly,
> T Carlyle

[3] The "Address at Manchester" was actually Ruskin's "Address to the Workmen at the Oxford Museum," delivered in Oxford on April 26, 1856. See *Works*, XVI, 431–36. Subsequently, on May 16, Carlyle wrote to Lord Ashburton (MS: Northampton), enclosing an "old newspaper" that Ruskin had given him, containing "Ruskin's speech at Oxford to his assembled mechanics."

[4] See Matthew 6:34.

Letter 15. MS: Duke University. Hitherto unpbd.

[1] George Rennie (1802–60), sculptor and politician. A Haddington man who had known Mrs. Carlyle from the time of his youth, he had just returned from the Falkland Islands, which he had governed since 1848. For a description of the event mentioned in this letter, see Wilson, V, 216–17.

[2] *Aeneid*, VI, 129: "hoc opus, hic labor est." The reference is to Aeneas' eventual return from Avernus.

16. Ruskin to Jane Carlyle

[ca. November 1857]

Dear Mrs. Carlyle,

I like this little composition very much, but it isn't quite right—nor can I suggest what would put it right—I can only do as you bid me, & mention the little things which seem to me wrong.

1st. Books too visible got up for colours sake—& too much in Harlequinad squares. Books should always be grave in colour, especially books behind the head of a historian's wife. Everybody would want to know what you *could* have been reading.

2. The masses of red in shawl a little too equal in weight, & buff corners of bookcase ditto.

3. Too much insistance [*sic*] on slender waist.

4. Angle here[1] very awkward. Three lines should never meet in this way.

5. People will say that Mrs. Carlyle is indolent.

6. Bar of bookcase horizontal above head too conspicuous.— That's all, I think. Nero[2] will be delightful.

Ever affectionately Yours and Mr. Carlyle's
J. Ruskin

17. Ruskin to Jane Carlyle

[ca. November 1857]

Dear Mrs. Carlyle,

The points to be stated in your interior-or finish [?] painter respecting his perspective are simply these. That if he stands at any point he choose in the room, and tries to get his canvas to hide from his eye all that he has drawn of it, he will find that he cannot do it. He thus violates the first rule of perspective by making his point of station imaginary, or rather impossible—the perspective is only true for a point

---

Letter 16. MS: NLS, 555.2. Hitherto unpbd. The letter has no date, but the watermark on the paper is dated 1857. This letter, and its successor, both describe a painting by R. Tait called "A Chelsea Interior." Tait began the painting in the spring of 1857 and finished it in late November or early December. Ruskin had been in Scotland with his parents until mid-October, and so could not have seen the picture until then.

[1] Ruskin draws a figure here. See the accompanying illustration.

[2] Mrs. Carlyle's dog, who was also in the picture.

Letter 17. MS: Alexander Turnbull Library, Wellington, New Zealand. Hitherto unpbd. See note to the previous letter.

4.

angle here very
awkward.
Three lines
should then
meet in
this way

5. People will say
Mrs Carlyle is indolent.

Bar
6. ~~Bar~~ of bookcase
horizontal above head
too conspicuous.

— That's all. I think.
Nero will be delightful.

Ever affectionately yours Jelly Carlyle

J Ruskin —

Letter from Ruskin to Jane Carlyle, ca. November 1857, page two (Letter 16). Courtesy of the National Library of Scotland.

within about six inches of the picture's surface which is at *least* a foot too little. This station point should have been a foot and a half from the surface at least.

The second point to be noted is that even in the supposition of his point of station being possible, I believe the returning distances are not drawn to true scale. I am not *quite* sure of this, but I think he has given the inner room too much recess by an inaccurate use of his measuring line. If he will cut three inches off the top and bottom of his picture however it will be very nearly right.

Kindest regards to Mr. Carlyle.

The book I sent yesterday is of no use to *me*, and is very highly spoken of by the French themselves; but if it is only like the rest—I will take it away again when I come next. Dear Mrs. Carlyle,

Most truly yours,
J. Ruskin

18. Ruskin to Thomas and Jane Carlyle

[after Thursday, March 17, 1859]

Dear Mr. & Mrs. Carlyle,

When may I come & see you?

Friday—Saturday—Monday—or Tuesday—evening?

I've been in Yorkshire. In, also, lands of figurative Rock and moor[1]— hard work—& peat bog puzzle.

No end visible.

Not getting on with German.

Frederick yet unread.

Nothing done.

All sorts of things undone— Stitches run down.

Entirely dim notions about what ought to be done. Except—that I ought to come and tell you all about it.

Always affectionately Yours,
J. Ruskin

Letter 18. MS: NLS, 555.3. Pbd: Ruskin's *Works*, XXXVI, 304. In a note on the same page, Cook and Wedderburn add: "The letter is undated; but the first two volumes of Carlyle's *Frederick* were published at the end of 1858, and in March of 1859 Ruskin was in Yorkshire! See Vol. XVI, p. lxvi." Ruskin, in fact, returned home from Yorkshire on Thursday, March 17, 1859.

[1] Ruskin had visited Yorkshire from February 25 to March 1, in order to check the topography of J. M. W. Turner's Yorkshire drawings. Before that, he stopped at Buxton Moors in Derbyshire, then went to Manchester on February 21 to deliver his lecture "The Unity of Art." See Burd, *Winnington*, p. 98 n. 3; p. 103 n. 2.

19. Carlyle to Ruskin

Chelsea, 19 April, 1859

Dear Ruskin,

We are in great misery here: my poor wife, after escaping all winter, has fallen into the worst cold I have ever seen her have; and suffers very much; *weak* too as an infant,—tho' I strive to flatter myself, *not* growing worse, but contrariwise. I caught a cold on the same occasion (last paroxysm of July-December weather),—or rather *renewed* a cold I have always obscurely had since a "bathe in the Baltic" last autumn;[1] but I try to keep it at the staff's end, and do not hithermore allow it to interfere with business. Absolute *silence* being the rule here just now.— I will come riding out to Denmark Hill, on Thursday (day after tomorrow): and call you over the coals for half an hour, if you will be at home. Near 5 P.M.;—no, let us say "4.20 or so", and be away before 5 again. Don't write, *unless* you have something to object.

That heaving about, and circling among the eddies, is not a pleasant process; but you will (to your astonishment perhaps) have various bouts of this kind in your wide voyage; and they are not unsalutory [*sic*], still less can be dispensed with, tho' so disagreeable to the natural man.

If the Natural Man is *totally* at a loss for a career, let him read with attention this American Letter wh^h came this morning;—surely that opens a career *talens qualens* [such as it is]! As the letter is not to be answered, you can burn it for the poor young Lady's sake.[2]

Yours always,
T. Carlyle

20. Ruskin to Jane Carlyle

23rd Nov. [1859]

Dear Mrs. Carlyle,

I have had to go down into the north since I came from abroad,[1] and have been sharply unwell since and am still confined to the house, but

---

Letter 19. MS: NLS, 1796.97. Pbd: Sanders, p. 215.
[1] Actually in late August of 1858.
[2] The young lady cannot be identified.
Letter 20. MS: NLS, 555.4. Hitherto unpbd.
[1] After his return from the Continent, Ruskin spent the latter part of October and the early part of November at Winnington Hall, a school for girls in Cheshire. He had first

unless I hear from you to the contrary I shall come the first evening in next week that I am well enough.— I have been nearly crushed by the badness of German painting, & all that it signifies of worse evil. "Vanity, the clearest Phasis of the Devil in these days."[2]

—I think I shall have to give up painting—writing—talking— everything but reading—and I read little now but Mr. Carlyle.— Fiction sickens me, because it is fiction. I am weary of it. Truth depresses me—because it is true. Not that one can find much very plainly written. And it depresses me also never to have had a line from you, though I heard you were both on the whole well, in Scotland.

I trust I may find you so in good truth, when I come.

Ever with sincere regards to Mr. Carlyle.

Faithfully and affectionately Yours,

J. Ruskin

21. *Ruskin to Jane Carlyle*

[December 3, 1859]

Dear Mrs. Carlyle,

I hope I shall hear that you are better—I have been looking over my Durer's and find an impression of the melencholia[1] which, though not a first rate one, is good enough to show the principal characters of the plate—and I having no better—(it is a matter of great difficulty to get fine impressions of this plate)—can only *hope* Mr. Carlyle may think it worth placing in a house where so much noble work has been done—this being, as I suppose, intended for the type of noble earth labour.

The next time I come, I will bring a number of Durers with me, to look over—I am so selfish as to want to hear what Mr. Carlyle says of them.

---

visited the school in the previous March, having apparently been invited to do so by Miss Margaret Alexis Bell, the headmistress. Ruskin enjoyed his visit there so much that he paid many calls there in future years, and the school became important to him. Two of his works—*The Elements of Perspective* and *Ethics of the Dust*—grew directly from his experiences there. For an admirable record and discussion of his entire experience at Winnington, see Burd, *Winnington*.

[2] The quotation is from *Sartor Resartus*: "It would go to the pocket of Vanity (which is your clearest phasis of the Devil, in these times)" (Carlyle's *Works*, I, 191). The thought was repeated in an earlier letter to Clarkson Stanfield on August 22, in which Ruskin said that German painters "have much real feeling and extensive knowledge and considerable power of thought, the whole rendered *utterly* valueless by the intensest, most naive, most ridiculous, most absorbing, most helplessly ineradicable vanity that ever paralysed Human art" (*Works*, VII, liii).

Letter 21. MS: NLS, 555.5. Hitherto unpbd.

[1] The famous *Melencholia I*, by Albrecht Dürer (1514).

—I hope Mr. Carlyle caught no cold by his unmanageable conduct at the door—that snowy evening.

(Best love to Nero—with *condolences*)[2]

Always affectionately both y's—
J. Ruskin

22. *Ruskin to Jane Carlyle*

[December 1859]

Dear Mrs. Carlyle,

I am so very glad you liked the things & especially the flowers—for indeed the Melancholy is not exactly likeable. What it means—no one *knows*. "Cavernous meaning" is just the word for it.

In the main, it evidently means the full sense of the terror-mystery—turmoil—responsibility of the world, ending in great awe & sadness—and perpetual labour—(as opposed to French legerete [*sic*]—lightly crowned with budding bay—winged—as in true angelic service—(The Wolf hound of fiercer sorrow laid asleep at her feet.) Strong bodied. Having the Keys of all knowledge. Compare Tennyson's—

> Seemed to touch it into leaf,
> The Words were hard to Understand[1]

Ever affectionately Yours,
J. Ruskin

Poor little Nero. But he will love you just as much, even when he is blind—and move his little paws just as prettily.

23. *Ruskin to Carlyle*

[Late December 1859]

Dear Mr. Carlyle,

This weather hardly lets one manage one's pen; much less one's horse: We never hoped for you on Sunday: I am only sorry you had the trouble of writing about it;—don't do so any more—I only want you to come precisely when you are in the way & the liking thereof. I am

---

[2]Nero, Mrs. Carlyle's dog, had been run over by a cart two months earlier, and was severely injured. He died in January 1860.

Letter 22. MS: NLS, 555.6. Pbd: Ruskin's *Works*, XXXVI, 328.

[1]See *In Memoriam*, lxix, 18–20. Ruskin has omitted line 19.

Letter 23. MS: NLS, 555.7. Hitherto unpbd.

always at home by dinner time on Sunday, at latest; my father generally all day: of course till the frost ends we have no hope: But I can't
come but at nights either in this bitter weather—at least unless it
drives one to extremities. I *must* come, somewhere about Tuesday or
Wednesday to wish you happy New Year. I'm going to make Christmas & New Years presents of "Past and Present" chiefly. I find everything that has to be said on any matter is all in that, and other people
may forever hold their Peace. (I'll hold mine;—if I can get a little to
hold.) My hands are too cold to write. Love to Mrs. Carlyle. Ever devotedly Yours,

J. Ruskin

24. *Ruskin to Carlyle*

3rd February [1860?]

Dear Mr. Carlyle

I should have come long ago—but it is really a shame to take horses
about in wet weather & on such ground. I cannot enough thank you
for your kind letter. I will come to tea the moment the weather breaks
a little— With sincere regards to Mrs Carlyle.

Ever respectfully & gratefully, Your
J. Ruskin

25. *Ruskin to Jane Carlyle*

Monday [1859 or 1860?]

Dear Mrs. Carlyle,

I am hindered this evening but hope to come tomorrow & to find
cold better. ever yours & *his* affectionately.

J. Ruskin

26. *Carlyle to Ruskin*

Chelsea, 15 March, 1860

Dear Ruskin,

The door had no sooner closed on you than the maid brought in her
Cigar Box,—the third that I have had from that cornucopia of a
House: a shame to think of! This is what may be called *cigarring* a

Letter 24. MS: Berg Collection, New York Public Library. Hitherto unpbd. Ruskin
does not give the year in which this note was written, and I have placed it in 1860 only
because of its slender meteorological relevance to the letter before it.
Letter 25. MS: NLS, 555.9. Hitherto unpbd.
Letter 26. MS: Rylands, English MS 1191/5. Pbd: Sanders, p. 216.

man for his difficult adventure, as they talk of "coaling" a steamer to go thro' the seas. Truth is, I am not yet half way thro' the First Box, tho' I carry something of it daily in my pocket; and the Horse of himself pauses at the fit places, inviting me to smoke and be thankful. I can only say, and think, you are very good.

The new *Dürer* is hung up in fine light, and I study to make acquaintance with it before it returns home. The invincible grave simple *Ritter*,[1] industriously riding on his way, with such a load of sorrow whh he makes not the least complaint of, pleases me more and more— less and less I am pleased with his two detestable companions;[2] who, I incline to think, lie beyond and below the real domain of Art, tho' they are very true to Nature, too, and attend any man, tragically visible to *him*, if *not* to others. The Picture I guess to have no other meaning than that universal symbolical one.— Of the other Dürers which you showed us, the Scarlet Woman, with the flames bursting out, and the universe all going to live rubbish (like a cheese to mites) under her guidance,—is his most vivid in my memory; but by far the most pleasant there, is St. Hubert in the primeval woods of Liege, so beautifully sculptured out, he and they, and what they contain for a devout simple heart. Excellent pious Dürer, who made himself an ornament to this world, in his day and generation! —

I wish you were not going off in May to paint pine needles! Are there not plenty of unpainted needle-woods and beautiful umbrageous creatures nearer home? "The finest trees that grow in the Temperate Zone" stand all about, not far from Denmark Hill, I am told! *Cor inquietum est* ["the heart is restless"].

I expect to ride out again, in the interim, some day soon.

Yours most truly

T. Carlyle

---

[1] Dürer's *Der Ritter* (generally known as *Knight, Death, and Devil*). Ruskin has a lengthy discussion of this and the *Melencholia I* in volume V of *Modern Painters*. See *Works*, VII, 310–12.

[2] I.e., Sin and Death.

II

A MINORITY OF TWO

"Meantime my joy is great to find myself henceforth
in a minority of *two* at any rate!—"
Carlyle to Ruskin, October 29, 1860
Letter 27

LETTERS 27-79

October 29, 1860, through June 25, 1867

Ruskin publishes *Unto This Last* and "Essays on Political Economy" (later *Munera Pulveris*). He travels to Switzerland. Publication of *The Cestus of Aglaia*, *Ethics of the Dust*, and *The Crown of Wild Olive*. Courtship of Rose La Touche. Quarrel with Carlyle during publication of *Time and Tide by Ware and Tyne*.

Carlyle finishes *Frederick the Great*. Jane Welsh Carlyle's declining health and death. The Governor Eyre Defense Committee. Trip to Menton. Work on the *Reminiscences* and "Shooting Niagara and After." Carlyle's niece, Mary Aitken, comes to live at Cheyne Row.

27. *Carlyle to Ruskin*

Chelsea, 29 Oct^r, 1860

Dear Ruskin,

You go down thro' those unfortunate Dismal-Science people,[1] like a Treble-x of Senna, Glauber and Aloes;[2] like a fit of British Cholera,—threatening to be fatal! I have read your Paper with exhilaration, exultation, often with laughter, with "Bravissimo!"— Such a thing flung suddenly into half a million dull British heads on the same day, will do a great deal of good.

I marvel, in parts, at the Lynx-eyed sharpness of y^r logic, at the *pincer*-grip (red hot pincers) you take of certain bloated cheeks and blown-up bellies:—more power to y^r elbow (tho' it is cruel in the extreme)! If you chose to stand to that kind of work for the next 7 years, and work out there a result like what you have done in painting: yes, there were a "something to do,"—not easily measurable in importance to these sunk ages. Meantime my joy is great to find myself henceforth in a minority of *two* at any rate!—

The Dismal-Science people will object that their Science expressly *abstracts* itself from moralities, from &c &c: but what you say, and show, is incontrovertibly true, that no "Science" worthy of men (and not worthier of dogs or of devils) has a right to call itself "Political Economy," or can exist at all except mainly as a fetid nuisance and public poison, on *other* terms than those you now shadow out to it for the first time.[3]

On y^r last page, and never till then, I pause slightly, not too sor-

Letter 27. MS: Yale University Library. Pbd with omissions in *English Illustrated Magazine*, IX (November 1891), 105–6, and in Wilson, V, 406–7. Pbd in full, with discussion of text, by M. H. Goldberg in *TLS*, May 16, 1935, p. 313, and by Van Akin Burd in *Boston University Studies in English*, III (1957), 51–57.

[1] Believers and preachers of utilitarian doctrines of political economy. Carlyle seems first to have used the phrase in 1849, in "The Nigger Question." See his *Works*, XXIX, 354.

[2] Senna, Glauber's salt, and aloes were three purgatives popular at the time. Carlyle is referring to Ruskin's *Unto This Last*, which was appearing in the *Cornhill Magazine*.

[3] Responding to Carlyle's evaluation in a letter to Dr. John Brown on November 11, 1860, Ruskin said that "the value of these papers on economy is in their having for the first time since money was set up for the English Dagon, declared that there never was nor will be any vitality nor godship in him, and that the value of your ship of the line is by no means according to the price you have given for your guns, but to the price you have given for your Captain. For the first time I say this is declared in purely accurate scientific terms; Carlyle having led the way, as he does in all noble insight in this generation." (MS: Bembridge.)

rowfully, and appeal to a time coming. Noble is the spirit then too, my friend; but alas it is not Philanthropisms that will do then,—it is Rhadamanthisms[4] (I sorrowfully see) wh^h are yet at a very great distance! Go on and prosper. I am yours always (sleeping a little better, & hoping an ev^{ng} soon)

T. Carlyle

28. Carlyle to Ruskin

Chelsea, 24 dec^r 1860

Dear Ruskin

I am very sorry I did not write on Saturday, as it was my tho^t to do; but the old groom predicted "a thaw tomorrow," and that there w^d be riding for an unroughened horse. *Hence*—these unpolite phenomena! I much regretted my bright Sunday; but in fact it w^d have been at night,—and please Heaven, there are others coming.

As y^r carriage horses must have got prepared before this,—the plan will now be that *you* come across (positively!) one of these silent evenings. No Xmas here; perfect seclusion,—but great readiness for a visitor of luminous type.

The wife is prisoner; I too in a sense,—but am to ride today, and hope to recover some. Yours ever truly

T. Carlyle

29. Carlyle to John James Ruskin

Chelsea, 4 March 1861

Dear Mr Ruskin,

Many thanks for y^r kind charities and good offices. I have sealed up the first Bottle of y^r exquisite Cognac, much more have left this second one under the wax, and have set them safe aside,—that this house, in case of real emergency, may never be with^t *Brandy that can be depended on.* Meanwhile, the Leith people, in return for my late questionable (or rather *un*questionable) stock, have sent me an *old* sort, deep brown, wh^h I was acquainted with;—wh^h, with^t the least pretension to fineness of flavour, is at least genuine grape-brandy (I be-

---

[4] Severe judges and judgments. Rhadamanthus was one of the judges of the underworld. For a repetition of both the word and the thought, see Carlyle's "Model Prisons," in *Works,* XX, 20.

Letter 28. MS: Yale University Library. Pbd: Sanders, p. 217.
Letter 29. MS: Bembridge. Hitherto unpbd.

lieve),—or at least does not give me a headache when I apply to it. That is the essential; and we may for the present rest thankfully there.

"Martel", I think, was the name given to that late spurious stuff, wh^h came from Leith;—evidently *whiskey* in good part. *Right* Brandy, I doubt, is hardly procurable at all just now. But as matters stand,— especially with such Tobacco as I boast,—one can in some measure defy an evil world!

With many sincere thanks for your ready helpfulness, and friendliness in this and other matters, I remain always,

Yours faithfully
T. Carlyle

30. Carlyle to John James Ruskin

Chelsea, 27 March, 1861

Dear Sir,

Many thanks for your new Gift of Brandy: surely you are very kind to take so much trouble about that matter for me. If it do rank at present among my necessaries of life (wh^h unluckily it does in a small way for the time being), I must admit that I am now well provided. I hope to report favourably of this new specimen when we next meet.

The absence of the Junior Mr. Ruskin has of late been frequently commented upon in this house: we request you to despatch him hitherward directly on his return from Cheshire.

With many thanks & regards,
T. Carlyle

31. Carlyle to John James Ruskin

Chelsea, 23 April 1861

Dear Mr. Ruskin,

The wife was not with me on Friday Ev^g last:—but if she had been? It is a literal fact, I, for my own part, found the Discourse[1] a genial, wholesome, welcome one,—and was very well *pleased*. A failure as a "Lecture" (if you will), as a Discourse tied all up into sheaves, and able to stuff itself mostly into the space of 60 minutes, filling that and no more;—failure that way; but otherwise, I can assure you, quite the reverse of "failure." It did contrive [?] to tear up the big subject (by *explosion* if not otherwise) for one's behoof; gave me the liveliest desire

---

Letter 30. MS: Yale University Library. Pbd: Sanders, p. 217.

Letter 31. MS: Rylands, English MS 1191/8. Pbd: Sanders, p. 218.

[1] Ruskin's lecture "Tree Twigs," delivered on April 19 at the Royal Institution on Albemarle Street. See *Works*, VIII, lix.

to hear that man talk *for a month* on "Newleaves";—and to me individually (tho' you must not mention it in Albemarle Street) gave, so far as I can calculate, more such satisfaction than any the neatest of the many neat Discourses I have heard in that place. "A failure" from over-opulence (*embarras des richesses*): Heaven send us many, very many, of precisely the like kind! These are facts I can myself bear witness to. I recommend, therefore, that everybody return to "the Arms of Murphy" as if nothing were wrong at all or had been: indeed it never struck me that the *Chief Culprit* cared the least ab^t it; or I sh^d have been distressed for the moment, in one transient particular; wh^h I was not at all. This is my affidavit; wh^h I could not have written except to yourself; but I had something else to write this night for the younger Mr. R.; & will now append it here; viz:

That he, said R. Junr is due, and overdue, for weeks back, at this House; and that we expect to *see* him within two or three nights, or *any* night he likes.

The Glasgow Brandy was exquisite,—perfect, so far as I c^n judge.

Yours sincerely,

T. Carlyle

32. *Ruskin to Carlyle*

Holyhead,

Wednesday, 28th August, '61

Dear Mr. Carlyle,

I was *so* glad to get Froude's letter, with your little endorsement[1] and I would have set to work instantly, but you can't think how ill I am; indeed I've not been able to do a sentence of anything all this summer. The heaviest depression is upon me I have ever gone through; the great questions about Nature and God and man have come on me in forms so strange and frightful—and it is so new to me to do everything expecting only Death,[2] though I see it is the right way—even to play—& *men* who are men, nearly always do it without talking about it.

But all my thoughts and ways are overturned—so is my health for the present—and I can do nothing this year.

I'll write to you and to Mrs. Carlyle from Ireland where I'm going today[3]—wind and weather serving.

Letter 32. MS: NLS 555.10. Pbd in Ruskin's *Works*, XXXVI, 382.

[1] At Carlyle's instigation, James Anthony Froude had written a letter to Ruskin in which he praised Ruskin's work on political economy. The MS is not available. For the results of this encouragement, see Letter 39.

[2] That is, without hope of life after death.

[3] Ruskin went there to pay his first visit to the home of Mr. and Mrs. John La Touche,

I have written to Mr. Froude by this post and I am ever your & Mrs. Carlyle's affectionate servant—(though you have Charlotte[4] too).

J. Ruskin

33. *Carlyle to John James Ruskin*

Chelsea, 29 Oct[r], 1861

My dear Sir;

You are abundantly kind and obliging. If it please Heaven, I will come to Denmark Hill some day again, and *stay* dinner![1] Sh[d] November 17th prove favourable in point of weather,—more especially a certain paltry little "breast-cold" wh[h] I have caught, be tolerably shaken off,—Nov[r] 17 shall be the day. In the opposite case, I will at least be punctual to give notice the day before. So that if *you hear nothing*, it is all right.

Yours sincerely
T. Carlyle

34. *Ruskin to Thomas and Jane Carlyle*

Lucerne, 7th November, '61

Dear Mr. and Mrs. Carlyle,

Two days before hearing from my father of Mr. Carlyle's kind little visit[1] I had sent an underlined charge of gravest character, to let me know how you both were. I should have written myself, but was for a month after leaving home this last time, in a state of stupid depression which there was no use in giving any account of. I am now settled here, with a bright room—fire—and view of lake. I draw and paint a

---

in Harristown, County Kildare. Since 1858 he had been engaged as art teacher for the three La Touche children. His interest in Rose La Touche, the youngest child, who was nine years old in 1858, grew and deepened so much that he proposed marriage to her in 1866 (see Introduction and Letter 78). Ruskin's description of his first visit to Harristown is in his *Works*, XXXV, lxvii; his brief but touching discussion of Rose is in pp. 525–34 of the same volume (*Praeterita*).

[4] Charlotte Southam, one of the Carlyles' servants.

Letter 33. MS: Yale University Library. Pbd: Sanders, p. 218.

[1] A sad little note in John James Ruskin's diary for November 14, 1861, says: "Carlyle was to dine with me. Bayne wanting to bring friends—spoil all." (MS: Bembridge.)

Letter 34. MS: NLS, 555.11. Pbd: Ruskin's *Works*, XXXVI, 391. Addr: Mr. Carlyle / 5 Cheyne Row / Chelsea, / London / Angleterre. Pm: Lozern, 8 Nov. 61, Nach M.

[1] A letter from Ruskin to his father on October 31 refers perhaps to this "kind little visit" and its questionable effects: "Account of Carlyles most pleasant. In general however with these sort of people I fancy you would be most comfortable of the two uncomfortablenesses by keeping them, but it did not matter a bit. I will write to them by next post." (MS: Yale University Library.)

little every day—very little, but what I do is now accumulative and I hope will come to something. I am gaining strength gradually;—and learning some Latin & Greek.[2] I do everything as quietly and mechanically as I can. I have little pleasure—and no pain—except toothache sometimes. I forget, resolvedly, all that human beings are doing of ridiculous, or suffering of its consequences; try to regret nothing—and to wish for nothing. I am obliged to pass much time in mere quiet— and standing with one's hands behind one's back is tiresome— I make up my mind to be tired and stand. The nights—if one wakes in them, are sadly long—one tries to think "after all—it is life—why should one wish it shorter"—and one is thankful, in spite of such philosophy, when the clock strikes— (I wonder if one would be—or will be— when it is a passing bell that strikes—which will be the same thing, once for all.) When I've read Xenophon's economist [*sic*], and Plato's republic and one or two more things carefully, I shall finish—if I can— my political economy—of other plans, or hopes, I have none for the present. There is enough, and a great deal too much of myself. Mr. Carlyle will be angry with me for not going on with German, but it is impossible among Germans; the people make me—(or *would* make me if I contemplated them) too angry to endure their language. Switzerland is degenerating—at least its people are—(and the lakes are not so clear as they used to be)— The peasantry seem still nearly what they were—(that is to say, little more than two-legged cattle). The towns-people imitate and hate the French, having neither dignity enough to stand on their own ground, nor beauty or modesty enough to respect these they borrow from. By rifle practice, and much drinking, and making disgusting noises in the streets at night, they are preparing themselves against French invasion. But what of silent and worthy is yet among them I do not see, and have no business to abuse them in general terms.

—I hope to get home before Christmas: but will write again as soon as I know about the time. It would be a great delight to me if Mrs. Carlyle would send me just the merest line to Schweizer Hof, Lucerne, saying how you are both—& that you still believe me to be affectionately yours,

J. Ruskin

[2] For the past few months Ruskin had been helping Rose La Touche learn Latin and Greek, and had been trying to learn German again. For a discussion of Ruskin's studies at this time, see Cook, II, 41.

35. *Carlyle to John James Ruskin*

Chelsea, 14 Nov^r, 1861

Dear Mr. Ruskin,

I really am ashamed under your munificences as to cigars! I was still *two Boxes* strong; and here has another come today. All I can say is, you are very kind; and I return you many thanks the best I have. The Flowers[1] also are praised as "superlative",—tho' my poor wife is not able to put them in their bottles herself today, as she w^d otherwise have taken a half-holiday in doing. She has caught cold, in these inclemencies of weather; & keeps her room, and even her bed, all day.

It is a poor return for such kindnesses to say, what has been forcing itself upon me as too probably lately, that I actually must not venture on Sunday. This weather is of such a raging character; that *bosom-friend* (in the windpipe) still keeps such hold; the poor wife is so ill &c &c: in short, I will postpone it till "the Prodigal" (so let us call him in figurative language) returns from his Swiss wanderings;—and then, I shall be seriously unwell, and things very perverse about me, if I fail! We had a Letter from Lucerne the other day; very kind and pleasant; shadowing out a *hermit*-life among the Mountains yonder,—solitary, affectionate, not without a trace of sadness, but wholesome, diligent, and leading towards *good* that I foresee. So soon as *he* returns—!—

Believe me always, Dear Sir,

Yours sincerely
T. Carlyle

36. *Ruskin to Jane Carlyle*

Lucerne, 24*th* Nov. 61.

Dear Mrs. Carlyle,

Indeed I was just going to write again, and did not expect any answer, for I knew you were ill,[1] but it's so good of you, and I'm sure it made you worse— Doing nice, good things always makes people

---

Letter 35. MS: Yale University Library. Pbd: Sanders, p. 219.

[1] In June of 1861, Ruskin had instructed his young friend George Allen to "let flowers be taken as often as possible to Mrs. Carlyle . . . ," who, he added, "has been very ill." See *Works*, XXXV, 541n. In December he repeated these instructions to his father (*Works*, XXXVI, 399).

Letter 36. MS: NLS, 555.12. Pbd: Ruskin's *Works*, XXXVI, 394.

[1] Ruskin's father had so informed him. "I'm glad to hear of Carlyle—must write again as Mrs. Carlyle is ill," Ruskin wrote to him on November 16, 1861 (MS: Yale University Library).

worse. Only it's wicked of you to teaze me so about that romantic thing—so perhaps it wouldn't hurt you after all.

No, I can't come home yet. There's a difference I assure you—not small—between dead leaves in London Fog—and living rocks, and waters—and clouds— I never saw anything so entirely and solemnly *divine* as the calm winter days are, here— Dead—or living—calm whichever you choose to feel—or call it— Intense sunshine—the fields green, as in summer, on the slopes sunward—but sparkling with dew, frost—and the white hoarfrost on their shadowy sides—mounded and mounded up and far to the pines— They all lost in avenues of light—and the great Alps clear—sharp—all strength and splendour— far round the horizon—the clear streams, still unchained, ringing about the rocks and eddying into green pools—and the lake, taking all deep into its heart under the hills. It is like the loveliest summer's morning at five o'clock—all day long. Then in ordinary weather, the colour of the beech woods and pine on the cliffs—and of the rocks in the midst of the frost clouds!— I never saw such things—didn't know what winter was made or meant for, before— I walked through the Reuss the day before yesterday, just for delight in its clear green water—not many people can say they've done that, for it is the fourth river of the Alps (Rhine—Rhone—Aar—Reuss): and it would have given a good account of me if I had tried it in the summer time—even as it was, it ran like a mill race in the middle, and needed steady walking. No—I can't come home yet—must manage it by New Year's Day, though, I believe.— Yes, it is quite true that I not only don't know that people care for me, but never can believe it somehow. I know I shouldn't care for myself if I were anybody else.— Yes, we'll bring home a Lion[2]—and I think we shall have some satisfaction in looking at it.

I'm just away to-morrow deeper into the Alps, to Altorf [*sic*]—to see how the grimmest of them look in the snow. I'm better than I was, a good deal.— Still very sulky—and reading Latin and Greek, or rather beginning to learn them—but a little comforted in feeling that I am really learning *something* and in the entire peace—and rest—and being able to swear at people and know they're out of hearing.

There's more cracking of whips and barking of dogs than I like— than Slender would have liked, and there are no Ann Pages.[3] The Swiss

[2] Probably a photograph or engraving of the *Lion of Lucerne*, a monument to the Swiss Guards by Thorwaldsen.
[3] See Shakespeare's *The Merry Wives of Windsor*, I.i.79–104: "How does your fallow greyhound, Sir?" etc.

are frightfully ugly—but when I get tired of it, I can always get away
into the pine woods—where it is quiet as the night—or row into the
middle of the lake—where there is often not a ripple. It would be good
for both of you to come here to finish Fredrick—you would have no
influenza—and Mr. Carlyle might enjoy his pipe in peace.

I'll write again from among the deeper Alps.— Mind & get the head
& martyrs all right.— Ever affectionately Mr. C's & yours,

J. Ruskin

37. *Carlyle to John James Ruskin*

Chelsea, 30 Nov^r, 1861

Dear Mr. Ruskin,

The Publisher has sent me the Book of "Selections",[1] as promised;
and it is my constant companion, these evenings, in the few leisure
hours I have;—awaking in me, seriously, the wish that every drawing-
room in her Majesty's dominions were provided with a Copy, and able
to read it with feelings similar to mine! It is many a day and year since
I met with any Book the spirit of wh^h (to say nothing of its lively felici-
tous expression) is so accordant with what I reckon best & truest.—
The idea of the Publisher was surely altogether good: multitudes of
people, who could not get access to the big expensive books, will be
furnished with this as a kind of manual; and no ingenuous soul will
read any bit of it (at least any bit I have fallen in with) wh^h will not
have a tendency to do him *good*, as well as give him pleasure. The
Book is well printed, unusually *correct* for most part; the Portrait has
a good resemblance *a la Richmond*:[2] it is altogether a pleasant little
companion, and a profitable in these bad times;—and I am much
obliged to you for my individual share in the adventure.

My wife continues *room*-fast, sometimes *bed*-fast (wh^h she does not
easily consent to be); but is never yet what we can call very ill. There

---

Letter 37. MS: Yale University Library. Pbd: Sanders, pp. 219–20.

[1] *Selections from the Writings of John Ruskin*, published by Smith, Elder in 1861.
Ruskin's disapproval of this book is expressed in a letter to his father on November 9,
where he calls the book "a form of mince-pie which I have no fancy for." On December
1, however, Ruskin's father sent him this letter from Carlyle, and Ruskin's answer reflects the measure of Carlyle's influence upon him: "I have your nice and kind letter of
1st December, enclosing Carlyle's most interesting and kind also (herewith returned). As
he says the extracts are right, I have not a word more to say against them. It is the books
which must be wrong." (Ruskin to his father, December 5, 1861; both letters are in
Cook, II, 42.)

[2] The portrait of Ruskin on the frontispiece was by George Richmond, Ruskin's
friend.

has been a sad tragedy next door to us (a poor Mr. Gilchrist,[3] a young literary man; one of his children took Scarlet fever, the mother w^d not send it away, others of them took it; and within 5 days illness, the Head of the House is himself lying dead of the disorder);—this of course has been an agitating circumstance on our side of the wall, and has done my own poor Patient a sensible mischief. I believe y^r last flask of perfect Brandy (let that be y^r Thanks for it) went across to poor Gilchrist as *medicine*. I do not think a nobler use c^d have been made of it, tho' it proved unavailing.— We had another Letter from Switzerl^d, with nothing but cheery news. Send my best regards when you write. Yours sincerely,

T. Carlyle

38. *Ruskin to Thomas and Jane Carlyle*

[Lucerne,]
[December 23, 1861]

Dear Mr. and Mrs. Carlyle,

Only to wish you as happy a Christmas as anybody has any business to have. Nice peace on earth and good will to men we have preached and practised—this many a day—have not we? But I do wish that people had feeling enough, when they want a word synonymous with beef and pudding, to use a less solemn one. My father sent me Mrs. Carlyle's love, and it came quite nicely.— I'm coming home for New year's Day at any rate, D.V.[1]

I write you cheerful scraps, because it makes me cheerful to think of you—but it was very cool of Mr. Carlyle to say I was leading a life "with a trace of sadness" in it. I'm entirely miserable—that's all; but it's all right—and I believe I'm stronger than I was.— It is not muscular power that I want so much, though I've no large allowance of that: but the least over thought—above all, the least mortification or anxiety—makes me ill so quickly that I shall have, I believe, to live the life of a monster for some years and care for nothing but grammar. If I

---

[3] Alexander Gilchrist (1824–61). Sanders (p. 220) adds that Gilchrist's *Life of Blake* was published in 1863, and that Gilchrist's "widow Anne Gilchrist wrote *Mary Lamb* (1883). See also *The Letters of Anne Gilchrist and Walt Whitman* (1918) and *The Letters of William Michael Rossetti to Anne Gilchrist*, ed. C. Ghodes and P. F. Baum (1934)."

Letter 38. MS: NLS, 555.13. Pbd: Ruskin's *Works*, XXXVI, 400. The letter is undated, but a letter from Ruskin to his father from Lucerne on December 23 seems to warrant my ascription of the same date here. In it, Ruskin starts by saying, "This was a beginning of a Christmas line to Mrs. Carlyle—I changed it to 'Dear Mr. & Mrs.' and forgot it was on this side of the sheet" (MS: Yale University Library).

[1] *Deo volente* ("God willing").

could make a toad of myself and get into a hole in a stone, and be quiet, I think it would do me good.— My eyes—(and toads have got those too) and ears—(which asses have also)—are too much for me.— "Non veder—non sentir m(e) (sarebbe) gran ventura." [2]

I can't write letters—but I love you both, and would if I could, and long ones. I've got the Lion,[3] photographed—and engraved—and neither are the least like—and it doesn't matter, for the real thing is good for nothing—like the useless "fidelity"—(query "stupidity" & "obstinacy"?) which it commemorates. I've no patience with the Swiss, now,—nor with anybody:—myself included. Goodbye— Ever your affectionate

J. Ruskin

39. Carlyle to Ruskin

Chelsea, 30 june, 1862

Dear Ruskin,

It was, and is, y^r duty to send some tidings of y^{r}self to this address. We are more concerned ab^t you than you seem in the heart to believe;—and therefore reigns no despair here upon the black state you are evidently in: nothing is considered the least *essential* but that your bodily health sh^d keep good, and clear itself of those superficial presences w^h have been annoying of late. Take every precaution *then*, I do earnestly counsel you! The want of every such counsel to myself, or of my following any such, has been such an item in the general invoice to me (invoice highly considerable, you w^d say if you knew it) as swallows *all* the others, and how fitly has with a shudder when I look back

---

[2] Roughly, "not seeing and not feeling would be very fortunate for me." The quotation is from a famous quatrain by Michelangelo entitled "La Notte" ("Night"), the third line of which reads "non veder, non sentir m'è gran ventura." Ruskin's allusion is most appropriate. The poem (written in 1545–46) is an answer to a quatrain by Giovanni Strozzi, which praised the lifelike qualities of Michelangelo's sculptured figure of *Night* on the tomb of Giuliano de' Medici, Duc de Nemours, youngest brother of Pope Leo X, in the New Sacristy of the church of San Lorenzo in Florence. The sleeping figure of *Night* awakes and says:

> While all about one harm and shame and woe,
> How good to sleep and be but marble block!
> Not to see, not to hear is my great luck;
> So do not rouse me then, but please, speak low.

The translation is by Joseph Tusiani, in his *The Complete Poems of Michelangelo* (New York, 1969), p. 96. For the Italian text see the edition of Michelangelo's *Rime* by E. N. Girardi (Bari, 1960), p. 117. See also Harold I. Shapiro, ed., *Ruskin in Italy: Letters to His Parents 1845* (Oxford, 1972), p. 154.

[3] A photograph Ruskin had promised the Carlyles. See Letter 36.

Letter 39. MS: Mr. L. E. Brown. Pbd: with omissions in Collingwood (rev.), p. 202.

on it! [. . . ?] *de expecto*. If you are wise you will.— For the rest, you ought to write *regularly* to Chelsea; some kind of answer will be sent (quite regular ans^r, if we were once thro' this Book); and if no ans^r come, still you are bound to write.

I am finishing vol IV; busy as a poor spent costermonger's ass getting its head over the *last* hill but *one*. For years past I have ceased writing Notes pretty nearly altogether:—not a wise step, I begin to see but it now cannot be mended. Well, and the case at present is: I have read, a month ago, your *First* in *Fraser*;[1] and ever since have had a wish to say to it and you, *Euge, macte nova virtute*.[2] I approved in every particular; calm, definite, clear; rising into the sphere *of Plato* (our almost best), wh^h in exchange for the sphere of *Macculloch* [*sic*],[3] *Mill and Co.* is a mighty improvement! Since that, I have seen the little *green* Book, too;[4] reprint of your *Cornhill* operations,—ab^t ⅔ of wh^h was read to me (*known* only from what the contradict^n of sinners had told me of it);—in every part of wh^h I find a high and noble sort of truth, not one doctrine that I can intrinsically dissent from, or count other than salutary in the extreme, and pressingly needed in Engl^d above all. This "wish" has been steering me more than ever since the green Book. So now I have written. We are tolerably well. Adieu, write!

Yours ever   T. Carlyle

40. *Ruskin to Thomas and Jane Carlyle*

Christmas Evening (not eve), '62

Dear Mr. and Mrs. Carlyle,

I'm sitting by a bright wood fire—which flickers on the walls of a little room about twelve feet square—somewhat stiff in finger, as you

---

[1] The first of Ruskin's "Essays in Political Economy" (later published in book form as *Munera Pulveris*) had come out in the June 1 issue of *Fraser's Magazine*. J. A. Froude, who was editor of the magazine, had already come to know Ruskin (see Letter 32, n. 1), and a letter from Carlyle to Froude on April 4 explains the reason for Ruskin's articles: "Ruskin, I have got to understand, is at last beginning upon his Political Economy. I think, if you were to send him a word or two of incitat^n, you might actually get a Paper out of him for y^r next N^o,—wh^h w^d be a beautiful thing to begin the Summer with!" (MS: Dr. Gordon N. Ray.) See also the Introduction.

[2] A significant and revealing quotation from Virgil's *Aeneid*, IX, 641–42. Apollo, addressing the young Ascanius after a victory, says, "Macte nove virtute, puer; sic itur ad astra!" ("May you prosper in your new-found virtue, boy; thus one goes to the stars!")

[3] John Ramsay McCulloch (1789–1864), Scottish economist and author of *Principles of Political Economy* (1825).

[4] Ruskin's *Unto This Last*, which had been published in book form in June.

Letter 40. MS: NLS, 555.14. Pbd: Ruskin's *Works*, XXXVI, 427.

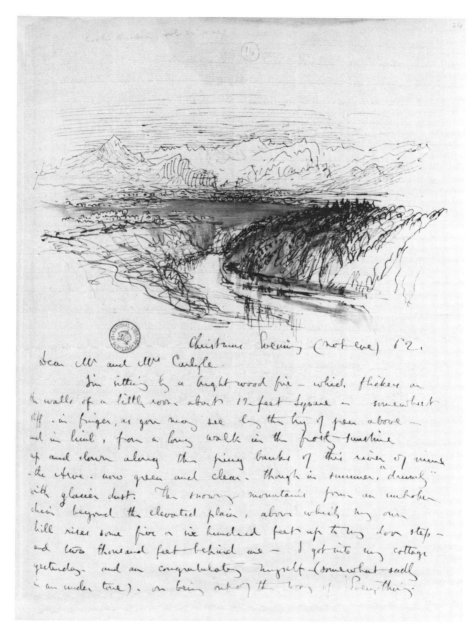

Christmas Evening (not eve) '62.

Dear Mr and Mrs Carlyle.

I'm sitting by a bright wood fire — which flickers on the walls of a little room about 12 feet square — somewhat stiff in finger, as you may see by the way of pen above — and in limb, from a long walk in the frosty sunshine up and down along the piney banks of this river of mine — the Arve — now green and clear — though in summer "dreamy" with glacier dust. The snowy mountains form an unbroken chain beyond the elevated plain, above which my own hill rises some five or six hundred feet up to my door steps — and two thousand feet behind me — I got into my cottage yesterday. and am congratulating myself (somewhat sadly in an undertone). on being out of the way of Everything

may see by the try of pen above¹—and in limb, from a long walk in the frosty sunshine up and down along the piny [*sic*] banks of this river of mine, the Arve, now green and clear, though in summer, "drumly"² with glacier dust. The snowy mountains form an unbroken chain beyond the elevated plain, above which my own hill rises some five or six hundred feet up to my doorstep—and two thousand feet behind me.—I got into my cottage yesterday, and am congratulating myself (somewhat sadly in an undertone) on being out of the way of—Everything.

The month in London was mischievous to me. I got "off" my quiet work, and now my books seem a little dull to me, and the evenings long—and yet life seems to pass in nothing but dressing and undressing—going to bed and getting up again, a night older.

I saw Lady Ashburton³ in Paris for a few moments, and promised to write to you, and did not—having no hope to give you, and thinking that you might as well be anxious as hopeless.

I then travelled on through the night and came in the grey of dawn to the roots of the Alps. While, I see by the papers, there were dreadful gales in England, a keen, but healthy north wind was breaking the Lake of Geneva into chequers of white and blue—dark blue—far laid under the rosy snows of Jura. Now it is quite calm, with clearest light, and soft mists among the pinewoods at morning.

I've been reading Latter days again—chiefly "Jesuitism."⁴ I can't think what Mr. Carlyle wants me to write anything more for—if people don't attend to that, what more is to be said? I feel very lazy, and think—in fact, I'm sure—that after February I shan't write anything more till Autumn again. I can't correct press in Spring time.

I wish you both a happy New Year with all my heart.

Ever your affectionate,
J. Ruskin

41. *Ruskin to Thomas and Jane Carlyle*

[Geneva,]
[January 5, 1863]

Dear Mr. & Mrs. Carlyle,

I mean Mrs., particularly, but I wish you both all feasible happiness, this New Year. But dear Mrs. Carlyle, I want you to be very kind and

---

¹Ruskin has drawn a sketch at the top of the page. See the accompanying illustration.
²Muddied, shadowed, or gloomy. See *Works*, XXVIII, 758.
³Louisa Caroline Mackenzie (1827–1903), the second wife of Lord Ashburton (see Letter 14, n. 2). She had been one of Ruskin's pupils before her marriage in 1858, and remained his close friend thereafter.
⁴The last of Carlyle's *Latter-Day Pamphlets* (1850).

Letter 41. MS: NLS, 555.15. Pbd: Burd, *Winnington*, pp. 392–93. In the upper left-

good, and to show that little miniature you did when you were 14 to a friend of mine—a wise, intelligent, energetic, schoolmistress, of a girls school,[1] where I go sometimes when I want to be—whatever you call it—flattered—or petted—or what not— But I've been much too sulky to stand petting this long while, and haven't been there, and have left all my pupils at a stand still— But I want Miss Bell, and one of the girl-governesses, if she can come too, to call on you, and to see that miniature, that it may show them what a child of 14 can do, when she's going to be a Mrs. Carlyle. And if you like them, I wish you would ask them to tea. You couldn't give a greater pleasure to two more deserving people, and you would give some to a very undeserving one, in Savoy. But this woman, Miss Bell—educated her two brothers—and they went, like idiots for missionaries, and died, and she's got the world to fight with by herself now—and does it nobly, and her school is thoroughly useful and nice. She talks perhaps a little too much generally—but won't with you, and its never nonsense.

I'm a little better— This weather marvellous for beauty and silence—no calm like winter calm. I was up 4,000 ft. above sea today, in deep snow, and was quite too hot when I got down again.

Ever your affectionate,
J. Ruskin

42. *Carlyle to Ruskin*

[early April, 1863]

. . . There is a felicity of utterance in it here and there, such as I remember in no other writer, living or dead, and it's all as true as gospel. . . . What enlightened public will make of it I know not. To be visited with such a dividing joint and marrow! so quiet, so sudden, fatal as

---

hand corner, the MS has "Switzerland, Jany 1863 (A. C.)? [PM^k Geneva 5 Jan^y, 63]" in another hand, probably Alexander Carlyle's. Addr (cited in Burd, *Winnington*, p. 393): Mr Carlyle / 5. Cheyne Row / Chelsea, / London / Angleterre. Pm (cited in Burd, *Winnington*): GENEVE / 3 JANU 63; [LOND] ON / JA 5 63.

[1] Miss Margaret A. Bell, headmistress of the Winnington Hall school for girls, which Ruskin visited frequently. See letter 20 and n. 1. Mrs. Carlyle's "little miniature" has not been identified, but a note in the margin of the MS says "* qu. The Little Tragedy wh' Miss Welsh wrote when 14 years old? A.C." If so this would be "The Rival Brothers," which Jane Welsh Carlyle wrote in 1815.

Letter 42. This is Ruskin's attempt to reconstruct a letter from Carlyle that he had accidentally destroyed. The letter was written soon after Ruskin's last *Munera Pulveris* essay appeared in *Fraser's Magazine* at the beginning of April, and Ruskin had copied some sentences to send home to his father. These sentences, and others he remembered, were included in letters from Ruskin to his father dated April 7 and 11, 1863, published in *Works*, XVII, lxx. The source for the first sentence of the text above is the MS of the April 7 letter in the Yale University Library. I have been unable to locate the MS of the April 11 letter.

the sword (here a proper name for sword I could not read)[1] to the un-happy smith who only knew he was killed by feeling the iron in his inside, and had to shake himself before he fell in two. *Euge!* I tell you I know nothing like it for felicity of expression; John Mill keeps not closer to his dialectics, and he but with one gift, while here are so many;—a man who comes on etymologically, phantastically, pro-phetically (I am not sure of this last word—could not decipher it; if it is right, it means 'eloquently,' but is stronger) all at once. Glad I am that you are in for a continuance—I care not now at what interval: I have lived to see it said clearly that government—(I forget the exact phrase following, but it meant the assertion of authority generally over mob.)

43. *Ruskin to Carlyle*

Denmark Hill
28th June [1863?]

Dear Mr. Carlyle,

The fine weather has really come at last, it seems, and I may claim your promise— I cannot tell you how much pleasure your letter gave me. Will you send me a single line to say when I may come and make prey of you. I should have done so months ago, only one does not like to be so importunate as to take the last excuse for staying at home out of the mouth of a revered friend—or I should have taken that of *the distance* out of yours, long ago.

—Any day next week—perhaps you had better give me choice of two, in case of any inevitableness turning itself up meanwhile—at your own time, I will come & carry you & Mrs. Carlyle off— Truly— our place here looks green, & the hay is deep—and we are on the whole at our best. With sincerest regards to Mrs. Carlyle—believe me most faithfully and gratefully Yours,

J. Ruskin

Thomas Carlyle Esq.

[1] The story of the sword Mimung (or Balmung) is told by Carlyle in his essay "The Niebelungen Lied." The sword was forged by Siegfried's foster father Mimer, who at one time was challenged by the smith Amalias to forge a sword that would pierce his "impenetrable mail." When the time came, Mimer struck Amalias with Mimung. The smith then said "there was a strange feeling of cold iron in his inwards. 'shake thyself,' said Mimer; the luckless Wight did so, and fell in two halves." (Carlyle's *Works*, XXVII, 233.)

Letter 43. MS: NLS, 555.8. Hitherto unpbd. Ruskin gives no year, and my dating of 1863 is admittedly arbitrary. Ruskin had not been at Denmark Hill during June since

44. *Carlyle to Ruskin*

Chelsea, Thursday, 8 p.m.
[late 1863]

Dear Ruskin,

Your benevolent Cousin[1] has been so very obliging as to call; and—I & the ill Chance, lo, we have made such a mess of it as was never seen!

At dusk when I came home from my ride, there was a whirlpool of people in and about the house, one of whom I privately learned was Dr. Quain.[2] I retired to the Kitchen, to smoke perdu, and waylay Dr. Quain. Having had a word from him, I stole up to my bedroom for the usual nap of sleep. I had not got to sleep there, when the maid came knocking with "a Letter, Sir" (your Letter, I did not learn *by* whom). I read the letter, with the bad candle and the bad eyes,—*failing* to make out the first line;—I conclude it was your man Crawley that had brot it; and I sent a verbal ansr as if *by* Crawley for *you*! Not till half an hour ago, on reading the Note deliberately after dinner, did I ascertain for myself what an unutterable absurdity there had been committed;—to my own and especially my poor Wife's very great disappointt:—with the question still in the rear, Is it forgivable and reparable, or is it?

I at once apprise you, at any rate and beg to make a thousand and a thousand apologies to the kind Dr. for what I unwittingly did.

Yours in great confusion
T. Carlyle

45. *Ruskin to Carlyle*

[February 26 or 27, 1864]

Dear Mr. Carlyle,

I have been very far from well—I meant to have come over today, but the weather is wretched & my father has been suffering very griev-

---

1857, and in the summer of 1864 John James Ruskin was dead, and Mrs. Carlyle was too ill to be asked to travel.

Letter 44. MS: Edinburgh University Library. Hitherto unpbd. The date of this letter is conjectural. The Dr. Quain mentioned in it is known to have attended Mrs. Carlyle from September to December of 1863, when she was suffering greatly from neuralgia and other ailments of her age.

[1] Probably a reference to Dr. William J. Richardson of Perth.

[2] Dr. Richard Quain (1800–87), surgeon and professor of anatomy. A member of the Royal College of Surgeons and a Fellow of the Royal Society, Richard Quain had been professor of general anatomy and physiology at University College, London, since 1830.

Letter 45. MS: NLS, 555.19. Hitherto unpbd. The MS has "P. Mk 27 Feb. '64" in another hand.

ously and made us even rather anxious—he is better, but I'm not sure when I can get over—would you send me the *merest* line to say how Mrs. Carlyle is? It would be *very* kind of you.

—Ever affectionately Yours,
J. Ruskin

46. *Ruskin to Carlyle*

[March 1, 1864]

Dear Mr. Carlyle,

So many thanks—I should have been over to see you, but my father is sharply ill and has needed me to be with him the past two or three days—it *was* all this dreadful frost.— I'll write again as soon as he is better.

Ever affectionately Yours,
J. Ruskin

47. *Ruskin to Carlyle*

12th March [1864]

Dear Mr. Carlyle,—You will not think it was out of thoughtlessness or disrespect that I have not written to you. You had enough sorrow of your own, and could by no means help us in ours.[1] To-day I have a note from Lady Trevelyan[2] saying Mrs. Carlyle is much better—this gives me courage to ask for you both. My mother and I are in all practical and necessary ways able for what has come upon us. *She* is very wonderful to me; I have little doubt but that I may yet, if I am spared, procure her some years of no false or slight, but peaceful and hopeful, *happiness*.

Ever affectionately yours,
J. Ruskin

Letter 46. MS: NLS, 555.16. Hitherto unpbd. The MS has "P. M^k.: 1st March '64" in another hand.

Letter 47. MS not located. Pbd: Ruskin's *Works*, XXXVI, 472.

[1] John James Ruskin died on March 3, 1864.

[2] Pauline, Lady Trevelyan, who, with her husband Sir Walter Trevelyan, had been a close friend of Ruskin since 1850. The Trevelyans also became close friends of the Carlyles.

48. Ruskin to Jane Carlyle

Denmark Hill, S.
[December 23, 1864?]

Dear Mrs. Carlyle,

This is the kind of thing I wondered how anybody could be got to print— One of them comes about once a month—here—to my great pride in the distinction above mortals who are beneath the level of prophecy.

Ever yours affect^{ly},
J. Ruskin

Dear love to Mr. Carlyle and happy Christmas to you both.

49. Ruskin to Jane Carlyle

Denmark Hill, S.
Wednesday [1865?]

Dear Mrs. Carlyle,

Indeed it is long, but I have just done a little bit of work which needed me to keep quietly at it: and I was ill in the middle of it which threw all back.

And I thought Mr. Carlyle would have enough to do, & be bothered:—and now it is all right, and I hope to bring him my bit of a book on Saturday, if I may come.

Don't write, if I may, only if I mayn't.

Ever affectionately Yours,
J. Ruskin

50. Carlyle to Ruskin

Chelsea, 22 February, 1865

Dear Ruskin,

You have sent me a munificent Box of Cigars; for wh^h what can I say in ans^r? It makes me both sad and glad. *Ay de mi.*[1]

Letter 48. MS: NLS, 555.18. Hitherto unpbd. The MS has "P.M^k. 23 Dec. '64" in another hand.

Letter 49. MS: NLS, 555.23. Hitherto unpbd. Over the date the MS has "perhaps 1866" in another hand.

Letter 50. MS not located. Pbd: Collingwood, II, 301.

[1] A favorite phrase of both the Carlyles. They first discovered it while reading a Span-

"We are such stuff,
    Gone with a puff—
Then think, and smoke Tobacco—"[2]

The Wife also has had her Flowers; and a letter wh^h has charmed
the female mind. You forgot only the first chapter of "Aglaia;"[3] don't
forget; and be a good boy for the future.

The Geology Book wasn't *Jukes*; I found it again in the Magazine,—reviewed there: "Phillips,"[4] is there such a name? It has ag^n es-
caped me. I have a notion to come out actually some day soon; and
take a serious Lecture from you on what you really know, and can give
me some intelligible outline of ab^t the Rocks,—*bones* of our poor old
Mother; wh^h have always been venerable and strange to me.[5] Next to

----

ish edition of LeSage's *Gil Blas* together in Craigenputtock during the first few years of
their marriage. The exact source is *Gil Blas*, book IX, chapter 5—"Ay de mi! Un año
felice," etc.—and the phrase can be roughly translated "Woe is me." See Wilson, VI,
84–85.

Years later, in a letter to C. E. Norton on October 7, 1884, Ruskin made a revealing
comment on the frequency of the phrase's appearance in Carlyle's letters and speech.
"The world's made up of morts and disses," he said, "and it's no use always saying 'ay
de mi' like Carlyle. I'm really ashamed of him in those letters to Emerson. My own diaries are indeed full of mewing and moaning all to myself, but I think my letters try to be
pleasant." (C. E. Norton, ed., *The Letters of John Ruskin to Charles Eliot Norton*
[Boston and New York, 1905], II, 204.)

[2] An excerpt from a popular poem by George Wither. Carlyle's quotation is inaccurate, though it is easy to understand why the original stanza stayed, however hazily, in
his memory:

> And when the smoke ascends on high,
> Then thou behold'st the vanity
>   Of worldly stuff—
>   Gone with a puff:
> Thus think, and smoke tobacco.

Another reference to this poem can be found in *Sartor Resartus*, ed. C. F. Harrold (New
York, 1937), p. 16.

[3] The first chapter of Ruskin's *The Cestus of Aglaia* had been published in the *Art
Journal* in February 1865.

[4] Joseph Beete Jukes, F.R.S. (1811–69), had been conducting a discussion of Alpine
geology with Ruskin in letters to *The Reader* during October and November 1864. See
Works, XXVI, 553 and n.

John Phillips (1800–74), professor of geology at Oxford, and a friend and teacher of
Ruskin.

[5] On March 1 Carlyle wrote to his brother John: "On Monday I had engaged myself
to Denmark Hill, for Ruskin's superb mineralogical collection and a free discourse upon
the same:—an adventure that proved pleasant enough while it lasted" (Alexander Carlyle, *New Letters of Thomas Carlyle* [1904], II, 225).

Ruskin's knowledge of the comparatively new field of geology was extensive. At the
age of fifteen he had published an essay on the rock strata of Mont Blanc—the first of

nothing of rational could I ever learn of the subject. That of a central fire, and molten sea, on wh^h all mountains, continents, and strata are spread floating like so many hides of leather, knocks in vain for admittance into me these forty years; who of mortals can really believe such a thing! And that, in descending into mines, these geological gent^n find themselves approaching *sensibly* their central fire by the sensible and undeniable *increase of temperature* as they step down, round after round,—have always appeared to argue a *length of ear* on the part of those gent^n, wh^h is the real miracle of the phenomenon. Alas, alas: we are dreadful ignoramuses all of us! Ans^r nothing; but don't be surprised if I turn up some day.

Yours ever,

T. Carlyle

51. *Ruskin to Carlyle*

[February 23 or 24, 1865]

Dear Mr. Carlyle,

Pray come—as you kindly think of doing, and let us have talks, and looks. Geology is just in its most interesting stage of youth—a little presumptuous, but full of strength and advancing life. Its general principles and primary facts are now as certain as those of astronomy, but of—Central fire we as yet know nothing. You shall look at stones, and give them *time*, and see what will come out of them for you, in your own way. I know you will find them interesting. But all the books are dismal, yet full of good work. I will stay in any day for you after Friday. You are sure to catch me before I go out any day, if you are as early as one.— Ever yours affecte,

J. Ruskin

I wish you would read the tenth chapter, especially pp. 112–113, in the book of Lyell's[1] which I send, with some care. The facts are those closest to us, and they are distinct, and very wonderful. If one once understands the relation of the formations of such an island as Ischia to the existing Fauna, all the after steps of geology are thereby measurable.

---

many such articles he was to write over the next fifty years. At Oxford he studied under some of the best geologists of the day, and since 1840 he had been an active member of the Geological Society. For a lengthier discussion of Ruskin's geological interests, see Collingwood (rev.), pp. 205–9, where this letter is also published.

Letter 51. MS: NLS, 555.20. Pbd: Ruskin's *Works*, XXXVI, 481.

[1] See Lyell's *Elements of Geology* (1865), chapter 10.

52. Ruskin to Jane Carlyle

Denmark Hill, S.
[July 13, 1865]

Dear Mrs. Carlyle,

Am I not glad to hear!—even though it is of such pain and though I have the sorrow of knowing you wrote all that with your lame hand.[1] After those last flowers, I went to Winnington where one of the younger governesses was ill of decline, she's now dying— And I never saw an entirely healthy and happy girl burned away like a wax candle before—so it gave me some thoughts, & left the others less time, and her sister less heart for their work, and the school was just at its busiest time so I stayed a day or two longer and gave them some talks by way of such help as I could; so when I came back in a fortnight my mother & I concocted a visit to you—and we got up really a nice flower, and away we went to Chelsea my mother so particular about her two cards! one to be for Mr. Carlyle's mythic presence. So when we got there they said you were in Scotland, but couldn't tell me where, or I should have written long ago.

Please come back and don't go to Folkstone[2] [*sic*]. I've found a doctor here who will make you well if anybody will, for he's so good to this poor girl and has helped her in all sorts of out of the way illness, that made the lungs worse.

—I've had one letter from lady Trevelyan—she's better, and soon coming home. I have not answered it. I can't talk—I've no ideas.— & I never seemed to have so much interrupting business—it drives me wild not to be able to go on with my life for perpetual "musts"—and I don't know what I shall come to, but I can't write for I'm always in bad humour. I'll see about this friend of yours, however. I wrote her last night. I don't remember any Mrs. Hawkes.[3] I remember Miss

---

Letter 52. MS: NLS, 555.21. Pbd in Burd, *Winnington*, pp. 562–63. Addr (cited in Burd, *Winnington*): Mrs. Carlyle / Nith Bank / *Thornhill* / Dumfries-Shire. Pm (cited in Burd, *Winnington*): LONDON / JY 13 65; THORNHILL / JY 14 [65]. The MS has "13 July, 1865" in another hand.

[1] Mrs. Carlyle's right hand had been occasionally lamed by her frequent attacks of neuralgia. See also Letter 53.

[2] In August, Mrs. Carlyle went to Folkestone to visit her friend, Miss Davenport Bromley.

[3] Emilie Hawkes, a friend of Mrs. Carlyle. She became the wife of Carlo Venturi, an Italian friend of Mazzini, who also knew the Carlyles. The MS of this letter has an asterisk after the name, and "Mrs. Hawkes, later Madame Venturi. A. C." penciled in the margin, possibly in the hand of Alexander Carlyle.

Jewsbury.[4] My mother is not well—nervous and dreamy—I am a little anxious—but hope it's only stomach.

Ever your affectionate,

J. Ruskin

53. *Jane Carlyle to Ruskin*

Holm Hill, Thornhill, Dumphriesshire

15 July [1865]

Oh how delightful! My dear Mr. Ruskin! That nice long letter and lovely little Book[1]— Imagine? They came to me the first thing on my Birthday morning![2] Came with all the charm of a Birthday present!— You once gave me strawberries and cream on my Birthday. Do you remember? (I have never seen such strawberries and cream since! nor have I had any such pleasant Birthday since! But all have passed in pain and sorrow!) I like the Book and letter far better, however, because these will *keep*! And, being superstitious a little, as a Scotch woman ought to be, I draw ever so many good omens from the Book and letter beginning a new year of Life for me. One piece of good I clearly divine therefrom; that *you* are not going to forget poor me in the pressure of your avocations and *distractions* but will care for me, and give me flowers now and then, as long as I last!

What a talent for *naming* you have!

"*Of King's Treasuries*

Of Queen's Gardens"[3]

The names lift me already into the sphere of Arabian Nights!

---

[4] Geraldine Endsor Jewsbury (1812–80), Mrs. Carlyle's friend and author of several novels. See also Letter 104.

Letter 53. MS: Yale University Library. Pbd: Sanders, p. 222.

[1] *Sesame and Lilies,* which had been published in June.

[2] July 14.

[3] The titles of two parts of *Sesame and Lilies.* The first part, "Of King's Treasuries," was first delivered as a lecture on the influence of good books at Manchester on December 6, 1864. The second part, "Of Queen's Gardens," was delivered in the same place on December 14, 1864, and was a lecture on the influence of good women.

Carlyle, writing to Jane from Scotland twelve days later, refers to Ruskin's gift, and makes an interesting comment on it. "Ruskin's *Sesame and Lilies*," he said, "must be a pretty little thing. Trollope, in reviewing it with considerable insolence and stupidity and vulgarity, produces little specimens far beyond any Trollope sphere of speculation." (T. Bliss, *Thomas Carlyle's Letters to His Wife* [1953], p. 381.) On pp. 404–5 of her book, Bliss has an extract of Trollope's review, which sheds some light on Carlyle's description. Trollope, after claiming that Ruskin's words do not contain Carlyle's "innate wisdom" and have "no definite tendency," goes on to lament Ruskin's "desire to preach sermons instead of making music with his bow," and wishes Ruskin would return to writing about art.

Please tell your Mother how much I am obliged to her for her call, altho' I was so unlucky as [to] miss it. And you may add, if you like, that I am sure she would not dislike me if she knew me: for the only time I ever saw her, I felt to *take to her* very much, because she said no superfluous or insincere word! And I have always found that those I take to at first sight take to *me* sooner or later if they give themselves a fair chance.

I cannot understand your persistence in forgetting Mrs. Hawkes (Madame Venturi)! She is to my mind perfectly charming! If you knew the romantic thing she once did for love of you, it would fix her in your mind forever!

"My lamed hand!" Alas no! It is not with *that* I write. *That* is quite past making any sort of writing whatsoever. It is too painful to attempt using *it* at all. So I have had to learn to write with my *left* hand, which protests against the unwonted exaction in taking every now and then the Cramp!

I hope to get home on the 24th or 25th.

Yours affectionately,
Jane Carlyle

I saw Mr. Carlyle Yesterday, entirely sick of "Solitude," which he had got to call "*Stagnation*"! He is about to start on further travels.

54. *Ruskin to Jane Carlyle*

Denmark Hill, S.
[July 18, 1865]

Dear Mrs. Carlyle,

I am so happy about the birthday,—and very proudly happy that I can give you pleasure on any day. My mother is very cock-ahoop too, about your pretty message, but that is good for her, for she's always snubbing *me* and then I say impertinent things to her, which she pretends not to mind, but does; and while she is always *saying* things which look as if she was the most conceited person in the world, she is really very uncomfortably humble, and glad of a bit of nice praise like this of yours.

I wrote "lame hand" carelessly, but I *had* read your letter. I meant the cramp-taking hand, not the disabled one.

Letter 54. MS: NLS, 555.22. Hitherto unpbd. The MS has "18 July, 1865" in another hand.

But you must get the hands into order, we can't have strikes right &
left like this.

I'm trying to draw flowers, and feel as if I was a cramp altogether
like Stefano[1] [*sic*]. But unremissedly in affection and duty to you always your,

J. Ruskin

The photograph is very sweet in expression— Keepable, which few
are.

55. *Carlyle to Ruskin*

Chelsea, 20 December, 1865

Dear Ruskin,—

Don't mind the *Bewick*; the indefatigable Dixon has sent me, yesterday, the Bewick's "Life" as well (hunted it up from the "Misses Bewick" or somebody, and threatens to involve me in still further bother
about nothing)—and I read the greater part of it last night before
going to bed.[1] Peace to Bewick: not a great man at all; but a very true
of his sort, a well complete, and a very enviable,—living there in communion with the skies and woods and brooks, not here in dᵒ with the
London Fogs, the roaring witchmongeries and railway yellings and
howlings.

The "Ethics of the Dust," whʰ I devoured withᵗ pause, and intend to
look at agⁿ, is a most shining Performance! Not for a long while have I
read anything tenth-part so radiant with talent, ingenuity, lambent fire
(*sheet*—and other lightnings) of all commendable kinds! Never was
such a lecture on *Crystallography* before, had there been nothing else
in it,—and there are all manner of things. In power of *expression* I
pronounce it to be supreme; never did anybody who had *such* things
to explain explain them better. And the bit of Egyptⁿ mythology, the
cunning *Dreams* abᵗ Pthah, Neith, &c, apart from their elucidative

---

[1] See Shakespeare's *The Tempest*, V.i.286.: "O touch me not! I am not Stephano, but a
cramp."

Letter 55. MS: not located. Pbd: Collingwood, II, 321–22.

[1] Thomas Dixon, the "philosophic corkcutter" whose discussions with Ruskin appear
in *Time and Tide*, had sent Carlyle a copy of *The History of British Birds*, by Thomas
Bewick (1753–1828), a famous English wood engraver and illustrator. It was a gift for
Carlyle's birthday (December 4). Dixon also sent Carlyle a copy of the *Memoir of
Thomas Bewick Written by Himself* (1862), edited by Jane Bewick, who is obviously the
"Misses Bewick" mentioned above. Ruskin was studying Bewick at the time, as part of
his research for *The Cestus of Aglaia*. See Wilson, VI, 39–40.

quality, wh^h is exquisite, have in them a *poetry* that might fill any Tennyson with despair. You are very dramatic too; nothing wanting in the stage-direct^{ns}, in the pretty little indicat^{ns}: a very pretty stage and *dramatis personae* altogether.[2] Such is my first feeling ab^t y^r Book, dear R.— Come soon, and I will tell you all the *faults* of it, if I gradually discover a great many. In fact, *come* at any rate!

Y^{rs} ever,

T. Carlyle

56. *John A. Carlyle to Ruskin*

The Hill, Dumfries

4th Jany 1866

Dear Sir,

By this day's post I have received your most welcome gift of a copy of your Ethics of the Dust, & I beg leave to thank you most cordially for sending it to me. I read nearly all of it yesterday, my brother having lent me a copy which I shall send back to Chelsea today. I also ordered a copy from London last night. I have recommended the book to friends who will be able to understand & appreciate it. I entirely agree with you in regard to all the things you teach in it, & admire the correct, easy & graceful style of the little book. It is one of the very best I have ever read, & I should be glad to have any "illustrated notes" you may be able to find time for—

Yours very truly,

J. A. Carlyle

[2] Ruskin's *The Ethics of the Dust* was first issued in December of 1865. Cast in the form of a dialogue between a kindly visiting lecturer (Ruskin) and an audience of young girls at Winnington school, the book is purportedly about crystals, but Ruskin's imaginative style carries him into the realms of the past, dreams, mythology, and social criticism. The "Egypt^n mythology" Carlyle mentions refers to Lecture II of the book, "The Pyramid Builders," which contains Ruskin's account of his dreams about Egyptian gods and goddesses—especially Neit and Ptah—and has three lengthy notes about the origins and meanings of these deities.

Some of the "faults" Carlyle may have discussed with Ruskin after his "first feeling" can be found in a letter to his brother John on December 21: "I have been reading a strange little Xmas Book of Ruskin's called *Ethics of the Dust*," he said, "it is all *abt*. crystallography; and seems to be, or is, geologically well-informed and correct; but it twists *symbolically*, in the strangest way, all its Geology into Morality, Theology, Egyptian Mythology, (with fiery cuts at Political Economy, etc!)—pretending not to know whether the forces and destinies and behaviours of crystals are not very like those of men! Wonderful to behold. Apart from this sad weakness of *backbone*, the Book is full of admirable talent; with such a faculty of *expression* in it (or of picturing what is meant) as beats all living rivals." (Froude, IV, 298, and MS: NLS, 526.35.)

Letter 56. MS: Bembridge. Hitherto unpbd.

Enclosed cutting from the Scotsman will show that your letter about Jamaica was also published in Edinburgh & would do some good there too[.]

57. *Ruskin to Carlyle*

> Denmark Hill, S.
> Wednesday morning [1866?]

Dear Mr. Carlyle

It must be Thursday, I find, not to day, but I hope for a happy chat. I shall bring you some eggs I've been putting by for you.

> Ever your affect.
> J. R.

58. *Ruskin to Carlyle*

> [1866?]

Dear Mr. Carlyle,

It breaks my heart to get such a letter from you, yet it is quite like you—very monumental of you— Only how could you think I did not understand your emphasis— I know how you feel things, and that what you were feeling was right, though you had not had time to see other things in the picture. What is that between thee & me?— Well, of course I'll come; but could not Mrs. Carlyle and you come here.— You see, if I ask you to dinner my mother will make a state-matter of it—and fatigue herself with thinking of all dishes on and out of the earth— If you will come earlier, & stay dinner by surprise good; but I think the best way would be to drive over here about ½ past six, to tea, & for chat in evening. Could you do this—would you like it? Then I'll come for another goodbye chat—at Chelsea— Any day would do for us except tomorrow?

> Ever your loving
> J. Ruskin

Letter 57. MS: NLS, 555.28. Hitherto unpbd.
Letter 58. MS: NLS, 555.17. Hitherto unpbd. The top of the MS has "*Before* April 1866" in another hand.

59. *Carlyle to Ruskin*

Chelsea, 16 Feb^y, 1866

Dear Ruskin,

You vanished in a moment, that Athenean night;[1] & I had not once thanked you, for y^r valiant punctuality both in signing and ag^n in voting. You are becoming a very evasive furtive kind of man; that night at Chelsea too, for instance, was not there a Box of Distinguished Cigars, wh^h told a strange story of you? For shame!— Where will that end? In *fact*, I know not what to say of it.

At the Athenean we were blackballed, as you perhaps know, lost by one ball it appears. A base envious Plebe delights here & there to squirt a drop of dirty water in the face of his betters: never mind it; it is the nature of the beast, and of the time it lives in.

Jane accepts you for Tuesday; and will this day warn the photograph people; indeed, is on the road thither at this moment. As to the lectures,[2] of wh^h the Program is abundantly seductive to us all, I had to prohibit *her* altogether: not to be tho^t of in such danger from cold. My Brother & I are extremely desirous; but even for us, such the distance, such the lateness of hour, I do not yet see any good possibility. The difficulty is not that of Dinner in the least; but that [of] getting home by ab^t 11 p.m. If *you* saw a practicable course in that particular and sent us tickets and indicate [?] &c. I almost believe we, even the lazier of us, w^d lift anchor and try.

Fair befall you in all your enterprises furtive & other.

Yours always truly

T. Carlyle

Letter 59. MS: Strouse Collection, University of California, Santa Cruz. Hitherto unpbd.
[1] Carlyle and Ruskin were members of the Athenaeum Club in London. Carlyle, through the efforts of Lord Ashburton, had been elected to the club in early March 1853; and Ruskin had been a member since 1851.
[2] Ruskin's lecture "War," which was delivered on the night of February 16 at the Royal Military Academy, Woolwich. It was later included in *The Crown of Wild Olive* (1866).

60. *Ruskin to Jane Carlyle*

Denmark Hill, S.

25th March [1866?]

Dear Mrs. Carlyle,

Could Mr. Carlyle and you dine with us on Tuesday? I could not ask you before, because I want you to see the child who was ill, (as I told you in posing up to the photographers the other day), and I was not sure if she would be able to come, but she's well now again and she's coming with her mother unless she gets ill again. So please come both, if you can. Just let me have one line by Crawly,[1] if possible saying if you can come. (½ past 6).

Ever his and your affectionate

J. Ruskin

61. *Carlyle to Ruskin*

Chelsea, London, 10th May 1866

Dear Ruskin,

Your kind words from Dijon were welcome to me: thanks. I did not doubt your sympathy in what has come;[1] but it is better that I see it laid before me. You are yourself very unhappy, as I too well discern— heavy-laden, obstructed and dispirited; but you have a great work still ahead, and will gradually have to gird yourself up against the *heat of the day*, which is coming on for you,—as the Night too is coming. Think valiantly of these things.

Letter 60. MS. NLS, 555.29. Hitherto unpbd.
[1] Frederick Crawley, whom Ruskin called "George," and who was Ruskin's devoted servant for many years.
Letter 61. MS not located. Pbd: Ruskin, *Works*, XVIII, xlvii; and (with omissions) in Cook, II, 113.
[1] Jane Welsh Carlyle had died on April 21, 1866. On the afternoon of that day Ruskin had come to Chelsea to call on Mrs. Carlyle, bringing flowers, only to be met at the door with news of her death. On April 24 Ruskin left England for a tour of the Continent with Lord and Lady Trevelyan, and he had reached Dijon on May 4. His diary says simply "I write to Mr. Carlyle" on May 6 (see *Diaries*, II, 587). This May 6 letter has not been found, but it is obviously the one Carlyle refers to here.
Carlyle's reference to Ruskin's "unhappy" state is probably a reference to Ruskin's alarming symptoms, since it was at this time that Ruskin first experienced fits of giddiness and clouded vision. It may also be a reference to Lady Trevelyan's declining health, for she was to die on May 13. The grief that Ruskin felt over the loss of both women was a deep and genuine one, as Carlyle knew, and some indication of it can be found in a letter from Ruskin to Rawdon Brown on June 11: "The deaths of Mrs. Carlyle and of Lady Trevelyan take from me my two best women friends of older power; and I am not very zealous about anything," he said (*Works*, XXXVI, 509).

I cannot write to you; I do not wish yet even to speak to anybody; find it more tolerable to gaze steadily in silence on the blackness of the abysses that have suddenly opened round me, and as it were swallowed up my poor little world. Day by day the stroke that has fallen, like a thunderbolt out of skies all *blue* (as I often think), becomes more immeasurable to me; my life all hid in ruins, and the one light of it as if gone out.[2] And yet there is an inexpressible beauty, and even an epic greatness (known only to God and me), in the Life of my victorious little Darling whom I shall see no more. Silence about all that; every word I speak or write of it seems to desecrate it,—so unworthy of the Fact now wrapt in the Eternities, as God has willed.

This day fortnight, about this hour (1 p.m.) we were lowering her dust to sleep with that of her Father, in the Abbey of Kirk of Haddington, as was our covenant for forty years back: since that day my life has been as *noiseless* as I could make it; and ought to continue so till I see farther. My Brother and Miss Welsh[3] are still with me; everybody is and has been kind as Humanity could be; help me farther nobody can. If by slow degrees I *can* really do some useful work for the poor remainder of my days, it shall be well and fit; if otherwise, I already seem to see I shall soon follow whither she has gone. That is yet all.

Come and see me when you get home; come *oftener* and see me, and speak *more* frankly to me (for I am very true to your highest interests and you) while I still remain here.

You can do nothing for me in Italy; except come home improved. If you pass through or near Montey (in the Valais, not far from Vevey, I think) you might call on (Dowager) Lady Ashburton,[4] and bring me some report of her. Adieu, my friend, adieu.

T. Carlyle

[2] A phrase Carlyle had used in the epitaph he composed for Mrs. Carlyle's tombstone. The last line of the inscription is: "She died at London, 21st April, 1866; suddenly snatched away from him, and the light of his life as if gone out."

[3] Dr. John Carlyle and "Maggie" Welsh, a cousin of Mrs. Carlyle.

[4] The second Lady Ashburton, who was now a widow, since Lord Ashburton had died in March 1864. See Letter 40.

62. *Ruskin to Carlyle*

Denmark Hill, S.

[September 14, 1866]

Dear Mr. Carlyle,

How can I ever thank you enough for being to me what this Milan letter[1] says (& your saying is like nature's—one with deed) that you are—& for trusting and loving me enough to be able to write so to me. *Then*—oh me—if I had lost this letter!

God keep you and give you back some of your care to use your inner strength—the strength is itself unbroken.

I cannot say more today.

Ever your loving

J. Ruskin

63. *Carlyle to Ruskin*

Chelsea, 27 Sept., 1866

Dear Ruskin,[1]

I have again read all those letters; but do not, from Mr. Price or his *Jamaica Standard*, get the least glimmer of new light ab^t "The Tramway Swindle"[2] or any of the other miracles alleged.— which I can only

---

Letter 62. MS: NLS, 555.24. Pbd: Ruskin's *Works*, XXXVI, 515. The MS has "PM^k. 14 Sept. '66" in another hand.

[1] Carlyle's letter of May 10 had been forwarded to Milan, but Ruskin decided not to go to that city, and the letter eventually reached him in London.

Letter 63. MS: Yale University Library. Pbd: Ruskin's *Works*, XXXVI, 517.

[1] This letter, and the three following it, deal with the "Eyre Defense Committee." In October 1865, a small uprising of blacks in Jamaica was suppressed with great speed and destruction by the governor of the island, Edward John Eyre. Soon a committee, led by John Stuart Mill, T. H. Huxley, Thomas Hughes, Charles Darwin, John Bright, Herbert Spencer, and Goldwin Smith, was formed to denounce and prosecute Eyre as an incompetent tyrant and murderer who violated the natural rights of all English subjects. Eyre was recalled to England and put on trial before Parliament. Carlyle, who had little sympathy for democracy, had already written disparagingly of the Jamaican natives in *Latter-Day Pamphlets* (see his *Works*, XX, 25–27; and XXIX, 355–57), and looked upon Eyre as a hero who had resolutely stopped a potentially dangerous rebellion. In the late summer and early fall of 1866, he helped form the Eyre Defense Committee, and served as its first chairman. He enlisted the aid of Charles Kingsley, Tennyson, Dickens, and Ruskin, whose speech in defense of Eyre can be found in his *Works*, XVIII, 552. Eyre was eventually acquitted, but was not allowed to return to his post in Jamaica. See Introduction. See also Bernard Semmel, *The Governor Eyre Controversy* (1962); G. H. Ford, "The Governor Eyre Case in England," *UTQ*, XVII (1947–48), 219–33; and Gillian Workman, "Thomas Carlyle and the Governor Eyre Controversy: An Account with Some New Material," *VS*, XVIII, no. 1 (September 1974), 77–102.

[2] In 1862, Eyre had been peripherally involved in an attempt by a colonial engineer to

conceive as more or less *natural* misbirths of that nearly *in*conceivable little *Chaos in a Coalbox* (probably very violent, and sure to be *fuliginous*) wh^h they call "House of Assembly"; all intent upon *talk* of various kinds, while their Governor was pushing towards work and result. A mere heap of flaming soot; abstrusely equal to zero for us! Mr. Price, I have no reason to doubt, was and is perfectly honest and *bona-fide*; but need not concern us farther.

The best thing you can now do is to consult seriously that practical Mr. Harris;[3] and if, unfortunately, he won't be of the Committee, get him to undertake that lucid Digest, or conclusive little Summary of facts and of principles, wh^h *must* be set forth, and addressed to the British People for their answer. Such a thing would have immense results, if rightly done; and, to all appearance, he is the one man for it. Be dilig^t. I bid you!—

The letter from Christie[4] (*ex-Brazilian* Excellency, and a very shrewd fellow) came this morn^g. I leave a memorandum of it with Hume;[5] to whom, if you chance to look in, you may give it *in corpore*;—otherwise, keep or return hither.— I expect ag^n ab^t Wedn^y; and hope to be alone and get more good of you. *Ay de mi*!—

Yours ever,
T. Carlyle

64. *Ruskin to Carlyle*

Denmark Hill, S.
29th Sept. 1866

Dear Mr. Carlyle,

I went in to Waterloo Place[1] and gave Mr. Hume that letter about Lord Russell,[2] yesterday, and the bearer of this had already delivered

---

embezzle government funds during the construction of a tramway in Jamaica. George Price, a member of Eyre's executive committee, had persuaded Eyre to prosecute the engineer by threatening to send a letter to the Duke of Newcastle exposing the whole affair. According to Semmel (*The Governor Eyre Controversy*, p. 112), Price wrote to Ruskin in September 1866, and gave all the information on the tramway episode. It is obviously these letters that have been shown to Carlyle.

[3] Actually Harrison. See Letter 64.

[4] William Dougal Christie (1816−74), who was ambassador to Brazil, 1858−63, and an advocate of black freedom.

[5] Hamilton Hume, who was writing his *Life of Governor Eyre* (1867).

Letter 64. MS: NLS, 555.25. Pbd: Ruskin's *Works*, XXXVI, 517−18.

[1] No. 9 Waterloo Place, Pall Mall, was where the committee met, and where Ruskin delivered his speech on September 7, 1866.

[2] Lord John Russell, who was foreign secretary under Palmerston from 1860 to 1865 and prime minister from October 1865 to July 1866.

his pamphlet to him today. I asked him also whether he might not be helped in his present work by the lawyer's precision of my friend Mr. Pattison[3]—(I heedlessly called him Harrison to you the other night—having another lawyer and politico-economist friend of that name).[4] But Mr. Hume looked a little disconcerted at the proposal, so it is best, I suppose, at present to leave matters in his very willing and active hands. I spoke to him about the Price matters; your kind note being, for the rest, quite enough for me;—however, I spoke to Hume about it, and he read me Eyre's own letter about Price—which is conclusive.

The reason I attached overdue weight to Price's letter you might partly guess from his niece's, which I left with you, not inadvertently. I do not know if you looked at it again or thought of it in any wise—but if you could be troubled to glance over this two-in-one letter enclosed, which you see bears (receptive) postmark, "Luzern, 28th Nov., 1861," you will see how it is that I can't work now so well as I used to do; and why you must not scold me for not always being able to "look valiantly upon these things."[5]

Ever your loving
J. Ruskin

The passage about governesses refers to a gallant thing she did in defiance of all scoldings by her friends—namely, nursing her children's sick governess herself, through a month's long illness requiring *closest* watching, during some part of it, night and day.

I have opened my letter to put in also one that has come by this post, which I think you will like—in answer to what I told her of your impression of Mr. Price.

I'll come over on Wednesday as usual. I am so glad you *like* to have me alone.

---

[3] This may be Dr. Pattison, a physician whom Ruskin saw on September 6, or (more probably) Mark Pattison, who was then rector of Lincoln College, Oxford, and who had dined with Ruskin on September 23. See Ruskin, *Diaries*, II, 598, 600.

[4] Frederic Harrison, who was actually serving on the Eyre prosecuting committee at the time.

[5] See Letter 61.

65. *Ruskin to Carlyle*

Denmark Hill, S.
[October 1, 1866]

Dear Mr. Carlyle,

Please, I'll come over and take you to the Committee on Wednesday. Then I'll come on *Thursday* evening for talk, if that will do—or Friday—as you like best.

I've been looking for accounts of Gustavus—Lutzen, etc.[1] can't get anything human about them.

It seems to be that a magnificent *closing* work for you to do would be to set your finger on the turning points and barriers in European history—to gather them into trains of light—to give, without troubling yourself about detail of proof, your own *final* impression of the courses and causes of things—and your thoughts of the leading men, *who* they were, and *what* they were. If you like to do this, I'll come and *write* for you a piece of every day, if after beginning it, you still found the mere hand work troublesome. I have a notion it would be very wholesome work for me, & it would be very proud & dear for me. But that's by the way—only think of the thing itself.

Ever your loving,
J. Ruskin

66. *Carlyle to Ruskin*

Chelsea, 11 Oct^r, 1866

Dear Ruskin,

I chanced to be a little out of sorts last night,—the cause inconceivably small, that of first drinking two mouthfuls of bad tea in a house where I called, and then of eating cauliflower instead of potato at dinner time, *inconceivably* small but suffic^t to keep me pointedly awake the greater part of last night! It is therefore probably as well that the second misfortune came,—tho' possibly too, y^r talk might have

---

Letter 65. MS: NLS, 555.26. Pbd: Ruskin's *Works*, XXXVI, 518. The MS has "P M^k. 1 Octr 1866" in another hand.

[1] In his *Life of Schiller*, Carlyle refers to Schiller's abilities as a historian and then gives "a few scenes from his [Schiller's] masterly description of the Battle of Lützen" and the death of Gustavus Adolphus as "a specimen of Schiller's historical style" (*Works*, XXV, 104, 317–20). Carlyle was revising his *Schiller* for a new edition, which, according to Isaac W. Dyer, ed., *A Bibliography of Thomas Carlyle's Writings and Ana* (Portland, Maine, 1928), p. 245, came out in 1867.

Letter 66. MS: NLS, Acc. 2773. Hitherto unpbd.

warmed the past morning [?] into genial heat, and *saved* me from the monsters of the Night, nobody can say for cert^n. Certain only that *thus* we now are—and that, so far as I can now judge, Wednesday Ev^g next will be the favourable time. Unless you prefer Monday or any other day of next week, *and* will take the trouble of announcing it to me? Otherwise silence (as to Wedn^y) shall mean assent.

Last night I drew Price from his doomed Limbo down in kitchen (happy to find him still *un*burnt), & sent him to you. Don't send him back, please!—

Interrupt^n of many hours, at this point, by a mass of printed slips from Ham^n Hume, part of his *Pamphlet on Eyre*. Facts dilig^tly *chosen*; but *presented* as if wrapt in bales of wool—or by the broadest end & even by the *side*, instead of the point! Ah me, I feel as if I had *douched* for hours in *dirty water*,—y^r own feeling, probably, in reading Price. For Hume's pamphlet, yes; but for Eyre's Committee, they will never do!— You will ultimately *have* to call in y^r Mr. Harrison, or man of real logic and law. Meanwhile, go to poor Hume, & help him a little— take *you* his printed slips & read them: can you? I must absolutely *shut up* in that direct^n, to save my sanity!—

Enough today;

Y^rs Ever

T. Carlyle

67. *Ruskin to Carlyle*

[December 1866]

Dear Mr. Carlyle,

I fear you have been expecting me. I have been expecting myself— every evening, but cold & hoarseness came after the toothache, & now I can't speak.

I'll come as soon as I can—I want so much to speak to you about that precious writing of yours, about old days. I had not courage when you did me the grace to speak of it, to say what I wanted to say. I must try, next time I come.

Ever your faithful & affectionate

J. Ruskin

Letter 67. MS: NLS, ۵۵۵.2/. Hitherto unpbd. The letter is dated "December, 1866" in another hand.

Letter from Carlyle to Ruskin, February 15, 1867, page one (Letter 68). Courtesy of the Ruskin Galleries, Bembridge School, Isle of Wight.

68. *Carlyle to Ruskin*

Mentone (The Dow^r Lady Ashburton's)
15 feb^y 1867—

Dear Ruskin,

If the few bits of letters I have written from this place had gone by the *natural* priority and sequence, this w^d have been the first or among the very first:—and indeed it is essentially so,—the first that I have written except upon Compulsion, or in answer to something written. My aversion to writing is at all times great. But I begin to feel a great want of having some news from you, at least of hearing that you are not fallen *unwell*; and there is no other method of arousing you to y^r duty.

I have done passably well since getting out hither; and cannot but count it a kind of benefit that the impetuous Tyndall[1] tore me out from the sleety mud-abysses of London, as if by the hair of the head; and dropped me here, on a shore where there is at least clean air to breathe, and a climate that is bright and cheerful to move about in,— and where if frost did fall, and the streets became all of glass, people w^d *not* be "fined for throwing ashes before their door", and trying to *save* one's bones or brains from being broken if one ventured out!— That is really hitherto the most unmanageable, or almost the one un-manageable point for me in the problem of my London Winter: com-pelled to take no exercise except under peril of life or limb; "most thinking people", was there ever the match of you for a power of "common sense" especially!—

I dare say you have been here; and descript^n of scenery, locality etc., w^d be quite thrown away on you. From Antibes on the west to Bor-dighera on the east, a stretch of perhaps forty miles diameter, is a beautiful semicircular alcove, guarded by the maritime Alps from all bad winds; included in this *big* bay (or *alcove*) are five or six smaller ones,—of wh^h *Mentone*, towards Bordighera, is the last but one:—no climate, you perceive, can have a better chance to be *good*: and indeed, ever since Xmas last, when I arrived, it has far surpassed all my expec-tat^{ns}, or requirem^{ts} in that partic^r; rather *too* hot for most part, and

---

Letter 68. MS: Bembridge. Pbd: Ruskin's *Works*, XVII, 339n., and with omissions in Collingwood, II, 340–41.

[1] Professor John Tyndall (1820–93), a famous scientist and an old friend of Carlyle. Through his instigation the trip was arranged, and he accompanied Carlyle across the Continent until they arrived at Menton, where the second Lady Ashburton kept a villa on the Riviera near Monaco.

driving me into the olive-woods and shaggy ravines, if the sun is still high. One's paths there are steep exceedingly and rough exceedingly (donkey-paths for the country people, paved into dreadful *stairs* in the bad places); but they are silent, solitary; a walk there is soothing to one's sad thots, instead of irritating, and does one good, tho' of a mournful kind. As to "scenery", you know me to care next to nothing for it; but I must own, these pinnacles that *stud* the back of *our* little Mentone "alcove," for example, are the strangest and grandest things of the mountain kind I ever saw; bare-rocks, sharp as steeples, jagged as if hewn by lightning; most grim, perilous, cruel; "sitting there", I sometimes say, "like so many witches of Endor,[2] *naked* to the waist, but therefrom with the amplest petticoats of dark or bright green" (for all is terraced, and covered with olives, or oranges and lemons, down almost to the sea),—a really fine scene, especially at morning and evg in light and shade, under a sky so clear and pure; scene whh I never yet raise my eyes to without something of surprise and recognitn.

The worst of my existence here is that I am thoroughly idle,—for the "work" I try at intervals is a mockery of work;—and my real task is to walk about four or five miles every day, and to guard myself vigilantly from being bored by surrounding black heads. For we are abt 800 here; and none of us has really anything to do. Patience, Vigilance,—and shirk off into the olive woods!

Often I begin to think of my route home agn; & what I shall next do there. Alas, all is abstruse and gloomy on that latter head; but surely something shd and must be settled as to all that too: while the days are, and any remnant of strength is, one ought not to wander in mere sadness of soul, doing nothing! The only point I look forward to with any fixed satisfactn as yet, is that of having Ruskin agn every Wedny evg, and tasting a little human conversatn once in the week, if oftener be not practicable!— But the very time of my returning is uncertn; though I care not for yr March tempests, and perhaps had better be at Chelsea even now: but there are grand speculatns abt seeing Rome first, Genoa at least and Florence first,—and many attempts to awaken my appetite that way, hitherto witht success perceptible. It is strange how one's love of travel perfects itself by simply sitting still, if [one] can do that long enough!—

Adieu, my Friend; I want a little note from you *quam* primum ["first thing"]. I send many regards to the good & dear old Lady;— and am ever

Yours gratefully   T. Carlyle

[2] See I Samuel 28.

69. *Ruskin to Carlyle*

Denmark Hill,
17th February, 1867

Dearest Mr. Carlyle,

I should indeed have written to you, as you bade me—long ago, if it had not been that I had nothing to say except either what you knew very well—(that I loved you—and because I did, was glad, for the time, I had lost you)—or—what it would have made you very angry with me to know. Which, as it must be told, may as well now be at once got confessed. Namely, that one day—soon after you left—I sat down gravely to consider what I could say about poetry, and finding after a forenoon that the sum of my labours amounted to four sentences, with the matter of two in them, that also my hands were hot—and my lips parched—and my heart heavy—I concluded that it was not the purpose of fate that I should lose any more days in such a manner, and wrote to the Oxford people a final and formal farewell.[1]

For which they have graciously expressed pretty regrets: but I have since felt none—except those which related to the letter I had some day to write to Mentone.

One pleasant thing I had to tell you of, however, was a most happy evening we had with your sister.[2] I think she enjoyed it too. My mother was entirely happy with her at once, and my cousin rejoiced in her, and I rejoiced in all three. Her modest gentleness of *power* is notable to me above anything I have yet seen of womankind.

She saved a little bit of Frederick the Great from the housemaid—and sent it me—for which I am ever her grateful servant.

She told me a little thing that touched me closely also—that you had thought it worth while to keep—labelled—that little scrawl of curved lines I made one evening. And I think I shall be able to show you, when you return, that my poor little gift, such as it is, *does* lie in eye and hand—not in brains—for, since I finally gave up the Oxford matter, I set myself (chiefly to put some too painful thoughts from me) to do in

Letter 69. MS: Carlyle House, Chelsea. Pbd: (with MS of first paragraph reproduced in facsimile) Ruskin's *Works*, XXXVI, 524. The upper left-hand corner of the MS has the following scrawl in Carlyle's hand: "Thinking to send only *a half*, I . . . [word illegible], but now Dissent."

[1] Carlyle was helping some of Ruskin's friends at Oxford who were trying to have Ruskin appointed to the professorship of poetry there, recently vacated by Matthew Arnold. After Ruskin withdrew his candidacy, the position was given to Sir Francis Doyle.

[2] Carlyle's sister Jean (Mrs. James Aitken, of Dumphries), who was taking care of the Carlyle house in Chelsea at the time. She was the mother of Mary Aitken, Carlyle's niece and helper in his old age (see Letter 93).

painting one or two little things as well as I could. (Which I never did before—for all my drawing hitherto has only been to collect data— never for its own sake.) And, doing as well as I could, I have done— not ill—several things—a dead partridge, and a wild drake, and a small twisted shell. That sounds despicable enough, I fear, to you in your olive woods at the feet of Witches of Endor;—nevertheless, poor as it may be, I think it *is* my work. For, Turner being dead, I am quite sure there is no one else in England now who could have painted that shell, but I; and it seems to me, therefore, I must have been meant to do it.

I need not say how happy the kind sentence about your wishing to have me again on Wednesday evenings made me. Nevertheless, I must still unselfishly pray that you may be enchanted away by magical "hair of the head"—to Florence at least, if not to Rome. That satiety of travel is surely a kind of lichenous overgrowing of one's thoughts when one has been *too* long at rest—very good for most people, if they would only have patience to take the colouring—but surely not for you? I think your interest in seeing would increase the more you were tempted to see, and that the mere change of air and of slope of sunray, by whatever endurance of irksome motion obtained, would be—of—so much better for you than the monotonous effluvium of Chelsea shore. The fog was so dark to-day that I had candles at nine- o'clock breakfast. Think of that! and look up to your sky "with recognition."

My mother thanks you much for your good message. I hope to have some interesting little gossip to write to you about my cousin, next week.[3]

I am so ashamed of my writing. I can't help it, unless I write so very slow that I should forget what I had to say. Sincere regards to Lady Ashburton.— Ever your affectionate

J. Ruskin

70. *Ruskin to Carlyle*

Denmark Hill, S.
31st March, 1867

Dear Mr. Carlyle,

I have had a heavy time of it since I wrote last, in various ways of which I cannot tell you; not that there is anything in my mind which I

[3] In Ruskin's diary for February 23 (*Diaries*, II, 611) he wrote "Saturday. The dread- ful day for poor Joan." This is obviously a reference to the fact that Rose La Touche's brother Percy had broken off his engagement with Joan Agnew.
Letter 70. MS: NLS, 555.30. Pbd: Ruskin's *Works*, XXXVI, 526.

would not trust you to know, but because there are some conditions of trouble for which one has no business to ask sympathy even from one's dearest friends.[1] I am now recovering some dim tranquility and writing a few letters on political econ., which I hope you will say it was better to write than not,—though I am too unwell to take pains with them: and the entirely frightful and ghastly series of unnatural storm and frost which lasted through the beginning of this month (far into it, indeed), followed by severe March blights and bleak swirlings of bitter rain, has kept me from any wholesome walking or breathing until I can hardly think or stand.

(4th April) And now I do not know if it is of the least use to send this to Mentone; but I will let it take its chance—the main thing that I wanted to say to you being that I have had to meditate somewhat closely over educational questions lately, and I am more than ever impressed with the sense of the greatness of the gift you could bestow in the good close of all your labour by a summary of your present vision of history, and of its causative forces: not writing the history of any country, but marking the conclusions to which you had come in reading its history yourself; and telling us the events that were of essential significance; & separating them in their true relations, from things useless.

Suppose I were to ask you, for instance, briefly (not being able to read for myself any history of Spain)—what had made the Spaniard of today what he is? You would sit down in your fender-corner, and roll me out an entirely clear and round statement of the main dealings of Providence and of the Devil with him—and of him with them. Now if you were to write down such an answer—of its quarter of an hour's length—and then amplify & illustrate it as you saw good, it would be a perfect guide to me, for such labour as I could undertake on the subject—but which without such a guide would be wholly thrown away—so that indeed I should never undertake it.

Do think of this, in your rambles under the olive trees. I hope, wherever you are, that this weather has found you still in Italy, and that you will outstay the Firefly time. I always think that nothing in the world

[1] Cook, II, 114, quotes Ruskin on his condition at this time: "In 1867 the first warning mischief to my health showed itself, giddiness and mistiness of head and eyes, which stopped alike my drawing and thinking to any good purpose." Ruskin's diary entries for this period confirm his remarks, and one must also remember that at this time he was feverishly counting the days until the 21st birthday of Rose La Touche, when he was to receive an answer to his proposal of marriage made in February 1866. J. L. Bradley, in his edition of *The Letters of John Ruskin to Lord and Lady Mount-Temple* (Columbus, Ohio, 1964), pp. 111 and 113, notes that Ruskin had received hostile letters from Rose's parents in February and March, and had been thus put in a state of "black anger."

can possibly be so touching, in its own natural sweetness, and in the
association with the pensive and glorious power of the scene, as the
space of spring time in Italy during which the firefly makes the meadows quiver at twilight. And then if you were to get up to the lakes, in
May! and go up the Val Formazza over the Gries and Grimsel, and so
to the Giesback Inn on the lake of Brientz, you would find that in early
June the happiest—coolest—warmest—cosiest—wildest work! and
two dear good Swiss girls would wait on you, who would remember
my two little girls[2] and me, last year—and do everything they could—
& they could a great deal—to make you comfortable.— And now I
must say good-bye—and please forgive this nothing of a letter. I might
have told you a great deal, that only would have vexed you,—
nothing—is better.

Ever your affectionate
J. Ruskin

71. *Carlyle to Ruskin*

Chelsea, 6 April, 1867

Dear Ruskin,

Y[r] letter reached me with warm welcome, at Mentone; but nothing
of the interesting "gossip," etc. wh[h] was promised for "next week"!
What has become of that?

About a fortnight ago, I got home (if this can now be called a
"home"), and have been lying strictly *perdu* ever since, in the hope of
recomposing myself a little;—have called literally on nobody, except
on Froude taking leave for Spain,[1] and on Forster[2] with whom I had
pecuniary "Bus[ss]"; nor has anybody (so to speak) called on me. I am
very quiet, of humor very somber;—looking, in these days, upon an
"April *last*," wh[h] must be forever memorable to me. My brother John,
who was here to receive me, still continues, for I suppose ten days yet;
and is the only company I have.

If you durst lift anchor ag[n] (Wed[y] night,[3] to be exact), you w[d] be a

---

[2] Joan Agnew, Ruskin's cousin, and Constance Hilliard, niece of Lady Trevelyan, both
of whom had accompanied Ruskin and the Trevelyans during their Continental trip in
April 1866.

Letter 71. MS: Rylands, English MS 1191/6. Pbd: Sanders, p. 225.

[1] J. A. Froude went to Spain to do more research for his *History of England*, which
was not completed until 1870. He had made a trip there in 1861 for the same reason.

[2] John Forster. See note to Letter 8.

[3] Ruskin, *Diaries*, II, 615 and 616, has the following: "April 10th. Wednesday . . . At
Carlyle's this evening." and "April 17th [1867] . . . At Carlyle's in evening. Tell him
about R[ose]."

very welcome appearance here! John, who knows you, and has sense to estimate you, will not be in our way at all;—if he be even *here* on any terms, wh^h is not cert^n for that ev^g.

If you *don't* write, I shall conclude you are coming.

Yours ever faithfully,
T. Carlyle

My kindest regards to the dear Old Lady & the d^o young.

72. *Ruskin to Carlyle*

30th May, [1867]

My Dear Carlyle,

I deeply regret, for many not trivial reasons, that you have been induced to write this letter.[1]

It seems to me that the only thing which now in justice remains for you to do, is to furnish me with a succinct statement of what you remember yourself to have said on the occasion in question; and to permit me to substitute that statement, in the edition of collected letters, for the one which has offended you. In any case I shall take no notice of the letter in the Pallmall Gazette, nor of any comments which may be made upon it.

Ever affectionately yours,
J. Ruskin

Letter 72. MS not located. Pbd: Ruskin's *Works*, XVII, 480–81. The text of this letter is based on the holograph of the first draft in Ruskin's diaries at Bembridge School, collated with the Cook and Wedderburn version.

[1] Ruskin was then publishing his *Time and Tide*, written in the form of letters to "a Working Man of Sunderland," in the Manchester newspapers. In one of the letters he reported a conversation in which Carlyle had said that he could not walk in the streets of Chelsea "without being insulted, chiefly because he is a grey, old man; and also because he is cleanly dressed. . . ." This paragraph was printed in many newspapers, and drew shocked inquiries from several working men to Carlyle. On May 22, Carlyle wrote a public letter to "a working man at Rochdale," in which he said that "the thing now 'going the rounds' is untrue, diverges from the fact throughout, and [is] . . . 'incredible.' " On May 28, he wrote the following letter "to The Editor of the Pall Mall Gazette": "In reference to a Newspaper Paragraph now idly circulating, with my name in it as connected with 'insults on the streets' and other such matter,—permit me to say that it is an untrue Paragraph, disagrees with the fact throughout, and in essentials is curiously the reverse of the fact; a Paragraph altogether erroneous, misfounded, and even absurd." (MS: Dr. Frederick W. Hilles.) The letter was printed in the *Gazette* on May 29, and Ruskin's diary for that date records a "foolish letter of C in papers" (*Diaries*, II, 619). The above letter is Ruskin's answer to it, starting a brief but bitter quarrel, which runs through the next few letters in their correspondence. See also the Introduction.

73. *Ruskin to Carlyle*

Denmark Hill, S.
1st June 1867

My dear Carlyle

I am under the sorrowful necessity of ignoring your present letter. You have given the lie publicly, and in the most insulting terms possible to you, to the man who probably of all men living, most honoured you. It is *first because* he so honours you, but ~~also~~ [*sic*] for many reasons besides—(and, as I said—none of them trivial) that he is compelled to require you to do right in this matter: and the right manifestly is that you either justify the terms of that letter in the Pallmall Gazette, or retract them, and that publicly; and with all convenient speed.

　　　　　　　　　　　　　　　　　　Always affectionately Yours,
Thos. Carlyle, Esq.　　　　　　　　　　　　　　　J. Ruskin

74. *Ruskin to Carlyle*

Denmark Hill, S.
[June 1, 1867]

Private

Dear Carlyle— I am fearfully sorry about this thing: more fatal and feminine incontinence never yet ruined cause than this of yours.— All the Edinburgh Professors and English Fools that live, bellowing with one accord in at my window, would not have made *me* write such words of a man who was my friend!—or of anything which could be indirectly traced or attributed to him. Not for my sake, but for a thousand sakes, you must either write the conversation—or retract or *yourself* explain, your letter— You may as soon avert Death, as my determination on this head.— Do not come to see me. We are both alike irritable. You *cannot* restrain your feelings,—& it would hurt me to use the strength necessary to restrain mine.

　　　　　　　　　　　　　　　　　　　　　[J. Ruskin]

Letter 73. Addr: Mr. Carlyle, Esq. / 5 Cheyne Row / Chelsea. Pm: London, June 1, 1867. MS: Bembridge. Pbd with omissions in Cook, II, 117. On the front of the envelope Carlyle has written: "The *Ruskin Newspr Rubbish* (june 1867)—judiciously trampled out!"

　　Letter 74. MS: Bembridge. Hitherto unpbd. The MS has "PMrk. 1 June 67" in another hand, and "After C's letter to Times?" in a third hand. Ruskin's signature is not on this one-page MS, and there may be a second page, which has not been located.

75. Carlyle to Ruskin

Chelsea, 8 June, 1867

Dear Ruskin,

Last night I sent away to *The Times* a paltry little Note (wh[h] ag[n], this morning, does not please me, and be hanged to it!)—after such concoction, rejecting, remodelling, nightly and daily botherat[n], and sheer waste of time and means as might have sufficed for a Book of the Iliad almost, instead of a Note to the Newspaper![1] For the beggarly Nothing is of a delicacy and difficulty almost infinite; like that of forging a horseshoe in the middle of crazy powder-barrels,—i.e. of the hardly yet "sleeping" whirlwinds of impious Newsp[r] rumour, capable of being re-awakened by a wrong word.— This wretched Note you will probably see on Monday morning; and from me, sure enough, it is intended to be *Finis* on the matter.

Letter 75. MS: Estate of Mrs. Helen Gill Viljoen. Hitherto unpbd.

[1] The letter was printed in the *Times* on June 8, and addressed to its editor this limited retraction:

Sir,

I could still wish, by way of marginal note to your friendly article of Monday last (the *Times* of June 3), to add, for my own sake, and for a much-valued friend's, the two following little bits of commentary:—

1st. That I by no means join in heavily blaming Mr. Ruskin, and, indeed, do not blame him at all, but the contrary, except for the almost inconceivable practical blunder of printing my name, and then of carelessly hurling topsy-turvy into wild incredibility all he had to report of me—of me, and indirectly of the whole vast multitude of harmless neighbors, whom I live with here—in London and its suburbs, more than 2,000,000 of us, I should think, who all behave by second nature in an obliging, peaceable, and perfectly human manner to each other, and are all struck with amazement at Mr. Ruskin's hasty paragraph upon us.

2nd. That in regard to the populace or *canaille* of London, to the class distinguishable by behaviour as our non-human, or half-human neighbors, which class is considerably more extensive and miscellaneous, and much more dismal and disgusting than you seem to think, I substantially agree with all that Mr. Ruskin has said of it.

I remain, Sir,
Your obedient servant,
T. Carlyle

See R. H. Shepherd, *Memoirs of the Life and Writings of Thomas Carlyle* (1881), II, 251–52. Excerpts are also given in Cook, II, 117. The MS of Carlyle's first draft of this letter is in the possession of Bembridge School, and is dated June 7, 1869, by Carlyle. Under this date, Carlyle has written two notes. The first seems to be addressed to J. A. Froude at a later date, and declares: "From *Ruskin* of 1 june in adjacent (I think there was one before, but I have by mistake destroyed it;—it essentially said (with . . . [word illegible] provocat[n]) 'Tell me what you did say then?'— Impossible!" The second note says: "No. 4 (Letter to 'Times,' in consequence of No. 3). Today (8 june) have sent a *Note to Ruskin* (rigorous but good-humoured—as absolute *Finis* to the paltriest absurdity I was ever dragged into as if in my sleep!)"

Your pres^t state of provocat^n does not surprise me at all, still less anger me at all. Excuse me if I say, there is even something of amiable in *it* too (as there has uniformly been in all you have ever done, said or intended towards me); something generous and *filial*; like the poignant sorrow on a very good, but far too headlong *son*, getting his rebuke from *papa*, with the consciousness as yet of only having meant the just [?] papa too well and too kindly; a poignant sorrow wh^h goes over into sparkles of wrath withal, for the time being. In ab^t 4 or 5 weeks of silence, I calculate that all this will have vanished and subsided; and the state of the case (one of the absurdest I was ever concerned in) will have become mathematically clear to you, on *both* sides of it; as it has, for the last fortnight or so, completely been to me,—mathematically clear, I answer you, after ample considering; and now *as* inflexible and unalterable "as the 47th of Euclid", or as the *Fifth of Euclid*, if we like that instance better! Believe me, my friend, you will find that that letter in the Pall Mall was a necessity and duty on me. Better still, you will find that nothing *I* c^d or can have written, or forbourne to write;—that not even the immortal gods, *can wash you clear of having done*, even thoughtlessly and with intention purely noble and kind, *an immense imprudence of its sort* (nothing *worse*, but for cert^n that); a deed done,—wh^h neither I nor the very gods can render *not* done! Of wh^h there is no conceivable remedy, but what (I hope) you are now on the way towards and will reach in ab^t 4 or 5 weeks hence, as above said.

If, by that time, you have arrived at complete contrit^n, resolut^n of amend^t, and mathematical clearness on both sides,—right happy shall I be to see y^r sunny face ag^n unclouded as before; but if not, I recommend that we both *wait* to try if you can't and won't;—and that in the meanwhile that accursed passage be *deleted* from your reprint of the Dixon *Letters*.[2] At pres^t this is all,—except unabated regard for you, of wh^h now you need no assurance. You see how mutinous my very hand and pen are!— Y^{rs} ever (whether you achieve "contrition" enough or not),

T. Carlyle

[2] *Time and Tide*, which was reprinted in book form later in the year, was addressed to "a workman," who proved to be Thomas Dixon. The passage was deleted in this edition.

76. *Ruskin to Carlyle*

Denmark Hill S.
10th June [1867]

My dear Carlyle

I have just come in from the country and seen your note to the Times, and I have your's—for both of which my thanks—but alas, you do not yet *in the least* see into this thing. I never denied the imprudence—discourtesy—Sin—whatever else you like to allege of my Dixon letter. But I emphatically deny its falsehood. And that is—to my utter sorrow—the one question which has to be settled—one way or another—harmfully either way—but the worst harm of all would be its remaining *un*settled.

—I write in haste—this is private—you will have my formal reply tomorrow. My *chief* wonder is to see how little you have known me all these years!— (No— Not my chief wonder—that is a far deeper one— but yet I am less—though more sorrowfully, surprised at your own conduct in this, than at your estimate of what mine would be.

Ever affectionately Yours
J. Ruskin

Do not fear any *hasty* proceeding on my part,—but my Dixon letters must remain unaltered now. You have put it wholly out of my power to withdraw a syllable. Of which tomorrow.

77. *Ruskin to Carlyle*

Denmark Hill, S.
12th June, [1867]

My dear Carlyle

I cannot write the formal letter to day, any more than I could yesterday, being variously occupied out in the sun:—but I more & more wonder at your not being able to distinguish between your lava-current of a mind—tumbling hither & thither and *cooling* in the odd corners of it at necessary periods—and my poor little leguminous-climbing-tendril of a vegetable-mind—subduable and flexible by a

Letter 76. MS: Bembridge. Hitherto unpbd.
Letter 77. Addr: Mr. Carlyle, Esq. / 5 Cheyne Row / Chelsea. Pm: London, June 12, 1867. MS: Bembridge. Hitherto unpbd. On the front of the envelope Carlyle has written: "(*Ultimate* last word!)."

touch—but utterly unchangeable and *implacable* in its poor wounded way—and changeless of temperature. One of the things that has struck deepest into me, in this, is the heartlessness with which, when I had told you that I was fighting a battle of bitterest pain, now at the very crisis when of all things it was [necessary?] that all probable honour should be done me by all who loved me, for my love's sake—that you should have forgotten and trampled all this under foot—just because you could not bear some newspaper gabble—and written the most dishonouring words that could be set down in public sight—

I know you did not mean them—and that you did the whole thing frantically. But see what a deadly *fact*, this phrenzy is to me, in the new reading it gives me of *all* your doings— Your books have from this one thing—become at once as a tinkling cymbal to me[1]—and whatever the commonest wretches now assert against them—I am powerless *now* to deny! What you have said of me—I know now, when the humour is on you—you would say of any one. It is the saddest thing.—

And I always suffer this kind of thing from those I have most cared for, and then I *cannot* forgive, just because I know I was the last person on earth they ought to have treated so. *Turner* did something of the same kind to me. I never forgave him, to his death.

Well, some day soon I will write the next necessary letter—you don't seem yet to understand that I intend the correspondence to be published, if necessary. Your two present letters are irrelevant, and shall not be held part of the series, unless you choose but *after this*—remember—answer, or refusal of answer, must be for possible publication.

J. R.

78. *Carlyle to Ruskin*

Chelsea, 13 June, 1867

Dear Ruskin,

With a Poet's temperament, you immensely exaggerate this miserable, but intrinsically small and paltry matter. "The most dishonouring words ever spoken of you" are, as you will understand by and by, simply to the effect, that you in y[r] headlong incautious way, with the best and truest intentions in the world, strode into one of the foolishest

[1] See I Corinthians 13:1

Letter 78. Addr: John Ruskin, Esq. / etc. etc. / Denmark Hill. Pm: London, S.W. June 14, 1867. MS: Yale University Library. Pbd: Sanders, pp. 227–29.

practical puddles recently heard of, and dragged a most unwitting friend along with you,—who refuses to lie there with you (especially to lie *undermost*, as he chanced to be), and, finding you took no steps and did not even recognize the puddle much, has striven honestly to save first himself, and then his more or less blameable compan^n too,— really with his best endeavour, and utmost stretch of faculty and skill, exerted in an element infinitely foreign and unpleas^t to him. So that *he* is now out, and getting his mind *cleaned*; and you too are out (if you will be wise) with only an infinitesimal minimum of *smutch* upon you,—such as all the sons of Adam catch to themselves from time to time, and are all absolved from *so soon* as they heartily acknowledge it. For the man that never made a "mistake" was not heard of hitherto.[1] And these are "the most dishonouring words that ever" &c &c. Oh dear, oh dear!—

But on the whole, I too, my friend, have had my abund^t vexation, botherat^n, and distresses ab^t this small and miserable matter—which is so extraneous, so infinitely *incongruous*, and comes intruding on me with such a ghastly contemptibility, amid the serious, sad and solemn matters wh^h are *my* constant occupat^n otherwise (especially sad in these weeks),—that I find it at last unbearable; and decide to have done with it at once, till it take a quite new figure! Please *don't* send me any "formal Letter"; but take this as my ans^r to it beforehand, and the only ans^r I will make to it or any other on that subject, as matters now stand bet^n us:

First, therefore, I never told you, nor c^d tell or have told any mortal, that "Mr. Carlyle" was liable to be insulted on the streets of London or Chelsea; the constant *fact* being that I have the natural liberty of all quiet persons to walk the streets unmolested, and if need were, protected & defended; and that in no street, lane or place of London or any other City, Town or region, did "Mr. Carlyle," when personally recognized, meet with anything hitherto but an evid^t respect far beyond what was his due, or what was in the least necessary to him. This is the steadfast fact; and this you have carelessly tumbled heels over head into a statement incredible to all who hear it, and monstrous to imagine. Secondly, I do tell you that, by order of the Doctor, I had *discontinued* my midnight walks, wh^h used to have a sombre soothing

---

[1] In the MS of the first draft of this letter, in the possession of Bembridge School, Carlyle has at this point written vertically across the rest of the sheet: "*ended* now, and be-hanged to it! (For the 4th and positively *last time!*)—(T.C.) 14 june." The rest of the MS of the first draft is written across the face of a blank proxy of the Great Eastern Railway Company.

charm, and to seem salutary, as the last work of the day. This I perfectly remember telling you. And what mad reversal you have made of this you cannot have forgotten! A domestic picture unexampled in British History or Biography. The wretched dreary old Dotard and Coward peering tremulously out of door at midnight, If he might now steal a little exercise,—and not substance enough left in him even to kill himself if he c^{d}n't alter such a state of matters. *Papae, proh pudor!* [Alas, the shame of it!] If a man were on the outlook for "dishonouring words," or cared much ab^t them when they came, here by accid^t they *are*, in richest measure for him.

In fine, so far as I can recollect those unlucky 10 minutes of loose talk, wh^h memory took so little charge of, and wh^h are now several weeks away, our discourse did not turn upon public streets, thoroughfares or *walking*, but almost wholly on my experiences in *riding*, thro' the unfrequented slums and waste-lying outskirts of London (tempted thither by the soft ground, or the immunity from wheels), where the lower populace or canaille inhabit: nor, ag^n, was my experience there the least definable as "Mr. Carlyle's," but simply as that of A. or B., riding, seemingly for his amusem^t, and from his age or gravity of aspect, not very likely to use his horsewhip in reply (wh^h more than once proved a miscalculat^n, too, and had firm effect on the individual two-legged *canis*, if he chanced to stand within reach). These are the precisest certain *facts* (as precise as I can now give them) of that bit of private dialogue bet^n us.

And had you, instead of carelessly, hastily and heedlessly *reversing* these, stated the whole of them with the accuracy of an affidavit, and then printed my name to them,—what c^d I have called it but the absurdest oversight, and foolishest "practical blunder" that ever dropped upon me of its own accord, from any man of sense, in all my days! And this is the last word I intend to write upon a subject, wh^h has already cost me a great deal too many.

For I have had, not on my own acc^t alone, to manipulate in my sad and sick Soul, this paltry bit of nonsense not a little, to tear it carefully down to its elemental fibres, and to sight and survey it on all sides till I c^d completely reckon it transparent to me, but something of *you* too, my friend, and of the mad world's ways with you and me; and in fine "to forge my miserable horse-shoe" (as I told you), nay in success^n my two horse-shoes, "in the middle of leaky powder-barrels": and I now thank God to have done with it altogether: Further words upon it, especially bet^n you and me, what good c^d be in them, till a considerable change come; till, as I once said already, we *both* of us come to see

John A. Carlyle, Thomas Carlyle, Mary Aitken, and Provost Swann, seated on the steps of St. Brycedale's House in Kirkcaldy in 1874. Photograph by J. Patrick. Courtesy of the Carlyle Society, Edinburgh.

both sides of the matter? Till each see, in a perfect and quietly transparent manner, not only his own grief and whether he brot it wholly on himself, but also on his neighbour's and whether *he* did so! If I am so egregiously in *error* to suppose that "six weeks" will work this salutary change in you, I shall be profoundly sorry (and much surprised withal, for it is still my belief); but the actual coming of the change does not now depend on me at all; and till it do come, we must wait.

The tone and new style of yr last Letters, especially of yr last but one, has been perhaps or seemed a little singular; and I want no more of that fashion soon. But as to *"implacability"* &c &c., it is, to myself, void of meaning or conceivability; and on such a score, as you assign, it wd savour to me of utter madness;—nor do I believe it of you at all, nor will unless forced. If I *had* in any degree injured a certn interest[2] (of whh I was not thinking at all), that wd indeed have been a cruel and most forbidding circ[umstanc]e in my necessity; but that was not there; nor do I now believe (whatr your wildly exaggerative mind may do) that it will have the weight of a fly's wing in the beautiful resolute and candid soul on whose vote you alone depend:—nay if it did, if she did see it to proceed from a too headlong habit &c, and to require a little censure and attempt at amendt, might it not be *better* that she know it now, before closure of the bargn than after it? There is for you!—

Adieu, my friend. Since you won't accept any counsel on that mutual plunge into the puddle, I must leave you to yr own. *Quod faustum sit* ["May it be beneficial"]. I consider it still possible that by this accidt we may become "better friends than ever"; more sincere, more frank, ruggedly *veracious*, much more humanly helpful to one another: But the chance depends now altogr on yrself, and I can't control it farther.[3] Adieu: none of yr fine qualities and talents, nor of yr uniformly amiable procedures, are forgotten by me at this moment, nor have much chance of ever being.

Yrs sincerely (so far as *you* will permit),

T. Carlyle

P.S. Please send me that Ms. of Edwd Irving[4] at yr convenience. I want it for a reason, but not till you have quite done with it.

---

[2] Rose La Touche, who was to decide upon Ruskin's marriage proposal in 1869. See Introduction.

[3] This letter evidently did not have the effect Carlyle wished for. Ruskin noted in his diary: "June 14th. Friday. . . . ugly letter from Carlyle in evening." (*Diaries*, II, 620.)

[4] On May 1, Carlyle had lent Ruskin the MS of the article on Edward Irving that he had written during the winter. See Ruskin's *Diaries*, II, 617.

79. *Ruskin to Carlyle*

Denmark Hill, S.
Tuesday 25th June, 1867

My dear Carlyle

I am going into Scotland for a week or two on Friday, and I want to see you before I go—if I may, without any reference to newspaper business. Don't think there is any change in my notions respecting *them*,—but between you and me, they ought not to come.

Only,—please understand this—I come to you, exactly as I should come to my Father, if he were alive—and I should say,

"Now, Father, if you are going to speak or teaze me, on such and such matters, I won't come; I have no mind to come, merely to be scolded—still less to find fault with you. If you were not my Father, I would not come at all, but being so, and because moreover you love me, and I love you, I want to see you—but you are not to say a word on such and such matters, nor to think that I shall in any wise act differently in them because I want to see you.

I have a great deal to see to and shall be a little later tomorrow evening.[1] Don't have tea for me, but I'll run in about nine o'clock and tell you where I'm going and anything else that I can, pleasant.

Ever affectionately yours.
J Ruskin

Letter 79. MS: Bembridge. Hitherto unpbd. Pm: London, June 25, 1867. Addr: Thomas Carlyle Esq. / 5 Cheyne Row / Chelsea, S.W. Carlyle has written on the envelope: "Ruskin: [Nichts, hardly read. June 25, 1867]."
[1] Ruskin, *Diaries*, II, 621: "June 26th. Wednesday [1867] . . . At Carlyle's in Evening with Scotch Provost."

III

NEARLY ALL MY CLOTHES
TO MAKE, FRESH

"I have nearly all my clothes to make, fresh—but more
shroud-shape than any other."
Ruskin to Carlyle, May 1, 1869
Letter 82

§❧

LETTERS 80-122

April 24, 1869, through October 9, 1873

Ruskin publishes *The Queen of the Air*. He visits Switzerland and
Italy. He becomes Slade Professor of Art at Oxford, begins monthly
publication of *Fors Clavigera* letters, and launches many different social welfare projects, including St. George's Guild. His dangerous illness at Matlock. Death of Ruskin's mother. Failing health of Rose La
Touche. Purchase of Brantwood home at Coniston.

Carlyle at home in Chelsea with Mary Aitken. He loses use of right
hand. He works on edition of his wife's letters and the "People's Edition" of his collected works.

80. *Ruskin to Carlyle*

Denmark Hill, S.E.
Saturday, 24th April, '69

Dear Mr. Carlyle

May I come to night a little after eight, for a talk in the old way? I am going to Verona, and back through Germany (Rhine east border) and want to tell you about some plans relating to the first volume of Frederick.

Ever affectionately Yours,
J. Ruskin

81. *Ruskin to Carlyle*

Denmark Hill, S.
[1869?]

Dear Mr. Carlyle,

If you *like* the book I send, I'll send you a copy—I should like you to have it from me—so would its author—if not—I'll bring it away in great discomfort, next Thursday.

Ever your loving
J. Ruskin

My remembrance to your little niece.[1]

82. *Ruskin to Carlyle*

Vevay. 1st May. 1869

Dear Mr Carlyle

I just got the Frederick in time; it is so nice to have it in this manageable form. with my own marked edition safe at home[1] I have been travelling every day since— I could not write before—nor now—for the sunshine and fresh air of the last four days have made me dull with their excess of brightness.— only just this word of thanks.

Letter 80. MS: Bembridge. Hitherto unpbd. The MS has, in Carlyle's hand: "Ruskin's *return* (By a messenger this morn^g (24 April 1869)."
Letter 81. MS: NLS, 555.36. Hitherto unpbd. The letter is undated, and the notation "? 1869" appears on the MS in another hand.
[1] Mary Aitken, who was staying with him.
Letter 82. MS: Bembridge. Pbd: Ruskin's *Works,* XXXVI, 565.
[1] Carlyle's *Frederick* was published by Chapman and Hall in London in 1869, in seven volumes (19cm., 12mo).

I have the Sartor with me ~~too~~ [*sic*] also—it belongs to me now—more than any other of your books.

I have nearly all my clothes to make, fresh—but more shroud-shape than any other.[2]

I'll write again soon.

I was very thankful to be with you again

Always affectionately Yours,
J Ruskin

83. *Carlyle to Ruskin*

Chelsea, August 17, 1869

Dear Ruskin,

Your excellent, kind, and loving note from Vevey reached me, but nothing since, not even precise news at second-hand, which I have much desired. The blame of my not answering and inditing was not mine, but that of my poor rebellious right hand, which oftenest refuses altogether to do any writing for me that can be read; having already done too much, it probably thinks! I did practically want a little thing of you at *Baireuth*, if you should pause there: *Photographs* of two portraits of Wilhelmina[1] which I had heard of;—but the *right hand* mumbled always, "You *can* do without them, you *know!*" and at length I lazily assented.

What I wish now is to know if you are at home, and to see you instantly, if so. *Instantly!* For I am not unlikely to be off in a few days (by *Steamer some* whither) and again miss you. Come, I beg, *quam primum!*—

Last week I got your "Queen of the Air," and read it. Euge, Euge! No such Book have I met with for long years past. The one soul now in the world who seems to feel as I do on the highest matters, and speaks *mir aus dem Herzen* ["to me from the heart"] exactly what I wanted to hear!— As to the natural history of those old Myths,[2] I remained here and there a little uncertain; but as to the meanings you put into

---

[2] A reference to the translated title of Carlyle's *Sartor Resartus*—"the Tailor Re-Tailored."

Letter 83. MS: Estate of Mrs. Helen Gill Viljoen. Pbd: Ruskin's *Works*, XIX, lxx–lxxi; and with omissions in Collingwood, II, 370–71.

[1] A reference to Wilhelmine (1709–58), sister of Frederick the Great, who married Friedrich, Markgraf von Brandenburg-Bayreuth in 1731. Her daughter, Friederike, was the first wife of Karl Eugen, Duke of Württemberg (1728–93).

[2] Ruskin's *Queen of the Air* is (nominally at least) a study of Greek myths of storm—especially the myth of Athena. Ruskin must have enjoyed Carlyle's praise well, for he had called this book "the best I ever wrote" and "the last which I took thorough loving pains with" (Cook, II, 159).

them, never anywhere. All these things I not only "agree" with, but would use Thor's Hammer, if I had it, to enforce and put in action on this rotten world. Well done, well done! and pluck up a heart, and continue again and again. And don't say "most great thoughts are dressed in *shrouds*:" many, many are the Phoebus Apollo celestial arrows you still have to shoot into the foul Pythons and poisonous abominable Megatheriums and Plesiosaurians that go staggering about, large as cathedrals, in our sunk Epoch again.

I have had a great deal to do with *insomnia*, etc., etc., since that last Wednesday evening;—come back, I tell you, while it is still time. With kind regards to the dear old Mother,

Yours ever,
T. Carlyle

84. *Ruskin to Carlyle*

Denmark Hill S.E.
2nd September [1869]

Dear Mr Carlyle

I am at home at last— I only got your lovely letter today—it was sent to a wrong address abroad—as well as Joan's[1] account of all your goodness to her.

I will come to morrow evening if I may.[2] I would have come to night, but it is my mother's birthday.

I should have written to you again and again from abroad, if all things had not been full of sadness to me—and of labour also—detaining me for this year from my happy work on your German castles. Italy is in a ghastly state of ruin and I did all I could on a few things I shall never see more.— Your German Castles will, I think, be yet long spared—but I hope to get some of them next year.

Just send a verbal "Yes" by the bearer if I may come to morrow.

Ever your affectionate,   J. Ruskin

Letter 84. MS: Bembridge. Pbd: Ruskin's *Works*, XXXVI, 589. The MS has "1869" in another hand.

[1] Joan Agnew (later Mrs. Arthur Severn), Ruskin's cousin. See Letter 107, n. 2.

[2] Carlyle probably refers to this visit in a letter to Froude on September 14, 1869: "One day, by express desire on both sides, I had Ruskin for some hours. Really interesting and entertaining, a much improved Ruskin since he went in May last. He is full of projects, of generous prospective activities, some of which, I opined to him, would prove chimerical. There is (in singular environment) a ray of real Heaven in poor Ruskin;—passages of that last book (Queen of the Air) went into my heart like arrows." (Cook, II, 164–65; also in Froude, IV, 383.) A letter written the next day to Lady Ashburton (MS: Marquess of Northampton) repeats this opinion, claiming Ruskin "much improved by his N. of Italy sojourn."

85. *Ruskin to Carlyle*

Denmark Hill S.E.
6th September 1869

Dear Mr. Carlyle,

I meant to come today but it is gusty & wet & I hope better for tomorrow— I will come tomorrow about ½ past one, be it wet or dry

Ever your affectionate
J Ruskin

86. *Carlyle to Ruskin*

Chelsea, 1 Octr 1869

Dear Ruskin,

We have been here, away bodily from Addiscombe,[1] since Monday gone a week,—situat^n a little "improved" by that change; I struggling, for my own poor hest [?], to beard [?] the faculty of *sleep*,—hitherto with quite imperfect success. Don't neglect to call on me the first time you are in Town—, the sight of y^r face will be a comfort; and I long for it, & a little farther talk on the problems you are occupied with.

At pres^t, after 2 p.m., I am not a certainty here;—note that, and *come*;—and let us settle for some [?] *weekly Ev^g* ag^n: why not!

Yrs ever Truly,
T. Carlyle

87. *Ruskin to Carlyle*

[October 2 or 3, 1869]

Dear Mr. Carlyle,

Thanks so much for kind note. I am so sorry for the sleeplessness.

—I cannot come on Thursday in the afternoon, but I will if I may, on Saturday.

I saw how wrong it was that you were disturbed that evening. You will think I never notice anything you say.— But when I came at 3 to the Croydon farm, it was the inevitable too late of an accident—and

Letter 85. MS: Bembridge. Hitherto unpbd. Addr: Tho. Carlyle, Esq. / Addiscombe Farm / *Croydon.* Pm: London S.E., X SP6, 69.

Letter 86. MS: Strouse Collection, University of California, Santa Cruz. Pbd: partially in Cook, II, 165. Addr: John Ruskin, Esq. / Denmark Hill. Pm: London, S.W., Oct. 1, 1869. A typescript of the MS is in the Bodleian Library at Oxford (*English Letters*, LII, 12).

[1] A country estate in Croydon owned by Lady Ashburton and frequently visited by Carlyle and Ruskin.

Letter 87. MS: NLS, 555.35. Hitherto unpbd.

last Thursday I had indeed *noticed*, but mistaken, your warning ½ past eight, and thought it was "eight," and put myself to some inconvenience that evening to come early!

Ever affectionately Yours,
J. Ruskin

88. *Ruskin to Carlyle*

Denmark Hill, S.E.
4 October [1869]

Dear Mr. Carlyle,

I am so *very* glad, always to have a note from you, but I *can't* get out in the evening now as I used to. I am always *so* weary; but I'll come some morning, when my poor wits are yet with me. I've so much to ask you about my work.

Ever your loving
J. Ruskin

89. *Ruskin to Carlyle*

Denmark Hill, S.E.
[November 30, 1869]

Dear Mr. Carlyle,

I have been unwell and Joanna has been in anxiety—ending in sorrow. Her newly married sister is dead.[1]— She was very good, and very useful, living. I wish I could think she was so still.

May I come and see you on Thursday—Friday—or Saturday evening?

Ever your loving
J. Ruskin

90. *Ruskin to Carlyle*

Denmark Hill, S.E.
[December 3, 1869]

Dear Mr. Carlyle,

I cannot venture to come out in this weather: I am so hard at work that the energy of me, such as it is—all spent in the morning—leaves me obliged to lie quiet in the afternoon unless the weather is warm and fine.— but I am often with you, in reality for I am reading the French

---

Letter 88. MS: NLS, 555.31. Hitherto unpbd. The MS has "1869" in another hand.
Letter 89. MS: NLS, 555.32. Hitherto unpbd.
[1] Joan's sister Kate, who had become Mrs. Simson. She died in November 1869.
Letter 90. MS: NLS, 555.33. Hitherto unpbd. The ellipsis in the middle of the letter indicates some words Ruskin omitted when he began a new page in the MS. The MS has "3 December 1869" in another hand.

Revolution again, to my mother.— It reminds her of old times, and I find more aphorism in that, at present useful to me [. . .] lectures for February[1]—to say to the schools of England what Painting means— and may be, if done by wise creatures.

—Enough to tire me?

[J. Ruskin]

91. *Ruskin to Carlyle*

Denmark Hill, S.E.
30th December
1869

Dear Mr. Carlyle,

Partly evil weather, partly my mother's more heavily pressing need of some evening comfort—and the equally pressing need, to *me*, of the unbroken morning, for what I have to prepare for very real duty at Oxford, have kept me from coming to you.

Might I come at ½ past 8 tomorrow, bringing with me a good, clear-headed, clearsighted—and to you most reverent and faithful—young English Merchant:—the son of my father's nephew[1]—who will I think work with me with all his heart in the sphere of a gradually widening West Indian Commerce—carrying it on, as English commerce should be done. His first ship he has named the "sesame",—she sails her first voyage early in the year. And he has no desire more earnest than that of being permitted to see your face—and hear your voice.

[1] The "Lectures on Art," delivered throughout February at Oxford.

Letter 91. MS: NLS, 555.34. Hitherto unpbd.

[1] Apparently William George Richardson (1839–77), the son of Dr. William J. Richardson and the grandson of Ruskin's "Aunt Jessie" Richardson of Perth. In a letter to J. R. Severn on December 30, 1869, (MS: Bembridge) Ruskin says, "Tomorrow George dines with me and we go together to Carlyle's, Bess having long wanted to go. Bess has bought a ship all his own—and calls it the 'Sesame.'" ("Bess" was Ruskin's nickname for George.) In Ruskin, *Diaries*, II, 692, he says, "Jan 1st. Saturday [1870]. Last night at Carlyle's with George."

The reference to the *Sesame* is tantalizing. The *Mercantile Navy List, Lloyd's Register*, and other sources say that she was built by John Crown's shipbuilders in Sunderland and launched in February of 1870 for the Sunderland to West Indies run. But the original owner of the ship is listed everywhere as "Hill & Co." of London, with no mention of a Richardson in any connection. Subsequent inquiries have also failed to establish any relationship between Richardson and the schooner. Yet searches in both published and unpublished Ruskin diaries reveal that between 1868 and 1877 Ruskin helped young George in some unidentified business dealings involving thousands of pounds, and the name "Sesame" clearly reveals a connection with Ruskin.

May I bring him?

The Woolwich lecture[2] went well.

> Ever your affectionate
> J. Ruskin

92. *Ruskin to Carlyle*

> Denmark Hill, S.E.
> Monday [1870]

Dear Mr. Carlyle,

Might I come about ½ past eight this evening?— I have not been able to get across in the middle of the day this week, to my sorrow.

> Your loving   J. R.

93. *Ruskin to Carlyle*

> Denmark Hill, S.E.
> [1870?]

Dear Mr. Carlyle,

We have all been so happy with Mary[1] that we are going to trust in your kindness so far as to keep her with us till tomorrow morning,— she wants herself to get back to you, but we all want her so much that I am going to assume your permission. I would not have done so, if I had been able to send to ask it, in time to make arrangements, but I have been hurried & confused to day.— She shall be back very early after breakfast tomorrow.

> Ever your affectionate
> J. Ruskin

94. *Ruskin to Carlyle*

> Denmark Hill, S.E.
> Saturday, 19th
> March, 1870

Dear Mr. Carlyle,

No, I have not forgotten Chelsea. But I have been doing all I could, and falling short of all I intended to do, at Oxford—(yet, it is well on the whole, hitherto) and for seven weeks, have had either cold— cough—face ache—or sore-throat—to work under and talk with.

---

[2] "The Future of England," delivered at the Woolwich Arsenal on December 14, 1869, and included in later editions of *The Crown of Wild Olive*.

Letter 92. MS: NLS, 555.56. Hitherto unpbd.

Letter 93. MS: NLS, 555.57. Hitherto unpbd.

[1] Mary Aitken, Carlyle's niece, who later married her cousin, Alexander Carlyle, editor of the Carlyle letters. See also Letter 69.

Letter 94. MS: NLS, 555.37. Hitherto unpbd.

It has been exactly as if the devil had been let worry me all he liked, provided only he didn't stop my speaking—for every lecture—hitherto—has been fairly well heard.— They are just going to press, at the Clarendon, and as soon as I have revised free from ludicrous misprints, I will send them you as they come from press, for I think you will be pleased by what I have got stated. There have been no reports in the least intelligible—for, as you suppose—they have not been without a plan. The Morning Post also made me say the exact reverse of what I meant.— but I've no chance of coming to Chelsea I fear till end of next week—my throat is sore & I must stay in at nights, till the last lecture is over, on Wednesday.

Ever lovingly Yours,
J. Ruskin

95. *Ruskin to Carlyle*

Denmark Hill, S.E.
[March 25, 1870]

Dear Mr. Carlyle,

I thought perhaps you might like to see this first proof—(see the vanity of me),—so I send it you as soon as I get it. I've got some hard work still in writing viva voce facts—but shall be over to see you next week.

Ever your loving   J. Ruskin

96. *Ruskin to Carlyle*

Denmark Hill, S.E.
Sunday 24th April
1870

Dear Mr. Carlyle,

Might I come at ½ past 8 to see you this evening. I have been entirely helpless lately through having planned twice as much as I could do, and getting my whole plan deranged like a campaign, again and again, by successive defeats. At last the best-worst is done—unless you are displeased by anything in the enclosed, pp. 105, 6. which please glance at before I come.

Ever your loving   J. R.

So sorry I was not to see you when you were so good as to come with Lady A.

Letter 95. MS: NLS, 555.38. Hitherto unpbd. The MS has "25 March 1870" in another hand.
    Letter 96. MS: NLS, 555.39. Hitherto unpbd.

97. *Ruskin to Carlyle*

Denmark Hill, S.E.
[ca. September 25, 1870]

Dear Mr. Carlyle,

I send you another, perhaps a little too long, study of Gotthelf's[1]—study—for it is hardly a story in any sense, but as you will see even from the first sentence, from "Je m'appelle Peter Koeser"—to "quittai la cuisine" a most finished piece of Dutch painting of two persons only—"*moi*, et Medeli"—the "Medeli", like the Aenneli of the miroir,[2] is better worth painting than most queens. The "Moi", I think you will much enjoy; and, first of all, these are some notes about the author, which will answer, better than I did, your questions of last night.

—I answered rashly also that I was always safe till 2. I should have said 1., though usually I am not out till 2.

—My day is—work at any rate till one—then, on fine days out till near 5—I dine at 5, and am *always* at home all the evening, unless I go to the theatre. I go nowhere else, but to Chelsea, which is my theatre of History—& Humanity.

On Monday next, Joanna[3] comes home, and we shall be in bustle; and on Wednesday next, I take her to Connie,[4] (the little lady I once brought to see you) and another sister, I hope, to the theatre,—but on all the rest of the days of next week am sure to be at home in the evening.

—Would you care to come with me by ourselves or with Joan only sometimes to a private box, to see anything absurd enough to be interesting? that may be played this winter?

Letter 97. MS: NLS, 555.41. Hitherto unpbd. The MS has "October 1870" in another hand.

[1]Jeremias Gotthelf, pseudonym of Albert Bitzius (1797–1854), a Swiss novelist. Ruskin is here quoting from a French translation of Gotthelf's *Leiden und Freuden eines Schulmeisters*, which was originally published in 1838–39, and begins with "Peter Kaser heisse ich. . . ." "Medeli," in German *Madele*, is Kaser's wife in the novel. See Gotthelf's *Sämtliche Werke* (Erlenbach-Zurich, 1921), II and III.

[2]Aenneli is a character in Gotthelf's *Der Bauernspiegel* (1836), which appeared in a French translation (Berne, 1854) under the title *Le Miroir des paysans*. For Ruskin's further discussion of her, see *Works*, VII, 429–30; and XXVII, 545.

[3]Joan Agnew.

[4]Constance Hilliard, daughter of the Reverend J. C. Hilliard, and niece of Sir Walter and Lady Trevelyan. Her sister's name was Ethel. Apparently Joan did not return in time, for Ruskin visited the Hilliards alone from the end of September to Thursday, October 6. See Burd, *Winnington*, 669–70; also Ruskin, *Diaries*, II, 703–4.

My sincere regards to your wise little niece.

Ever your affectionate
J. Ruskin

98. *Ruskin to Carlyle*

Denmark Hill, S.E.
[October 1870]

Why did not you come in?

I'll be with you at 8 ½ tomorrow. I don't mourn over time wasted on "Friedrich" *now*.[1]— It is the brightest among the few brightnesses left to us.

Ever your loving   J. R.

99. *Ruskin to Carlyle*

Denmark Hill, S.E.
Saturday,
[October 10, 1870]

Dear Mr. Carlyle,

I've been in a misery of provocation against myself ever since the note to you yesterday was sent off—for the stupidity of its wording, as if I meant Joan only to come with us, & not your niece—it would be so nice for us to go altogether—only first I was thinking only of going quite by ourselves—& then—I said to myself in a web of parentheses—"Joan wouldn't perhaps be merely in the way."

But even if you won't come, I want your niece to come with me & Joanna (moi et Medeli!), to see something pretty, when I hear or know of anything really pretty being played.

I send two daily Telegraphs with a word or two which you may care to glance at.

Ever your affᵉ,   J. R.

Letter 98. MS: NLS, 555.42. Hitherto unpbd.

[1] A reference to the Franco-Prussian War, which was going on at the time. In a letter to C. E. Norton on August 26, 1870, Ruskin exclaimed, "Dear old Carlyle—how thankful I am that he did his Friedrich exactly at the right time!" (C. E. Norton, ed., *The Letters of John Ruskin to Charles Eliot Norton* [Boston and New York, 1905], II, 24).

Letter 99. MS: NLS, 555.40. Hitherto unpbd.

100. *Carlyle to Ruskin*

5 Cheyne Row, Chelsea
10 October 1870

Dear Ruskin,

On Saturday morning, on my first sally out into the open air, I noticed on a Newsvendor's Placard that there was a "Letter from Mr. Ruskin",[1] which it would be necessary for me to see. Not having the copper penny in my pocket, I took the necessary steps immediately on my return home; and, along with my Coffee, comfortably swallowed the *Ruskin Letter* accordingly,—more comfortably than I did my coffee, for which, alas, as for all other material things (tho' *not* for things spiritual, thank God) there is now a clearly decaying appetite.

In the course of the day, I learnt that there had been another *Letter*, which somehow must be attained here; and, by our last post, came your beneficent announcement that both *Letters* had been duly put under way by you. By you duly; but not by the Postoffice Authorities, who did not, till our second post *this* day, forward your two *Daily Telegraphs* at all;—and now further, to my confusion, I discover that they are *both* copies of the Saturday's *Telegraph*, which I had already possessed, and given away several copies of, before the week ended! Letter First, therefore, still stands as a lonely *Desideratum* in that waste-howling Wilderness of human mismanagement, disloyalties and infidelities!— You see then, what is at once to be done. Pray clip out Letter First for one, and dispatch it *quam primum*.— Your Second Letter, full of holy indignation was as if it came from my own heart; at the end, however, I think you do the Germans wrong. My notion is: Bismarck knows very well what he is aiming at; & I find withal that it is a perfectly just thing; likewise that all the World cannot prevent him from getting it; and that he is calmly taking all the necessary steps for coercing an inarticulate, mad and furious Wasps' Nest of thirty five million delirious Mountebanks to quietly grant it him, with the *Minimum* of Sulphur applied. He seems to me at this moment to have power to cut France into thongs, and, in a few days, to convert Paris, if he liked, into a red hot Cinder; but is far from intending anything beyond the strictly necessary for his objects.[2]

Letter 100. MS: Yale University Library. Pbd: Sanders, pp. 231–32.

[1] This and the letter mentioned in the next paragraph were both entitled "The Franco-Prussian War," and appeared in the *Daily Telegraph* on October 7 and 8 (see *Works*, XXXIV, 499–500).

[2] Carlyle further expounded these ideas in his letter "On the French-German War" in the *Times*, November 18.

I am reading Bitzius, with astonishment at the dull gritty strength of him; also at his cruelty, limitation, dimness, narrowness: but there is the charm in him of a rugged Veracity; strange Dutch Picture, as you say, of an object curious to me and unknown to me. With great pleasure my little Niece will be of your party to the Theatre whenever you see good. Whether her poor old Uncle, who also would *like* much, can accompany or not will depend on the complexion of the Nervous System for that evening;—The willing mind for many things is still partially here; but the Man is way-worn, weary, and rigorously ordered to be aware of the fact.

Send me the Newspaper Clipping, dear Ruskin; and believe me

Ever yours,
T. Carlyle

101. *Ruskin to Mary Aitken*

Oxford, 26th
—Nov. 70.

Dear Miss Aitken,

I've been ill, and besides, looking after some love affairs for both my daughters—Lily and Joan[1]—at once, and Oxford lectures are very difficult—and my own temper difficulter—and so—and so.— I haven't come— I'll soon come now.

The Times letter[2] was delicious to me beyond beyond [*sic*].

Dear love to your Uncle

Ever your affectionate Friend
J. Ruskin

102. *Ruskin to Mary Aitken*

Denmark Hill, S.E.
27th Dec. 70

I am so glad of your kind note. Lily has gone back to her moorlands; but I shall gratefully bring Joanna with me on Friday evening[1]—if that evening would be open—though it has not been because I would not leave the two girls, but because I have only now taken breath after a

Letter 101. MS: NLS, 555.44. Hitherto unpbd.

[1] Lily Armstrong, a pupil at Winnington school and the "Lily" of *Ethics of the Dust*, who was to become Mrs. William T. S. Kevill-Davies in 1875. For additional details see Burd, *Winnington*, p. 442, n. 4, and *passim*. Joan Agnew was soon to become Mrs. Arthur Severn. See Letter 107, n. 2.

[2] See Letter 100, n. 1.

Letter 102. MS: NLS, 555.47. Hitherto unpbd.

[1] On Saturday morning, December 31, Carlyle wrote to his brother John: "Last night he [Ruskin] was here, he and two extremely insipid young women; but the result to me was . . . zero or at least considerable *minus* quantities" (MS: NLS, 527.37).

very difficult piece of work at Oxford,[2] that the year is thus so nearly ended before I again see your uncle.

I have more things of a more or less satisfactory nature to myself,[3] and therefore I trust to *him* also, (for I am always best pleased with what I think he is likely to like,) on hands at this moment, than for some years. I hope for a happy evening in getting his counsel about them.

Ever with Joanna's love & thanks.

affectionately Yours,
J. Ruskin

103. Ruskin to Mary Aitken

Denmark Hill, S.E.
2nd January, [1871]

My dear Miss Aitken,

It is very dear & kind of your Uncle to wish to see me. I will be at Chelsea tomorrow by one o'clock.

—affectionately Yours
J. Ruskin

104. Ruskin to Mary Aitken

Denmark Hill, S.E.
[January 18, 1871]

Dear Miss Aitken,

I was on the point of writing to say I had got a *quite* private, large, comfortable box for Drury Lane Pantomime on Saturday evening.

Would your uncle come with us. Nobody would see him, and he would see, I believe really some fairly good fooling,—but I'm going tonight to look myself, to tell him. If he won't come, you at least we *must* have.— Of course I shall be more than glad and proud to be of any help I can to Miss Jewsberry [*sic*].[1] Ever your uncle's and yours faithfully & lovingly,

J. Ruskin

---

[2] The lectures on "The Elements of Sculpture," delivered in November and December, and later published as *Aratra Pentelici* in 1871.

[3] Among other things, Letter 1 of *Fors Clavigera*, which was published the next month. For Carlyle's comments on it (which were unfavorable), see Introduction.

Letter 103. MS: NLS, 555.48. Hitherto unpbd.

Letter 104. MS: NLS, 555.49. Hitherto unpbd.

[1] Mary Aitken had undertaken the responsibility of trying to get signatures for a Civil List Pension for Geraldine Jewsbury, novelist and close friend of Mrs. Carlyle. See also Letter 52, n. 4.

105. *Ruskin to Carlyle*

Denmark Hill, S.E.
January [21], 1871

Dear Mr. Carlyle,

I don't quite know what to say about the Pantomime.[1] I think you might get so *very* angry! and poor little Mary, who would only think it amusingly foolish, herself, might think it—as it is—wickedly foolish, if she saw you angry. You know I want you to come with us, if you can *at all* enjoy a foolish thing, well done in its way in some parts. But I'm a little frightened. We will be with you at 20 minutes past six—or soon after—and will of course bring Mary home to you, if she comes alone with us, and if you will be *good*, and come too, we'll all come home to Chelsea together.

Ever your affe.
J. Ruskin

106. *Ruskin to Carlyle*

[April 8, 1871]

Dear Mr. Carlyle,

I have been more busy than I can tell you, at Oxford,[1] and when I came home, my old nurse[2] died—and since, I have had cold—and have still. But may I come & see you tomorrow Easter Sunday Evening? and assure you how devotedly I am still your affectionate

John Ruskin

Letter 105. MS: NLS, 555.50. Pbd: Ruskin's *Works*, XXXVII, 27–28. The date, January 21, is based upon internal evidence from this and the previous letter. January 18 was a Wednesday, and Ruskin's mention of "Saturday" would probably place the date of this letter at Saturday, January 21.

[1] Ruskin, having gone to the performance at Drury Lane Theatre on January 18, has enclosed a programme with his letter. It announces a "New and Original Farce" entitled "Rule Britannia" and a "New Grand Comic Christmas Annual" called "The Dragon of Wantley; or, Harlequin & Old Mother Shipton," featuring tableaux called "Workshop of Time," "Haunt of the Water Nymphs," and (preceded by a "Grand Ballet of One Hundred Coryphees") "Mother Shipton's Abode by the Dripping Well." Carlyle, as one might expect, chose not to go.

Letter 106. MS: NLS, 555.45. Hitherto unpbd.

[1] Ruskin delivered his "Lectures on Landscape" at Oxford in January and February 1871. He had also endowed a drawing mastership there, and was working hard arranging an art collection to accompany it.

[2] Anne Strachan, who had been Ruskin's nurse in his infancy, died in April 1871.

107. *Ruskin to Mary Aitken*

Denmark Hill, S.F..
28th April, 1871

My dear Mary,

You *must* let me thank you for your lovely letter, and say that you were entirely right in yielding to Madame Venturi,[1]—as I think you always are in everything, & therefore, I am sure you will forgive my disobeying your request that I would not answer.— It was a most true joy to me—(I had few, on the day)—to see your gentle and firm face shining amidst the variously weak & discordant elements of London amiability on the day of the wedding.[2] Faithful love to your uncle.

Your affectionate, John Ruskin

108. *Carlyle to Ruskin*

5 Cheyne Row, Chelsea, *April* 30, 1871

Dear Ruskin,—

This *Fors Clavigera*, Letter 5th,[1] which I have just finished reading, is incomparable; a quasi-sacred consolation to me, which almost brings tears into my eyes! Every word of it is as if spoken, not out of my poor heart only, but out of the eternal skies; words winged with Empyrean wisdom, piercing as lightning,—and which I really do not remember to have heard the like of. *Continue*, while you still have such utterances in you, to give them voice. They will find and force entrance into human hearts, *whatever* the "angle of incidence" may be; that is to say, whether, for the degraded and *in*human Blockhead-ism we, so-called "Men," have mostly now become, you come in upon them at the broadside, at the top, or even at the bottom. *Euge, Euge!*

[Yours ever,
T. Carlyle]

Letter 107. MS: NLS, 555.51. Hitherto unpbd.
[1] See Letter 52.
[2] Joan Agnew married Arthur Severn, youngest son of Keats' friend Joseph Severn, in April 1871.
Letter 108. MS: Estate of Mrs. Helen Gill Viljoen. Pbd: Collingwood, II, 411; and in Ruskin's *Works*, XXVII, lxxxvi. Carlyle's complimentary close and signature have been cut away. Beneath the cut the MS has, in Mrs. Viljoen's hand, "Hand of Mrs. Severn:" then "Signed 'yrs. ever / T. Carlyle' in TC's own hand. The signature / given to young Harvey goodwin [*sic*] / of Olton Hall," in Joan Agnew's hand.
[1] This is the famous letter in which Ruskin deplores modern science and mechanism and describes his ideals for the "St. George's Guild." Every man in the guild, he says,

109. *Ruskin to Carlyle*

Denmark Hill, S.E.
1st May, 1871

Dear Mr. Carlyle,

I am deeply thankful to have your letter on this day itself. I think the great help it gives me is not so much in the actual encouragement, great as that is,—as in the pleasure of giving you pleasure—and knowing that you accept what I am doing as the fulfilment [*sic*] so far as in me is, of what you have taught me.

Also, I needed your letter much, for I am at a strain in all directions at once—and was despondent, not for cause, but by over-work, about my work; and I have nothing else to fall back upon now, and can scarcely rest.

So many thanks to you.—

Ever your loving
J. Ruskin

Dear love to Mary

110. *Ruskin to Mary Aitken*

Denmark Hill, S.E.
10th May, [1871]

My dear Mary,

I have just come home & have your letter—the Fors, with another for you, will come, I hope by next post, I have not one by me.

How thankful I am for your account of your uncle.

Ever your affectionate,
J. Ruskin

I send you a wood hyacinth I painted before my class last week—but it was only to show them how to work, & is itself poor enough—but you may perhaps like to have it.

---

will be a "minute squire," and throughout the guild there will be "none wretched but the sick; none idle but the dead." In a sentence that must have especially delighted Carlyle, Ruskin then insists that the land of the guild "will have no liberty upon it; but instant obedience to known law, and appointed persons: no equality upon it; but recognition of every betterness that we can find." (*Works*, XXVII, 96.)

Letter 109. MS: NLS, 555.52. Pbd: Ruskin's *Works*, XXXVII, 30–31.

Letter 110. MS: NLS, 555.53. Hitherto unpbd. The MS has "P.M^k. 1871" in another hand.

111. *Carlyle to Ruskin*

5 Cheyne Walk, Chelsea,
21 October, 1871

Dear Ruskin,

I cannot explain to myself the strange, and indeed lamentable, fact that I have not seen you, or heard a distinct word from you, for, I think, seven or eight months. It is a fact that has become not only surprising to me, but distressing, and the source latterly of continual anxieties both about myself and you. For three months I had no amanuensis[1] (I in the Highlands; Mary in Dumfries-shire, far away), and without a hand could not write to you myself; about the middle of that period, too, there came the most alarming rumours of your illness at Matlock,[2] and both Lady Ashburton and myself (especially the latter party, for whom I can answer best) were in a state really deserving pity on your account, till the very newspapers took compassion on us, and announced the immediate danger to be past. All this is wrong, and *not* as it should be. I beg earnestly that, wherever this may find you, you would at once devote one serious half-hour to me, and write a few words of authentic news concerning yourself, and especially a work of *prediction* as to when I may expect to see you again, if ever. The *Fors Clavigera* sufficiently assures me, from time to time, that it is not want of the old goodwill towards me which keeps you silent, but the *Fors Clavigera* itself (which very few can get hold of, though many are seeking it) awakens anxieties in me instead of satisfying them all. In short, a deliberate bit of letter is indispensable to me for all manner of reasons.

It is four weeks today since I returned hither; said by sanguine friends to be visibly "improved in health"; felt by myself to be only invisibly so, if at all. Now, as formerly, I have my daily (especially my *nightly*) battle to fight with the innumerable Beasts at Ephesus[3]—human, diabolical, and also of the inanimate sort—which never quit a poor fellow till they have brought him to the ground altogether;

Letter *111*. MS: Estate of Mrs. Helen Gill Viljoen. Pbd: Ruskin's *Works*, XXII, xix–xx.

[1] Since 1865, Carlyle had gradually lost the use of his right hand. Most of the letters from this date on are in Mary Aitken's hand. See Letter 83.

[2] In July, Ruskin caught a severe chill, followed by a severe attack of internal inflammation, and at one time he came near death. See Cook, II, 216–18.

[3] See I Corinthians 15:32: "If after the manner of men I have fought with beasts at Ephesus, what advantageth it me, if the dead rise not?"

against which I faintly, but really sometimes with an earnest wish, endeavour to make fight, though of course with weaker and weaker effect. Froude has returned, and is often asking about you; as indeed are many others, to whom the radiant qualities which the gods have given you, and set you to work with in such an *element*, are not unknown. Write me a word at once, dear Ruskin. Mary sends her love to you. The most mournful tragedy has happened in her and my circle—the death of her eldest Brother by the accident of leaping down from a coach here, probably with too much trust in his nimbleness of limb; an excellent, completely faithful, and valiant young man, whose loss has thrown a gloom over us all. No more today. *Do* swiftly what I have begged of you.

I remain, ever and always,
Heartily yours,
T. Carlyle

112. *Ruskin to Carlyle*

Denmark Hill, S.E.
Monday, 23rd Oct., 71

My dear Mr. Carlyle,

Your loving letter greeted me returning today from Oxford. My illness indeed very nearly ended me, and left me heavy in limb and otherwise helpless for some weeks. Gradually—(people say with unusual rapidity)—my strength came back—but I cannot yet run or climb as I could before.

As soon as I could use my hand or head, I had to get ready for press two books at once—lectures on Sculpture, and the old Fraser's magazine polit. econ.[1] This last I had to read & revise, & the Sculpture lectures—to *think* much as I finished them.— My mother was, and is still slowly declining, and liked to have me near her for a little while in the evenings—so passed, with great fear of relapse into illness, the month of August.

In the course of the month, a letter came to me from America. In my illness, at most feverish fit, my one saying was, "If only I could lie down in Coniston water." The letter from America was from a friend,[2]

Letter 112. MS: NLS, 555.54. Pbd: Ruskin's *Works*, XXXVII, 39–40.

[1] *Aratra Pentelici* and *Munera Pulveris*, both published in 1872. *Munera Pulveris* had originally appeared in *Fraser's Magazine* as "Essays on Political Economy": see Letter 38.

[2] W. J. Linton, a poet, wood engraver, and husband of the novelist, Mrs. Lynn Linton. Ruskin paid £1,500 for the sixteen-acre property.

in need of money, to ask if I would buy his cottage by Coniston water, and a few acres of copse and rock with it. I answered, yes, without having seen the place,—sent to his lawyer—concluded the purchase—and went down early in September—like the wicked person who wouldn't come to supper[3]—to see my piece of ground.

It is a bit of steep hillside facing West—commanding from the brow of it, all Coniston lake and the mass of hills of south Cumberland.—The slope is half copse—half moor and rock—a pretty field beneath, less steep, a white two-storied cottage, and a bank of turf in front of it—, then a narrow mountain road—and on the other side of that—Naboth's vineyard[4]—my neighbour's field, to the water's edge. My neighbour will lease me enough of field and shore to build a boathouse, & reach it.

If I could write better, I should have told you all this before, but I am ashamed to inflict my writing on my friends.

—From Coniston, I went on to see the coast of the Antiquary at Arbroath[5]—and then back to superintend the putting of roof on my house: No workmen could be had—and it is but begun now. I had given 5000 pounds to found a drawing Mastership at Oxford.— To set this rightly on foot, I had to prepare an entire system of elementary teaching,[6] and am at work on the material of that—drawings and the like—still, and have just been to Oxford, and have returned much tired and send this miserable written letter to you with my love, and will come, if I may, to see you, at ½ past 8 tomorrow evening.

Ever your loving

J. Ruskin

I need not say I am grieved at what you tell me about poor Mary.[7] My mother is, I fear, more than slowly sinking, now, and other sad things have happened to me.

[3] See Luke 14:18.

[4] See I Kings 21:1–16 and II Kings 9:26.

[5] Arbroath, a small port on the Tay about seventeen miles northeast of Dundee. It is called "Fairport" in Sir Walter Scott's *The Antiquary* (1816). Under the disguise of "Redlintie" it was also the site of Sir James M. Barrie's *Sentimental Tommy* (1896).

[6] The "Educational Series." See *Works*, XXI, xxiv–xxxviii.

[7] In the margin of the MS another hand—probably Cook's—has written "Miss Aitken had lost her elder brother."

Brantwood, Ruskin's home in Coniston, in the 1880's. Courtesy of the Ruskin Galleries, Bembridge School, Isle of Wight.

113. *Ruskin to Carlyle*

Denmark Hill, S.E.
[October 24?, 1871]

Dear Mr. Carlyle,

Dr. Acland[1] has relieved me from all instant fear about my mother's state—and I hope, tonight without fail, to be with you a little before nine.

Ever your loving   J. R.

Love to Mary. She was so sweet & kind to my cousin[2] last night.

114. *Carlyle to Ruskin*

5 Cheyne Row, Chelsea
6 Decr., 1871

Dear Ruskin,

—My heart is sore for you in these dreary moments.[1] A great change has befallen; irrevocable, inexorable,—the lot of all the world since it was first made, and yet so strangely original, as it were miraculous, to each of us, when it comes home to himself. The Wearied one has gone to her welcome Rest; and to you there is a strange regretful, mournful desolation in looking before and back;—to all of us the loss of our Mother is a new epoch in our Life-pilgrimage, now fallen lonelier and sterner than it ever seemed before.— I cannot come to you; nor would it be proper or permissible, for reasons evident. But I beg you very much to come to me at any hour, and let me see you for a little, after those sad and solemn duties now fallen to you are performed. Believe always that my heart's sympathies are with you, and that I love you well.

Yours,
T. Carlyle

Letter *113*. MS: NLS, 555.55. Hitherto unpbd.

[1] Dr. (later Sir) Henry Wentworth Acland (1815–1900), Ruskin's intimate friend and family physician. During a lifetime of various professional positions at Oxford, Acland not only led the study of medicine at his university into the modern world but also was in the forefront of the new curriculum in the humanities established in the 1860's and 1870's. He was one of Ruskin's closest friends for more than half a century.

[2] Joan Agnew.

Letter *114*. MS: Luis Gordon of Luis Gordon and Sons, Ltd, London. Pbd: Ruskin's *Works*, XXXVI, xxiii; and in Cook, II, 223.

[1] Mrs. Margaret Ruskin died on December 5, 1871. "Poor Ruskin has lost his mother," wrote Carlyle, "she died Tuesday about 2 p.m. A note came from him of three

115. *Ruskin to Carlyle*

Wednesday
[December 1871]

Dear Mr. Carlyle,

Your lovely letter made me very sad—in some ways happy, too, in your sympathy.

—You must not cease enjoying your coffee. All your work is grandly done, and it is just time for coffee, & pipe, and peace. If one could do good by being unpeaceful—it would be another thing. But what's the use of dying uselessly— Better to live uselessly, but for the joy of one's friends.

I enclose a letter from Joanna to your niece. I sincerely hope you can spare her to us to-morrow. I've a bright Irish girl here; and the two Scotch ones will make the delightfullest trefoil possible—and I'll do what I can to make her happy, for writing me your letter.

Tell her, and she will tell me, why you call Bitzius "cruel"[1]—he seems to me an entirely sweet and loving person.

Ever your loving
J. Ruskin

P.S. I sent the slip yesterday at last. It wasn't worth [much].

116. *Ruskin to Carlyle*

Denmark Hill, S.E.
23rd Dec. 1871

Dear Mr. Carlyle,

Only to tell you I'm thinking of you.

I am getting some work—of I hope—detonating character, charged for January.[1]—I *must* come to see you next week.

Ever your loving
J. Ruskin

---

short lines that night, mournful as if every word were a tear." (Letter to his brother John, December 7, 1871; MS: NLS, 527.56.)

    Letter 115. MS: NLS, 555.43. Pbd: Ruskin's *Works*, XXXVII, 44–45.

[1] See last paragraph of Letter 100.

    Letter 116. MS: NLS, 555.46. Hitherto unpbd.

[1] Either the notorious "street-sweeping experiment" that took place in London in January 1872, or the preparation of a series of ten lectures Ruskin was to deliver at Oxford in February and later publish as *The Eagle's Nest*.

117. *Ruskin to Mary Aitken*

Denmark Hill, S.E.
3rd January. 72

My dear Mary,

I was very glad of your note, as you may well think, it is so dear of your uncle wanting to see me.

He likes me better, does he not, to come in the forenoon? tell me this,—(and say this letter is between you & me, and he is not to see it.) I've sent him some books. Get him to look at the preface to Munera Pulveris,[1] and the sentence at the end of the appendix which I think is very pretty.

I've sent you a little Venetian chain, which my mother used to wear.* The gold is very pure, and if you will be at the pretty pains of washing it, will I hope gleam out with Venetian light.

Ever your affectionate
John Ruskin

* She liked it best of all her chains.

118. *Ruskin to Carlyle*

Brantwood
Monk-Coniston
Lancashire
30th August, 1872

Dear Mr. Carlyle,

I have this moment received Dr. Carlyle's letter. I should have written to you long since, but had only horrible things to write.[1] I am under more kindly stars, now, but have much pain & doubt to bear

Letter 117. MS: NLS, 555.58. Hitherto unpbd.

[1] *Munera Pulveris*, which had just been published, was dedicated to "the friend and guide who has urged me to all chief labour, Thomas Carlyle."

The books Ruskin sent were read with Carlyle's usual critical appreciation. On February 24, 1872, Carlyle wrote to his brother John: "I am reading Ruskin's books in these evenings. . . . I find a real spiritual comfort in the noble fire, wrath, and inexorability with which he smites upon all base things, and wide-spread public delusions; and insists relentlessly in having the ideal aimed at everywhere: for the rest I do not find him wise—headlong rather, and I might even say weak. But there is nothing like him in England in these other respects." (Alexander Carlyle, *New Letters of Thomas Carlyle* [1904], II, 283–84.)

Letter 118. MS: NLS, 555.59. Hitherto unpbd.

[1] Earlier that month, Rose La Touche had definitely refused to marry Ruskin, after making him wait an additional three years (over six in all) for her answer.

yet.— I am to be here, arranging rooms in my new house, till the middle of October I believe, but will write soon again. This is to catch post

Ever your loving

John Ruskin

119. *Ruskin to Carlyle*

Brantwood, Coniston
Sunday, 15th Feb. 73

Dear Mr. Carlyle,

I can't in the least make out why you wished me to look at this enclosed letter. It seems to me out of quite one of the wooly-headiest of sheep's heads, and by no means to be noticed in any wise— It is the sort of thing that makes me feel as if I had to fight a scarecrow stuffed with dirty cotton—that choked one with fluff if one cut it. You are too good natured to put up with such people.

And I was a little surprised, also, (I must speak true you know), by the book you gave,—or I should have written of it before. It is boastful and pompous—not the sort of thing I should have thought you would have been pleased with—the more as I have heard you laugh at Humboldt for an old woman,—though his little finger was thicker than this man's loins.[1]

I got down here yesterday in the evening, and at five o'clock—crossing Lancaster Sands—saw what I thought the most wonderful thunderclouds in the sunset light that I had ever seen in my life.— In five minutes more, I saw they were my own opposite snowy mountains!— I had no conception any thing so beautiful was possible, with such low elevation. I would rather have drawn that view over Lancaster bay than any I ever saw from Venice.

Thanks, so much, for what you told me of your grandmother and mother.

Happy, this northern land—in snow of lofty soul—as of sweet hillside.

Ever your loving

John Ruskin

Letter 119. MS: NLS, 555.60. Pbd: Ruskin's *Works,* XXXVII, 61.

[1] See I Kings 12:10. I have been unable to identify either the "book" or the letter mentioned in the first paragraph.

120. *Ruskin to Carlyle*

Brantwood, Coniston
8th August 1873

Dear Carlyle,

I've been putting off writing to you till I could send you my notes on Friedrich;[1] but I've got so deep into it that I can't get it done yet awhile.— Some of your bits of small print have so much in them. One I'm going to take bodily out, and print in gold—and I think you will like that I am about, generally.

One great question forces itself daily on me more and more. "Throw a quilt over it."[2] They are beautiful last words. But why is Friedrich never, apparently, solicitous about the succeeding reign? when solicitous about his dog's comfort?

I am working hard at many things. Much at old chivalresque French,[3] which is full of things—as you know.

And always love you more and more every day and am ever more and more devotedly yours,

J. Ruskin

121. *Ruskin to Carlyle*

Brantwood, Coniston
9th Oct. 73

My dearest Carlyle,

I sent a letter of loving thanks—with begging for news, to the address of this one, some two months ago. Ever since I've been going to write—everyday. Are you still there & little Mary?

Ever your lovingest   J. R.

This is only to know where to send you a letter.

Letter 120. MS: NLS, 555.61. Pbd: Ruskin's *Works*, XXXVII, 70–71.

[1] Published in December 1873 as appendix I to a revised edition of *The Crown of Wild Olive*. See *Works*, XVIII, 515–17.

[2] "One of his dogs sat on its stool near him; about midnight he noticed it shivering for cold: 'Throw a quilt over it,' said or beckoned he; that, I think, was his last completely-conscious utterance" (Carlyle's *Frederick*, book XXI, chapter ix; in *Works*, XIX, 298).

[3] On August 13, 1870, Ruskin had purchased and was now reading "the *Romance of the Rose* in fourteenth-century MS, a little before Chaucer; the very text he translated—delicious old French—worse than Joinville to make out, a great deal" (Letter to C. E. Norton, July 15, 1873, in *Works*, XXXVII, 70).

Letter 121. MS: NLS, 555.62. Hitherto unpbd.

122. *Ruskin to Carlyle*

Brantwood, Coniston
9th Oct. 73

Dearest Carlyle,

I wrote to the hill Dumfries—some six weeks ago, and ever since have been wanting to write again—& put off from day to day. If you are now in London I hope soon to see you, but I've some little books to send you where shall they come?

Love to little Mary if with you. Your lovingest

J. Ruskin

Letter 122. MS: NLS, 555.63. Hitherto unpbd.

IV

EVER YOUR LOVING FILIUS

"I must get to my work. Ever your loving filius."
Ruskin to Carlyle, August 17, 1874
Letter 158

ട്ടം

LETTERS 123-166

October 1873 through December 7, 1874

Ruskin continues publication of *Fors Clavigera* letters. Publication of *Val D'Arno*. He travels widely in Italy, where he writes almost daily to Carlyle, whom he now calls "Papa."
Carlyle travels twice to Scotland.

123. *Ruskin to Carlyle*

Corpus Christi College, Oxford
Nov. [actually October], 1873

My Dearest Carlyle,

If I were in good heart, or felt happy either for you or for your poor scholar, I should write often. But my own discouragement, and my sorrow at the silence to the public which mere bodily weakness now imposes on you, still in the full strength of your intellect, prevent my ever writing with joy—& practically, my own hands and eyes have generally of late been past writing, before the day was over.

I have not the least pleasure in my work any more, except because you and Froude and one or two other friends still care for it. One might as well talk to the March dust as to the English of today—young or old; nor can they help it, poor things—any more than the dust can;—the general dustman will deposit them I suppose, some day where something will grow on them—if some beneficent wateringpan, or Aquarius ex machina, lay them in the "mud-deluge"[1] at rest.

—Besides this, the loss of my mother and my old nurse leaves me without any root, or, in the depth of the word any home, and what pleasant things I have, seem to me only a kind of museum of which I have now merely to arrange the bequest,—while, so long as I *do* keep at work at all, the forms of it are too many and too heavy for my digestion (Literal)—& therefore only increase, instead of relieving despondency.

I am very careful however about not doing too much.— If I do not write to *you*, think how many things I must leave undone—of duty and comfort.

—I have ordered two copies of the lectures[2] to be sent to you and one to Froude. (There will be ten altogether, I hope—two a week till 28th Nov.)

Ever, with love to Mary, your affectionate

J. Ruskin

Letter 123. MS: NLS, 555.64. Pbd: Ruskin's *Works*, XXXVII, 72–73.

[1] See *Latter-Day Pamphlets*, in Carlyle's *Works*, XX, 65. Carlyle's sympathy with Ruskin's dark views is expressed in a letter written a few days later (November 3) to C. E. Norton: "Ruskin is treading the winepress alone; and sometimes feels his labours very heavy. God be with him, poor fellow. I hear at the present time, no other Voice like him in this dreary Mother of dead dogs which is still commonly called a world." (MS: Harvard College Library, 5.)

[2] A series of ten lectures on Tuscan art, delivered at Oxford in October and November of 1873. They were published in 1874 as *Val d'Arno*, but they had been printed in quarto form before the lecture series began, and in this form were sent to Carlyle.

I read the bit about Servant Tenure in Shooting Niagara[3] to my class yesterday—with much (for the moment) effect on them.

124. *Carlyle to Ruskin*

5 Cheyne Row, Chelsea
31 October, 1873

Dear Ruskin,

After several weeks of eager expectation, I received, morning before yesterday, the sequel to your kind little note, in the shape of four bright 4to lectures (forwarded by an Aylesbury printer) on the Historical and Artistic development of Val d'Arno. Many thanks to you for so pleasant and instructive a gift. The work is full of beautiful and delicate perceptions, new ideas, both new and true, which throw a bright illumination over that important piece of History, and awake fresh curiosities and speculations on that and on other much wider subjects. It is all written with the old nobleness and fire, in which no other living voice to my knowledge equals yours *Perge, perge* ["continue, continue"];—and, as the Irish say, "more power to your elbow!"—

I have yet read this *Val d'Arno* only once. Froude snatched it away from me yesterday; and it has then to go to my Brother at Dumfries. After that I shall have it back. Your visit to me still hangs in the vague; your very pen to me-wards continues uncomfortably stingy; but we will hope, we will hope. I am not very well; but it is mainly Old Age that ails me, so that there is nothing to be said, or complained of. Have you read poor Mill's *Autobiography*; and did you ever before read such a book?[1]

Adieu, dear Ruskin; work while it is called today!

Yours affectionately,
T. Carlyle

[3] Carlyle's "Shooting Niagara: and After?" See *Works*, XXX, 5–6.
Letter 124. MS: Estate of Mrs. Helen Gill Viljoen. Pbd: Ruskin's *Works*, XXIII, iv; and (incomplete) in Collingwood, II, 431–32.
[1] The *Autobiography* of John Stuart Mill had recently been published. Elsewhere Carlyle calls it "the autobiography of a Steam-engine."

125. Ruskin to Carlyle

Corpus Christi College, Oxford
Early Nov. '73

Dearest Carlyle,

I have sent you none of the enclosed proof[1] before, because I thought it my highest duty to you to act in absolute independence in this case, and not to allow myself the pleasure even of obedience.

I to day send the sheets for press,—and, this larger portion seeming to me in fair type enough, and as it will be a month's job, probably before I get out the book, I send you these, trusting that you will forgive what may displease you in them in the knowledge you cannot but have now securely, that I am in all things your faithful and loving servant

J. Ruskin

Thomas Carlyle, Esq.

126. Mary Aitken to Ruskin

5 Cheyne Row, Chelsea
12 Nov. 1873

Dear Mr Ruskin

My uncle bids me say how very much he has been surprised and gratified about your Appendix. He says that the work is beautifully done; that you have seen into the very heart of the matter; and that he is more flattered than he can express by the trouble you have taken in this matter.

My uncle thinks that it would be much better to refer to the people's edition (which is only 2/ a vol., and is extremely popular) than to the little 1869 edit^n. I have therefore in each case substituted the page of *it* in the parenthesis for that of the one you had chosen; so that should you agree with him, and not have time to look it over, you could send the proof direct to the printer,—the numbers are perfectly correct (I have been used to doing work of the kind for him). If you in the least

Letter 125. MS: NLS, 555.65. Hitherto unpbd.

[1] The appendix (no. 1) Ruskin was adding to an edition of *The Crown of Wild Olive* that was to be published in December 1873. The appendix, which Ruskin mentions in his next letter to Carlyle, was entitled "Notes on the Political Economy of Prussia," and was based on the early chapters of Carlyle's *Frederick*. See *Works*, XVIII, 515–33.

Letter 126. MS: Yale University Library. Hitherto unpbd.

care for a copy of this edition, which is very pleasant to read, being in small voll. easily carried about & light to hold, he would be delighted to send you one at once. If your Ms. is already in the printer's hands, I should be so very happy to alter the numbers in the parenthesis of the proofs which are still to come.

With all kind messages to you from Uncle,

Yours affectionately & respectfully,
Mary Carlyle Aitken

127. Ruskin to Mary Aitken

[November 13, 1873]

My dear Mary,

It is a great relief to my mind that your uncle likes the Appendix. I was resolved it should be done clearly, so far before he saw it, but I was very nervous.

So many thanks for the beautifully made alterations. I've sent them straight to printers.

Ever affectionately Yours
J. Ruskin

Dear love to Mr. Carlyle

128. Ruskin to Carlyle

Corpus Christi College,
Oxford
3rd December, '73

My Dearest Carlyle,

It is a wonderful thing to me, that I do not know your birthday,[1]— that I write this evening, only because a good girl who loves you[2]— though not so much—I hope—as I do—wrote to me of it, thinking it was as it ought to be, a festival with me always. I have been irreligious in these things and would fain have a little altar tomorrow to be wreathed with vervain—and the good girl for a pretty priestess to

Letter 127. MS: NLS, 555.66. Hitherto unpbd. The MS has "P.M^k. 13 November 1873" in another hand.

Letter 128. MS: NLS, 555.67. Pbd: Ruskin's *Works*, XXXVII, 74–75.

[1] Which was on December 4.

[2] Probably Miss Blanche Atkinson, a young member of St. George's Guild, who later (1900) published *Ruskin's Social Experiment at Barmouth*. See also Letters 130 and 166.

make a little sacred feast for me, and a— Well, I don't think there's anybody else I would feast with on your birthday—because there's no one who is so entirely thankful for it as I am.

Accept my faithful love on all days—in that largeness of it—pardon its want of care for one—hitherto—I hope not hereafter.

Ever your loving disciple—son—I have almost now a right to say—in what is best of power in me

J. Ruskin

129. *Ruskin to Carlyle*

[December 1873]

Dearest Papa,[1]

Here's the book—I do hope you'll like some little bits in it. I'm not sure that you even have the end of the Future of England, which is all yours as much as this Frederick part.[2]

—I find Saturday will be the best day for me to come after all.

Ever your lovingest.
J. R.

130. *Ruskin to Carlyle*

[December 30, 1873]

Dearest Carlyle,

I hope you will enjoy reading the enclosed letter,[1] a little. The "extinguisher" it speaks of was a lovely one of yours, which has borne good fruit. I've never seen this girl, but I hope she will be one of my best helpers henceforward, and find happiness in becoming so,—instead of a merely "harmless" member of society. Alas—if only one

Letter 129. MS: NLS, 555.69. Hitherto unpbd.

[1] Ruskin here uses for the first time the salutation "Papa" in writing to Carlyle. He laid the foundation for this by calling himself Carlyle's "son" in the last paragraph of the previous letter. See Letter 128.

[2] "The Future of England" was the last section of *The Crown of Wild Olive* to come before the appendix mentioned in Letter 125. Carlyle identifies it as volume VII (though it was actually volume VI) of the "Works Series" Ruskin was editing from 1871 to 1880: "Ruskin has been here again and is coming back, I think, Saturday; full to overflowing with far glancing projects and speculations; a beautiful new vol. of his, beautifully bound in blue morocco with gilded edge (vol vii of his *Works*) is by far the most interesting I have received; but except that part of it which is new and relates to Friedrich of Prussia I can get no part of it read at present" (to Dr. John A. Carlyle, January 8, 1874; MS: NLS, 2509).

Letter 130. MS: NLS, 555.68. Hitherto unpbd. The MS has "30 December, 1873" in another hand.

[1] From Blanche Atkinson. See Letter 128, n. 2.

could reduce nine tenths of everybody about us to "harmlessness" what a world it would be.

I'm soon coming to Chelsea again. If I could but remember all you say to me, in its own words! That bit about the ordering a new world at *their* shop, was so delicious.

Ever your lovingest

J. Ruskin

When Miss Blanche says I *"can't* give her up", she means that I've promised to answer her letters if there's anything to be answered in them and she does what I bid.— in the meantime I've made a secretary of her, to keep list and order of now too fast accumulating letters needing reference afterwards.

131. Ruskin to Carlyle

March 1874

[actually February 1874]

Dearest Carlyle,

Both you and Froude must know what I feel to you both. I have not written to Froude—nor called. He will know it was not in neglect.

—*You* may well wonder—(but you have been with Froude very constantly, since, I believe?) why I have been so long from Chelsea— and even a day or two now in town without coming.

—Pardon me for speaking selfishly, of what must seem a poor matter, after Froude's sorrow.[1]— But I've had a bad tormenting one to bear as I best could—

—the girl whom I've been so long devoted to had to come to London,[2] very nearly dying,—at the best in great danger—half mad and half starved—(and eating nothing but everything she liked—chiefly sugar almonds I believe)— Well, she had to be forbidden food & I don't know what, and,[3]

Never mind that, its so ill written. She's been physically and gravely

---

Letter 131. MS: NLS, 556.70. Hitherto unpbd. Ruskin has dated the letter "March" in hasty error. Above the date, the MS has "Feb. 1874" in another hand.

[1] J. A. Froude's second wife, Henrietta Elizabeth, died on February 12, 1874.

[2] Rose La Touche, who was nearing the final stages of a fatal illness, had been placed in a nursing home in London.

[3] Ruskin here writes, and then crosses out, a second version of this paragraph: "—the girl whom I've been so long devoted to had to move to London—very nearly dying—at the best in great danger—half mad and half starved—& eating nothing but everything she liked—(chiefly sugar and almonds, I believe)— Well—she had to be forbidden food & I don't know what—and."

ill;—wanted to see Joan—and not to see me.— Joan goes and nurses her, and I let her do all she can, of course,—and the girl's getting better; but I can't stand the Tantalus life, in London: so went down home to Coniston and have done good work there, and am now going to Italy tomorrow, and shall do good work there, I trust, too.

I want to see you, and I can't get into town twice, today; and I'm to dine with John Simon[4] at Kennington at 6. Might I come to you at ½ past four?

I'm not ill, but I can't master my thoughts in London; and I find the little more pain is rather good for me than bad in many ways, if I'm far enough off. I've done a lot of work on Frederick—do you know—I think you haven't said enough of his Dogs. The "throw a quilt over it" at the last is so lovely.

So, I want to ask you about more Frederick things, and to see you and get a word of benediction before I go—and assure you of my true duty, and that I'm

Ever your loving son
John Ruskin

Just say yes, if it may be yes, to bearer, or No, which I'll know meant only that you can't not that you won't.

Thomas Carlyle, Esq.

132. *Ruskin to Carlyle*

Naples, 20th April [1874]

Dearest Papa,

I would write to you often,—and thankfully, if I had pleasant things to tell you, but every time I come abroad, I have a deeper sense of the advancing ruin of every country except your Germany,—nor do I believe that it will escape unpunished for its cruelty.

I have felt that more than ever, in passing through France this last time. Had Germany in her great strength, held herself on the defensive patiently, contented with crushing back every Frenchman who crossed Rhine, the humiliation to France would have been greater; but the shame would have been wholesome.— Now, blind with rage and pain like a dog beaten till it is mad, she will find her time.

Italy is in rapidly advancing decay;—this place was bad enough 30

---

[4]Sir John Simon, M.D., F.R.S. (1816–1904), a friend of Ruskin since 1856.
Letter 132. MS: NLS, 556.71. Hitherto unpbd.

years ago; but now!—what little animal beauty the people had left is, in the upper classes, exchanged for a sodden pallor of malignant vice; and in the lower,—darkened with gradual loss of all that they once believed or delighted in. English companies, over-buying each other ten times succeed as proprietors of the share, and all along the bay is one wilderness of beaten down houses and dustheaps to be sold in lots. Everything is dearer by the double at least, for strangers,—and the taxes are heavier—(I hear) under the new government for the peasantry.[1] The fault of *all*, to my thinking, is with England. Ever since I was able to understand or see,—this Naples has been the theme of all artistic, romantic, or pleasure loving creatures;—how many millions of English people of the upper classes have past winter upon winter here,—and yet, they have been absolutely without influence on the country, except to encourage manufactures of the foolishest rubbish—and any kind of amusing beggary.

I leave this afternoon at six, for Palermo; and hope to arrive there tomorrow morning.— I can only afford a week for Sicily, for I must be back and at my work in Rome this day fortnight. If Mary can send me a little line, to tell me anything you would like to hear of, Hotel de Russie, Rome, is, and will remain for some time, a safe address.

I am going to do what will be ill-thought of by many of my friends; but I do it after a fortnights very careful thought,—to refuse the gold medal of the Architects' institute, saying that in the present state of Architecture I cannot think it a time either for bestowing or receiving honours.

—I shall explain in a private letter to the Secretary, that it is simply impossible for me at present to say anything in public that would be thought due to such a Society on such an occasion. Which is the fact.— I cannot accept medals from people who let themselves out to build Gothic Advertisements for Railroads—Greek Advertisements for firms in the city—and—whatever Lord Palmerston or Mr. Gladstone chose to order opposite Whitehall—while they allow every beautiful building in France and Italy to be destroyed, for the "job" of its restoration.[2]

I hope I may have some better subject for a letter from Palermo,—this is merely to tell you I am ever and ever your affectionate

John Ruskin

---

[1] The kingdom of the Two Sicilies, with Naples as its capital, had been subsumed into the new kingdom of Italy after Giuseppe Garibaldi's recognition of Victor Emmanuel II on October 26, 1860.

[2] Ruskin had for years been incensed over the destruction of valuable buildings and

133. *Carlyle to Ruskin*

5 Cheyne Row, Chelsea, 13 May 1874

Dear Ruskin;

Your Naples letter was a welcome appearance here, & all the more as testifying (I hope) the intention of promise *fulfilled* by performance, & that other letters from you will follow this! I well comprehend the incessant business you have, leaving you only minutes of leisure; so that no impatience is permitted me, though as much desire as I like. All I will say is, that I read this Naples letter with a pleasure & interest entirely unusual in these late years, & that it will be very charitable in you to write as often as you fairly can.

Your con-spectus of the Foreign nations is gloomy & mournful, & I doubt but too well-founded: I suppose this long while they are all, like ourselves, got into the Niagara Rapids, & hastening towards a nameless doom. Not towards absolute destruction, I always hope, but towards black centuries of Anarchy & agony, & sordid tribulation, till a better spirit rise in them. Sometimes in late months I have been fancying the poor English Nation to be getting faintly sensible of this & the other long-continued delusion, & feebly preparing to get rid of it: but the curse of Boundless wealth which they call "unexampled prosperity" lies heavy on them; giving such unbounded arena to the development of all their low desires & endeavors, that nothing of real spiritual health is likely to be possible for a long while yet. God help them, poor wretches,—& us too ditto, ditto!

As is now, alas, nearly inevitable for me, I have been *doing* nothing, merely reading mostly idle books (not one book in twenty can be called other than a bad book), & drowsily musing over them with many silent-feelings; among which, willingness to close up shop on signal given is constantly present,—mixed also with other still more

---

works of art in the name of "progress" and "restoration," and he blamed all those who had anything to do with the situation, either actively or passively. Thus he refused the Gold Medal of the Royal Institute of British Architects, which had been offered to him in March 1874. His letter to the institute can be found in *Works*, XXXIV, 513–14.

Ruskin's remarks about "Gothic" and "Greek" refer to the famous "Battle of the Styles," in which English architects championed both Neo-Gothic and Neo-Renaissance styles during the late 1850's and 1860's. Gilbert Scott, one of Ruskin's friends and president of the Royal Institute of Architects in 1874, was once forced by Lord Palmerston to change his Gothic design for the India Office (opposite Whitehall) to Italian Classical—an act that did not endear Palmerston to Ruskin. For more information, see *Works*, XVI, xxxi–xxxiv; and Cook, I, 441–54.

Letter 133. MS: Bembridge. Hitherto unpbd.

inarticulate, unutterable glimpses of things that have a certain dignity & even blessedness, which would be lost by speaking of them.— Latterly I have lost my chief walking companion, Froude having gone to Wales for the Summer; solitary walking, which is next-best, seldom falls to my share, though in general I rather do avoid what is clearly foolish, insincere & frivolous in my collocutors, peripatetic or other. In short, I am grown very old, & have made, I notice, very rapid progress in that operation during the last year. If you did not so unjustly dislike the Germans, I would translate for you a beautiful "Tame *Xenion* [*sic*]" of Goethe's[1] which is often privately in my mouth while contemplating the Finale of my affairs.

You appear to me to be clearly in the right in reference to your Architectural Society Medal. The offer of it I find to be a decidedly pretty little thing; but,—for a name so clothed with lightning & quack-devouring Fire, it is at least equally becoming & imperative to decline speech or acceptance on any terms which exist at present in that quarter. Architecture, down to the very art of making bricks, has fallen fatuous at present,—fatuous & false, to be shunned by every one who is sane, & not under clear compulsion to it.

One thing will perhaps seem curious to you: the real excellency, in a kindred province, of our Chelsea Embankment, which was at last opened the other day. It was done by our Board of Works; essentially, so far as I can find, by one Bazalgette;[2]—& my testimony is that it

---

[1] The "tame Xenia" (*zahm Xenien*) are a series of 161 classical distichs on literature and art composed jointly by Goethe and Schiller for publication in the latter's journal, *Musenalmanach*, in 1795–96. The adjective "tame" was to distinguish them from another series of 414 epigrams published in the same journal, which were aggressive replies to hostile criticism of the work of both poets. The title of the whole collection is taken from the thirteenth book of Martial's *Epigrams*.

Ruskin, *Diaries*, III, 819, records a conversation with Carlyle on October 25, 1874, in which Carlyle translated one of the "tame Xenia," which begins with the line "*Hätte Gott mich anders gewolt. . . .*" Carlyle's impromptu translation, which Ruskin took down at the time, reads in the entry as follows:

> Had God wished me otherwise
> He would have built me otherwise,
> But as he put talent into me
> He has greatly trusted me.
> I use it to the right and to the left,
> Know not what comes of it,
> But when there's no good to be got more of it
> He will surely give me the sign.

[2] Sir Joseph William Bazalgette (1819–91), civil engineer. Though best remembered for his design of London's modern sewer system while chief engineer of the Metropolitan Board of Works (1855–89) Bazalgette also designed the Thames Embankment in three distinct sections, the Victoria, Chelsea, and Albert embankments, as well as the new Northumberland Avenue. He was knighted in 1874, on completion of the Chelsea Embankment.

entirely surprises me. Miles of the noblest Promenade. The Thames pushing grandly past you, & even at low-water leaving a foot or two of *pure* gravel; a labarynthic [*sic*] flower-garden, with all manner of planted young trees, green spaces, subsidiary walks, & grand pavements; Cheyne Walk looking altogether royal on you through the old umbrage & the new; I was obliged to say, & still repeat, I have never seen anything, of any description whatever, nearly so well done in this monstrous City since I knew it first. I long to shew it you, & hear your judgment of it. To me it will be a great resource for the rest of my appointed days here. In another 50 years, were the shrubs & saplings all grown, I think it will be admitted universally that there is no other such pretty region in all London & its environs. This Bazalgette I have heard the name of before, but will henceforth attach a meaning to it, such as to that of few others in any line of business like his.

Your "Fors," two numbers of it at once, came punctually on May 1st, & were, as always, eagerly read. Winged Words, tipped with empyrean fire. Not in my time has the dark weltering, blind & base mass of things been visited by such showers & torrents of an Element altogether amazing to it. *Euge, Euge.*

Adieu dear Ruskin. Do not forget me, in your Grotto, or other Italian Studies;—& write a line or two when you have a minute of leisure. Mary, you see, is gone from me; on a visit of some few weeks to her mother; I am sitting (by compulsion) for a statuette to one Boehm,[3] who is worth your knowing, if I do not altogether mistake his artistic talent. The one sitting more will set free [*sic*] from him. All good be with you dear R.— Yours Ever

T. Carlyle

134. *Ruskin to Carlyle*

Rome. 19th May [1874]

Dearest Papa

I had yesterday your most kind and long letter, for a treat, on returning from a vexed expedition to Assisi where I could do nothing for the cold. Please, you must translate that song of Goethe's for me, and you must not get old, this long while yet.

I have not been so much pleased by anything this many a day as by

[3] Sir Joseph Edgar Boehm (1834–90). Though born in Vienna of Hungarian parents, Boehm made his artistic reputation in England. He would later be commissioned to do the portrait statue on the Chelsea Embankment of the seated Carlyle. He also designed the renowned "Jubilee" coinage of Queen Victoria.

Letter 134. MS: NLS, 556.72. Hitherto unpbd.

what you tell me of the Thames embankment,—for—steady grumbler as I am, there is really nothing that gives me so much comfort as hearing of anything well done. And also I was afraid that change at Chelsea was all for the worse for you.

I am going to write for a little while to you, as I used to my own father,—who had his letter every day, whether there was anything in it or not.— So, sometimes, I may tell you of things which I do not remember when I sit down for a regular letter, (and alas—too often—the proposed "regularity" becomes—emptiness, at last)—

I am almost paralyzed in my own work, now, by horror and pity at the state of all things here. Chiefly, the aspect taken by religion,—staggering me in what I most want to be strong in faith of, and giving me endless problems and difficulty. If only I could enter into the hearts of one or two of these friars!

More tomorrow, I hope. Ever your loving,

J. R.

135. *Ruskin to Carlyle*

Rome, 20th May, '74

Dearest Papa,

This is merely to be a Papa's scrap of a letter, for I've had to draw up my formal letter to the Architects' Institute,—and must get to my work by the morning light.— little enough of that I've had lately, but here is some.

I chanced, this morning, upon Hosea—no, Amos, VIII, 4 and 9:—I am thinking of drawing up some meteorological views founded on those two verses.[1]— I've got so much in my head if I had only time to take it out!—time and strength,—the latter I believe much diminished by overeating myself. I'm drawing in the Sistine chapel, *before* Michael Angelo's Last Judgment which disgusts me more and more every day (as I turn casually to it from my own work on Sandro Botticelli's maid—Zipporah)[2]—and I think continually how strange it is that none of the great old and true painters really worked out that subject in any detail. Fancy the look of a person with some good in him, con-

---

Letter 135. MS: NLS, 556.73. Hitherto unpbd.

[1] "Hear this, O ye that swallow up the needy, even to make the poor of the land to fail," and "it shall come to pass in that day, saith the Lord God, that I will cause the sun to go down at noon, and I will darken the earth in the clear day."

[2] Ruskin's sketch of a part of Botticelli's "Life of Moses." The drawing was exhibited at Brighton in April 1876. See the catalogue of Ruskin's drawings in *Works,* XXXVIII, 234, no. 253.

vinced of all he had lost in *this* life—certainly, in the next, if any, probably,—merely for the sake of green pease and rasberry [*sic*] tarts.
—More tomorrow Papa, if you don't mind scraps.

Ever your loving
John Ruskin

136. *Ruskin to Carlyle*

Rome, 21st May, '74

Dearest Papa,

I am greatly exercised in mind about the monks here. One sees more
of them than in other towns; and last night, close by the temple of
Vesta, in a little eleventh century church (Sta. M. in Cosmedin),[1] a
priest was preaching energetically standing on a raised platform
only,—no desk or anything before him, but as an actor from a small
stage—Energetically—vociferously—it seemed in sincerity. But if one
could only be in their hearts for one moment. What puzzles me is that
the rougher monks certainly live entirely wretched lives. What do they
gain by hypocrisy? My life is one of swollen luxury and selfishness
compared with theirs; and yet it seems to me that I see what is right
and *they* don't. How is it—how *can* it be?

Anything so dismal as the state of transitional and galvanized Rome
I never saw. Two kinds of digging go on side by side—antiquarian
excavations—and foundations of factories and lodging-houses. The
ground, torn newly up in every direction, yawns dusty and raw round
the feet of the ruins of Imperial—that is to say, of clumsy, monstrous,
and even then dying Rome.— New chimneys and the white front of
the Pope's new Tobacco manufactory,[2] tower up and glare beside the

---

Letter 136. MS: NLS, 556.74. Pbd: Ruskin's *Works*, XXXVII, 99.

[1] This church is one of the most ancient in Rome, dating from the sixth century, with
its foundation resting on the remains of the temple of Hercules. The public grain-distri-
bution center that replaced the temple under Theodosius the Great was later trans-
formed into a church for the use of the Greek community in Rome and was for centuries
called Santa Maria in Schola Graeca. By the tenth century it had become the seat of a
cardinal-deacon, and when, in 1064, it was largely destroyed by the forces of Robert
Guiscard, its titulars began the long rebuilding program that gave the building its present appearance. Much of the medieval architecture was invisible during Ruskin's time
because of extensive restoration carried out in the early eighteenth century by Cardinal
Annibale Albani, but this was removed in 1899, exposing the older construction.

The sermon Ruskin describes was that of the octave of the Ascension, delivered by
the vicar capitular or his deputy, as the church had no cardinal assigned to it from 1858
to 1875.

[2] "The Pope's new tobacco manufactory under the Palatine," as Ruskin calls it in *Fors
Clavigera*, letter 44 (*Works*, XXVIII, 125). The Fabbrica de' Tabacchi was erected during the reign of Pius IX, in 1863, before Rome fell to Italian troops, thus causing Ruskin

arches of the Palatine—the lower Roman mob distributing its ordure indiscriminately about both—and the priests—singing and moaning all day long in any shady church not yet turned into barracks—

What *will* it come to?

Ever your loving

J. R.

137. *Ruskin to Carlyle*

Rome, WhitSunday [May 24], 1874

My dearest Papa,

I've just been correcting the introduction and bit of first chapter of my Botany book, Proserpina[1]—that I've been underground with so long; and I hope it will be a little refreshing to you after the sulky Fors. I shall order the printer to send you the clear revise.

I've had a little comfort to day in seeing the peasants come driving in to their festa in festa dress. Not much of the common pictorial costume, but the dresses strong and fresh and clean; firmly and decently put on, and always flowers in the hair, not for vanity, but in honour to the day, and with true enjoyment in the look of *each other*: and therefore, a really wilful use of the decoration they had, setting themselves off to real, natural, and wise advantage. The men, with a feather or two and flower in their hats looked like gentlemen, and not the least like our "foresters"[2] or the like.

I never was glad to see flies before—two or three are plaguing me to day, to my great contentment.— it is the first *not cold* day I have had here. But I think it will be long before I shall have had enough of the sun.

I have good news too of my Oxford roadmakers.[3] I believe my class in *that* art will be the good one, and go on with me to all others.

Ever your loving,

J. Ruskin

---

to call it "the Pope's." It was located in the Via Anicia just beyond the church of Santa Maria dell' Orto.

Letter 137. MS: NLS, 556.75. Hitherto unpbd.

[1] Parts one and two of *Proserpina* were published in December 1875.

[2] From the Italian *forestiere, forestiero*, meaning "foreigner, visitor, guest."

[3] A group of Oxford undergraduates who, under Ruskin's direction, had been constructing a short rural road to Ferry Hinksey since the spring of 1874.

138. *Ruskin to Carlyle*

Rome, Wednesday
27th May, '74

My dearest Papa,

On Whitsunday, and last night I was at a church-service entirely beautiful and satisfactory to me, as far as anything human ought to be—that of the nuns of the Trinita di Monte,[1] (of the Sacred Heart). It is an educational Convent, and for all the years I can remember— (now thirty five) has been notable for its beautifully sung service, organ and women's voices only, but very highly trained, yet remaining entirely modest and quiet, strong in effortless execution and perfectly right doing of the duty of sweet voices what charm may justly belong to the externals of such things—what allowable picturesqueness and romance of association, in the true remnant of a piece of old religion, really serviceable is all here added to the pleasant sense that all is for the patient and secluded preparation for active life; and not merely the refusal, or the weary close of it.[2]

The perfect order, reverence, and loveliness of the thing throughout, were a great comfort to me, the rest of my day being necessarily spent either with the sad wrecks of a good past, or under the intrusion of frightful and unseemly modern life.

I am sorely puzzled what element of this kind to try for, in the education which I ought very soon now to be more specially describing in Fors. But I can't think it out, yet, and am resting with my botany a little.

Steady darkness and rain again, to day, all day long.

Ever my dear Papa,
Your affectionate filius,
John Ruskin

Letter 138. MS: NLS, 556.76. Hitherto unpbd.

[1] The church of Santissima Trinità de' Monti, the French parish in Rome, was erected under the patronage of Charles VIII of France in 1495 in reparation for his occupation of Rome. In 1587 it became the title church of a cardinal-priest. Having been devastated by riots during the French Revolution, it was restored in 1816 at the expense of Louis XVIII.

[2] See Letter 139, n. 3.

139. Ruskin to Carlyle

Rome, 1st June, [1874]

Dearest Papa,

I haven't written for a day or two because I had nothing to tell you—but yesterday I saw what may interest you—a buried—or (properly), *dug* church of the 2nd or 3rd century.¹ Most of the *show* churches here have been altered by half a dozen popes,² and finally gone all over with new paint and putty by a modern upholsterer—But this little church has just been dug down into, in a hill of the Campagna. I suppose it *fell* in first, and so showed where it was, or rather, the roof having fallen and brought down the aisle pillars, ages ago, there remained a depression in the soil which attracted the excavators.

There, however, one stood among the fallen pillars and broken tombs, not one touched—nor one added—since the last tomb was closed—and one saw exactly how far the first thoughts of Christianity changed the temper and work of the Roman. One sculpture of "the good shepherd" in the midst of a group of sheep and cattle—the same that were grazing in the Campagna at that moment—overhead—with the same long horns, and great effort on the part of the rude sculptor to show the projecting balls of the large eyes, would have been impressive to me, if anything could be impressive, now. But all things have become to me so ghastly a confusion, and grotesque mistake and misery, that I *feel* nothing,—(except that the man with the grinding organ outside is a nuisance at seven in the morning and not in the same order of things as my singing nuns at seven in the evening),³ and enjoy nothing. All dawn light seems to me only on the smoke of Etna.

Letter 139. MS: NLS, 556.77. Hitherto unpbd.

¹Ruskin's subsequent description makes it almost unquestionable that he is referring to the little basilica of Santa Petronilla built in the center of the upper level of the Catacombs of Domitilla, one of the most ancient Christian burial grounds in Rome. The structure, originally constructed to contain the body of the saint venerated as Saint Peter's principal Roman disciple, had a nave and aisles on an approximately square ground plan. It was in use as a place of public worship from the fifth to the eighth century, when the body of the saint was translated to the Vatican and the old site forgotten. It was rediscovered in 1874 and was fully excavated the following year. For additional details see G. B. De Rossi, "Sepolcro di S. Petronilla nella basilica in via Ardeatina e sua translazione al Vaticano," in *Bulletino di archeologia cristiana*, 1878, pp. 125–46, and 1879, pp. 5–20; and August Urbain, *Ein Martyrologium der christliche Gemeinde zu Rom* (Leipzig, 1901), p. 152.

²Compare Ruskin's impressions in Santa Maria in Cosmedin. See Letter 136.

³A reference to the famous Vespers service of the French nuns of the convent of the Dames du Sacré-Coeur, attached to the church of Santissima Trinità de' Monti (See Let-

Etna is in a mess, because I had nearly written, the smoke of *dinner*; for I was thinking, in advance, whether my views this morning were not a little more desperate than usual, in consequence of having eaten green pease as well as asparagus, last night.

—Ever my dearest papa
Your inconsistent and ashamed filius
J. Ruskin

140. *Carlyle to Ruskin*

5 Cheyne Row, Chelsea
20 June, 1874

Dear Ruskin,

That was an excellent scheme you had of writing to me daily a detached bit of thought, observation, or experience,—excellent, had you but been able to continue. The three or four you sent came duly, each of them a blazing fire's flake, or direct photograph of the minute passing over Rome and you; altogether strengthening and pleasant to the mind of the recipient. But, alas, it could not continue; with that wildly touching, and as if tragic disinterment of the poor old Christian Church of "the third century" into the closing epoch of Pio Nono and company, your fire flakes or quasi-living photographs suddenly ceased, and I have remained ever since, not from that cause alone though doubtless that helped, one of the most indolent, torpid and useless souls now extant on this Planet. In sad truth, except walking every morning to the end of our embankment and back on the finest sleekest most undisturbed and soothing promenade I ever had, *nothing* has been done by me but another rather longer walk or crawl, latish in the afternoon, into one or other of the Parks, and idle reading or slumber and sleep all day and all night. I say to myself, but not too angrily, is this what they call euthanasia? *eu*thanasia? Well, well! In fact there is no end to the cloudy musings I have,—especially on that benignant Chelsea embankment; unluckily until Death itself come there is no escaping the dismal necessity to eat food and the still more dismal and almost impossible ditto to digest the same. Patience, patience; Hope, too, a little; and thanks always and loyal reverence to the Almighty Builder. Amen.

---

ter 138). Mendelssohn was so impressed by the performance of these "singing nuns" that he dedicated his three motets, opus 39, to them after hearing them in 1830. See Lady (Grace) Wallace, *Letters from Italy and Switzerland* (1862), pp. 85–86, letter of December 30, 1830.

Letter 140. MS: Bembridge. Hitherto unpbd.

About a week ago, I got from Aylesbury,[1] the promised first proof sheet of your Book on Botany, which, to judge from this first sample, will be a most welcome Book to me, such as I have never met with before in my struggles, completely fruitless hitherto, to get any insight into the "Science of Botany" or those strange and beautiful fellow creatures of ours that make lovely every year the face of this "rugged all-supporting Earth." What a long-eared people that Guild of scientific gentlemen is and has been here below!—

Your Architect Gold Medal, left stranded on the waste beach, had an immense rumour for some days in London; and I doubt not is still standing like a fateful Sphinx-riddle in the minutes of many men. The blame I think was not laid heavily on you, but the astonishment, the mocking pity for the Medal and its authors was large and loud. I continue to discern that in your situation and in that of Architecture there could nothing else be done. I have heard a great deal also about your volunteer young gentlemen, delvers & diggers, now busy about Oxford; really an almost miraculous thing; proof such as was not seen for long ages of the influence of an earnest man upon earnest youths; at which even the penny-a-liner pauses for a moment, uncertain what to say or do. In fact it becomes clearer to the world than ever that there is but one Ruskin in the world; an unguidable man, but with quantities of lightning in the interior of him, which are strange and probably dangerous to behold. Well, well; unguidable to outsiders you surely are; and you justly may pretend to spend your own lightning in the way you find suitablest to this wildly anarchic condition of affairs. Continue only for a quarter of a century yet as you may fairly hope to do; there will be something of result visible, something of combustion, kindling here and there in the dark, boundless belly of our Chaos; and meanwhile the clang of the silver bow will be cheering to all the select of men.

I wish you would write to me at once again, and say clearly what your address is, and is to be in the now-current weeks: what your describable employments are and when we may look for you home. Adieu, dear Ruskin; you know well enough what my thoughts towards you are. With my whole soul I wish you noble victory and success.

Yours ever,
T. Carlyle

[1]The Aylesbury works of Messrs. Hazell, Watson & Viney, where Ruskin's later books were printed.

141. *Ruskin to Carlyle*

Assisi, June 24th, [1874]

My Dearest Papa,

I am so very glad of your letter and Mary's. I did not stop in the daily news because I couldn't go on, but because I was afraid you were away from home and would only find an unreadable mass of dead letters when you came back. Now I can go on again nicely. Your pleasure in the embankment[1] is a great joy to me, what else you tell me—of your too quiet time, may well be sad. But it seems to me there are some subjects of thought, connected with your own past work, which such too sorrowful leisure might nevertheless be grandly spent in. None of your readers, I believe,—none even of the most careful—know precisely, in anything *like* practical approximation—what sympathy you have with the faith of Abbot Samson, or St. Adalbert[2]—I don't know myself; to me, the question of their faith is a fearful mystery, but one which I am sure is to be solved;—I mean that we shall either live up to Christianity, or refuse it. But I don't know what your own inner thoughts are of the faith—such as you told me of your mother—and such as so many noble souls have had in Scotland.

What final sayings you would leave to men on this, now quite near and dreadful arbitration which England has to make—& which you have left her as yet but with dim assertion upon; Truely, this might well occupy many an otherwise valuless [*sic*] hour?

I can't write of myself today—being tired—I am so glad of all you give me of encouragement and sympathy. The Oxford movement[3] was, of course, long since planned by me; but I did not intend to begin it till the close of my drawing work: (the wholly ineffectual trouble of which prevented all other energy). But one or two of the men themselves asked me to begin now—so I let them.— And truly, I think it will grow.— Next October, I go out myself with them, and hope to get other tutors to join. Gradually, I mean to develop a plan for the draining of the Oxford fields, which are under water at present all winter; and— Well, enough for today.— Ever your loving

J. Ruskin

Best love to Mary.

Letter 141. MS: NLS, 556.78. Pbd: Ruskin's *Works*, XXXVII, 115–16.
[1] The Chelsea Embankment. See Letter 133, n. 2.
[2] Figures discussed by Carlyle in *Past and Present* (*Works*, X, 39–126) and *Frederick the Great* (*Works*, XII, 66, 94).
[3] Ruskin's Hinksey road makers. See Letter 137, n. 3.

142. *Ruskin to Carlyle*

Sacristan's Cell
Monastery of Assisi
June 26th, '74 Morning

My dearest Papa,

I come down here to write, every morning now. The Sacristan makes me a cup of coffee, and then leaves me quiet for three hours, from 7 to 10,—and I get much done. The room is precisely that of a Highland cottage but too windowed,—whitewashed walls—the windows in deep recesses, three feet high by two wide, looking out on—not Scottish, but nevertheless, true Highlands—a deep valley set with olives, running up into limestone hills covered with pasture and forest, 2 to 3000 feet—then above,—rising in rocky and arid slopes of Apennine.

St. Francis lies in his grave about thirty yards from me, across the cloister—it is (for a marvel,) a sweet summer morning, and the birds sing at the windows—or at least in the wood underneath them—for the monastery is built on a slope as steep as that under Stirling castle.[1]

I have just been having a wonderfully interesting piece of passionate legend-telling, from the Sacristan.[2] He couldn't find Isaiah the other day and was looking for it hopelessly in the "index" to a commented Bible—but, set him off on the story of St. Anthony preaching to the fishes—on this lake—and he is delicious. And his heart is in it.— Also—he agrees wholly with Papa and me, that there never was on earth yet such a horrible age as this, for corruption and madness.

"Remember," he says, "what Fra Antonio tells you—I may die or live to see it, but, before this age is over, (questo secolo) ["this century or age"] there will be such a plague, or war as has not been yet in the world,—and few men left, from the chastisement of God."— And truly—things are too horrible to last long now. I am tired with many thoughts about what I have to do, and my own feebleness or worthlessness.

—Can't write more this morning.

Ever your loving   J. R.

Letter 142. MS: NLS, 556.79. Hitherto unpbd.
[1]The castle in the Scottish town of Stirling. Ruskin mentions it in *Fors Clavigera*, letter 10 (*Works*, XXVII, 170).
[2]The same Fra Antonio who is described discussing Isaiah in *Fors Clavigera*, letter 45 (*Works*, XXVIII, 145). His full name was Antonio Coletti, and he served as the sacristan of the basilica of San Francesco at Assisi for many years before his death on August 16, 1897, at the age of seventy-one. The *Liber Defunctorum* of the diocese (p. 7) contains the following marginalium: "Fu amico del critico d'arte inglese Ruskin, al quale spesso

143. Ruskin to Carlyle

Assisi, Sacristan's Cell
27th June '74

My dearest Papa,

There is the prettiest portrait of you here, close by me, in the lower church, as the leading Wise King, kissing the feet of Christ. It is by Taddeo Gaddi, not Giotto[1]—Terribly high up—I only can see it through my glass,—nobody in general sees anything here—or knows even what they come to see, for the monks added chapels all round, and put in dark painted glass, in the 15th century, and the frescoes, ever since, have been absolutely invisible except on perfectly fine afternoons in June and July. What I wanted to say yesterday[2] was, more distinctly this—

You have perfectly shown the value of sincerity in *any* faith moderately concurrent with the laws of nature and humanity. Faith in Allah—or Jupiter—or Christ.—

You have also shown the power of living without any faith—in charity and utility—as Frederick.

And what you say of Friedrick's [*sic*] sorrowful surroundings and impossibilities of believing anything is to me the most precious passage of the whole book,[3]—many though there be—priceless.

But you don't say what you would have Frederick *be*? You don't say what a Master ought now to teach his pupils to believe, or at least, wish them to believe.

And this, remember is now a quite vital and practical question for me at Oxford.—

Ever your loving
J. Ruskin

---

offri' la sua stanza per fare studiare il critico nella sua permanenza in Assisi" ["he was a friend to the English art critic Ruskin, and many times offered him his own bedroom so that the critic could study while staying in Assisi"]. Brother Antonio was assisted by Brother Giovanni Ferrata, who died on January 10, 1897, at the age of seventy-six. Both are interred in the cemetery near the basilica.

Letter 143. MS: NLS, 556.80. Pbd: Ruskin's *Works*, XXXVII, 118–19. Addr: Thomas Carlyle, Esq. / 5 Cheyne Row / Chelsea Inghilterra.

[1] This painting is one of a cycle of eight frescoes in the right transept of the lower church of the basilica of San Francesco at Assisi. Ruskin is incorrect in ascribing the painting to Taddeo Gaddi. Recent scholarship suggests that the work is by a follower of Giotto, whose name is unknown and who is now called the *Maestro delle vele*. For a further discussion of this painter and his work at Assisi, see Emma Zocca, ed., *Catalogo delle cose d'arte e di antichita d'Italia—Assisi* (Rome, 1936), pp. 56–58.

[2] Actually June 24, three days previously. See Letter 142.

[3] See Carlyle's *Frederick*, book XXI, chapter ix (*Works*, XIX, 290–91).

I don't want you to write about these things to me, but to tell me when I come.

I was so grateful to you for seeing my good bookseller—the enclosed scrap shows what pleasure you gave:[4]—

144. *Ruskin to Carlyle*

[Assisi] 29th June, '74

My Dearest Papa,

I can't easily answer your question, what I am doing;—it is so mixed; but, mainly writing a patient and true account of this place,[1] the source of so much religious passion throughout Europe, and drawing bits that I think nobody but I can draw affectionately enough. I have been at work today on Love, Death, and the Devil.[2] The latter is the perfect likeness of an average "practical" Englishman. Giotto has the most intense hatred of that sort of person.

Love is blind, with a string of hearts round his neck, and lovely rose and violet wings—"Penitence" is flogging him and Death out of the way. I hope to let you see something, very like it, for my drawing is coming well.

Ever your loving   J. R.

145. *Ruskin to Carlyle*

Sacristan's Cell, Assisi
Last day of June [1874]

Dearest Papa,

It is the first pure day of summer here. There is no cloud, and no poison wind. I think you will like to know the view out of my little windows.

As I sit—the cloudless sky and green-and-gold Apennine;—cornfield with grass—clumps of olive, grey, and dark spots of ilex. If I rise, under the window the hill falls steeply about 500 feet, clothed with

[4] Mr. George Allen, one of Ruskin's former students, who had begun printing Ruskin's works at Orpington. The "enclosed scrap" is part of a letter from Allen, and reads as follows: "I thought the best way to determine about Mr. Carlyle's health and whereabouts was to run down to Chelsea and ask after him. He very kindly told his housekeeper to ask me upstairs, and to have exchanged a few words with him will be one of the memories of my life. He is, I am happy to say, very well, and he said that it would not be long before you heard from him but he had been somewhat uncertain as to how. . . ."

Letter 144. MS: NLS, 556.81. Pbd: Ruskin's *Works*, XXXVII, 120–21.

[1] See *Works*, XXIII, xliv and 205 ff.

[2] Giotto's allegory of Chastity in the lower church of the basilica of San Francesco at Assisi.

Letter 145. MS: NLS, 556.82. Pbd: Ruskin's *Works*, XXXVII, 121–22.

broken wood—near the window, fig and Spanish chestnut, below—
ilex, down to the stream bed—the Tescio [*sic*]; (see Dante's account of
St. Francis in the Paradiso. No, I've got confused, I see Dante doesn't
name it. *L'acqua*, etc., in Canto xi. is it, I believe, but I don't know
Tupino)[1] which is all but dry; it runs beneath, *across* the window, but
fronting me, comes down to it, winding for a couple of miles, a pretty
tributary brook between low thickets, with rich cornfields on each
side of it, and, in the whole visible space of country up to the hills,
there are countable eleven rough farmsteads or cottages and roofs of
them—(too broken—for the good of the owners—or virtue).

Beside the brook, five reapers have begun their work in a golden
field—the white specks of them gleam changefully in the sunshine.—
A bird or two is singing a little.*

The room has a summer murmur of flies in it—(just a fly or two too
many—brother Anthony, the Sacristan not being careful about washing up) and I'm writing down the measures of this upper church—
very difficult to get accurately.— I've been reading Lamentations IV.
and thinking that I'm precious son of Zion comparable to fine gold,[2]
but I can't make out who "they" is, and who "them" is in the 15th and
16th verses.

Love to Mary always and kindest regards to Mrs. Warren,[3] and I'm
your loving

J. R.

* Also the frogs down at the edge of the Tescio [*sic*] are talking loudly
every now and then. One can always hear *them*, any distance.

146. *Ruskin to Carlyle*

Monastery of Assisi
2nd July, '73 [actually 1874]

My dearest Papa,

I'm not so comfortable in my cell, this morning, for it being quite
cloudless, and very hot, the cicadas are delighted, and the consequence

---

[1] See Dante's *Paradiso*, canto xi, lines 43–45, where Saint Thomas Aquinas describes
the environs of Assisi preparatory to his praise of Saint Francis: "Intra Tupino e l'acqua,
che discende / Del colle eletto dal beato Ubaldo." The town is situated between the
streams of Tupino, on the east, and Chiasi, on the slopes of Monte Subaso to the west,
where Saint Ubaldus had his hermitage. The Teschio is the local stream within Assisi
itself.

[2] See Lamentations 4:2: "The precious sons of Zion, comparable to fine gold, how
are they esteemed as earthen pitchers, the work of the hands of the potter!"

[3] Mrs. Carlyle's housekeeper, who had stayed on in Chelsea.

Letter 146. MS: NLS, 556.83. Hitherto unpbd.

is that the Spanish chestnut under the window is filled with a quantity of small watchman's rattles, which never stop going for an instant. Also I'm a little out of temper,—for all the beggars in Assisi,—that's five sixths of its population, know me, now; and the stupid and vile ones come at me like wasps at a rotten nectarine—wherever I move. Their unfathomable stupidity is the thing that torments me most, thinking to get money by importunity at every corner, bearing up against being sent to the Devil—with exactly the sort of obstinancy [*sic*] that flies have—or goats—

In other respects, my presence here is on the whole, healthy for the place. I made them wash down their cloister thoroughly the other day,—and got the sacristan to stop the blackguard boys of the town from playing bowls at the church door. The boys returning again and again, when he was out of the way, he took courage, under my adjuration, to confiscate three of the bowls. This ended the business satisfactorily. Two of the boys laid wait afterwards to throw stones at me, in my morning walk.— I didn't see them—but as Fors would have it,[1] the Syndic—looking early out of his window—did; and put them both in prison. The church porch is now left in peace, and the respectable people touch their hats to me— So much for Liberty and Equality.

I wonder what you'll say to the July Fors![2] and the French and German bits!

I'm so ashamed of having written so ill, but am tired this morning.

Ever your loving   J. R.

147. *Ruskin to Carlyle*

Assisi, 7th July, '74

My dearest Papa,

It is getting very hot here, and if I had not a cave to work in, I should have to come away. But the lower church is always cool. You can imagine it easily as two large chimney pots cut in half and dovetailed so forming nave and transepts only instead of crossing simply at the same height—like that,[1] where they cross, the *diagonal* arches are

---

[1] One of Ruskin's favorite phrases. One of the meanings of "Fors" given in *Fors Clavigera*, letter 2 (*Works*, XXVII, 27–28) is "Fortune," which, Ruskin says, "means the necessary fate of the man: the ordinance of his life which cannot be changed."

[2] Letter 43, entitled "The Chateau-Rouge. French Freedom." It speaks of the "selfishness of the German temper" and the "deeds and virtues of the French." See *Works*, XXVIII, 106–20.

Letter 147. MS: NLS, 556.84. Pbd: Ruskin's *Works*, XXXVII, 122, with facsimile reproduction of MS.

[1] See the accompanying illustrations.

semicircular also, which gives a vault like that lifted in the middle—on the four compartments of this vault, as at thus, the pictures which I've mainly got to work on are painted, the figures all sloping together to the points of them.

Then the upper church is built over this lower railway tunnel one like that and finally the tunnel mouths are stopped up and the cloister and convent added and there you are on the top of the hill, like Stirling Castle.— I'm writing to day in the convent lumber room, the coolest place I can find.— Here's my table and chair, look, on enclosed leaf, and all my books before me. I'm sadly ashamed of writing this so badly, but somehow when I'm thinking I can't shape the letters.

Ever your loving   J. R.

148. Ruskin to Carlyle

Monastery of Assisi
8th July, '74

Dearest Papa,

If you have any word to me, now, direct to Perugia, for I am driven away from here by the noise at night, and beggars in the day. I have done two pieces of kindness, which have buzzed all over the town and produced the impression of my being either a fool, or an angel with unlimited command of money, in either case to be made the most of. And the thirsty, lazy, hungry, miserable and totally uncared for population is coming upon me like a swarm of rats.

The proper practical English conclusion upon this would be,— "there, you see what it is to give money. Never give anybody anything,"—&c. Whereas my own feeling—or better than feeling—knowledge, is exactly that of a man on a raft in the midst of a wreck, who has rescued two wretches and sees all the sea full of hands held up.

"Kick them away," says the practical Englishman—"Haven't they wrecked themselves"? "Yes, of course they have. They had no pilot—no captain—no compass—and no port. They drifted here—and drank all the rum in the hold before they came ashore— You wise-acre—don't I know all that as well as you—but what's to be done now"?

Meantime, the sense of the extreme and utterly hopeless misery of the country almost unfits me for doing any work in it at all. While the

Letter 148. MS: NLS, 556.85. Hitherto unpbd.

158

Assisi 7ᵗʰ July .74

My dearest Papa

It is getting very hot here, and if I had not a cave to work in, I should have to come away. But the lower church is always cool. You can imagine it easily as two large chimney pots cut in half and dovetailed to frames nave and transepts only instead of crossing straight at the same height — like that, when they cross, the diagonal arches are semicircular also, which gives a vault letter than lifted in the middle — on the four compartments of this vault — as at this , the fractures,

Letter from Ruskin to Carlyle, July 7, 1874, page one (Letter 147). Courtesy of the National Library of Scotland.

which I've mania[n]g got to work on
are painted, the figure[s] all slopi[ng]
to getter to th point[s] of them.
Then the upper church is built
over this lower railway tunnel one

like that
and finally
th tunnel
mouth[s] are
stopped up and
th cloister and
convent added

and there you are
on th top of th hill, like
Stirling Castle. — I'm writ[ing]
to day in the convent lumber room
th coolest place I can find — Here
my table and chair, look — in a noland
leaf. and all my books before me.

Letter from Ruskin to Carlyle, July 7, 1874, page two. Courtesy of the National Library of Scotland.

Letter from Ruskin to Carlyle, July 7, 1874, last page. Courtesy of the National Library of Scotland.

cheerful English tourist goes dancing and coquetting about—and has been fifty years finding his pleasure and education in Italy—and never done it one pennyworth of good— How much *harm*, the devil only knows.

Ever your poor savage J. R.

149. *Ruskin to Carlyle*

Perugia, 13th July [1874]

My dearest Papa,

You have never sent me that translation from Goethe[1] yet, and I am very faithfully and deeply desirous of it. I tremble for what you will say about the German bits in July Fors.[2]

I am worried here as Fors will have it, by an inflexible German artist to whom I can teach nothing,—and who contrasts unfavorably with a flexible young Italian, who expects me to teach him everything.[3] Seriously, a receptive, docile, eager youth, very thankful to be shown a thing or two. The German is only anxious to prove that what he does is the best that can be done,—and it is very poor, and very narrow.

The heat has come heavy at last and I begin to think of home. I want to see the "Mont" of Simon de Montfort, by Seine side,[4] as I come back, and if France is pleasant may linger there—but this is only a scratch today because I was getting out of my morning habit of writing, and was thinking of that translation.

Ever your loving,

J. R.

Letter 149. MS: NLS, 556.86. Hitherto unpbd. The MS has "P.Mark 1874" in another hand.

[1] Running vertically up the left margin of the MS is "The 'Gerotes-Exochier', I think A. C." (probably Alexander Carlyle). See Letter 133, n. 1.

[2] See Letter 146, n. 2.

[3] The two young artists are unidentified, but were connected with the Arundel Society, for which Ruskin was doing much work.

[4] Simon de Montfort, Earl of Leicester (c. 1208–65), was a friend and minister of Henry III of England, and was famous as a rebellious baron who was instrumental in the early stages of the development of Parliament. Francis Espinasse, in his *Literary Recollections* (London, 1893, p. 189), quotes Froude as saying that in 1851 Carlyle planned a biography of Montfort, but abandoned the project in favor of the subject of Frederick the Great.

The "Mont" in question is the ruin of the tenth century castle of the counts of Montfort at Montfort-l'Amaury, about thirty miles downriver from Paris. The Earl of Leicester was a member of this family and was probably born in the castle.

150. Carlyle to Ruskin

5 Cheyne Row, Chelsea
15 July, 1874

Dear Ruskin,

We have been bountifully furnished with these precious little showers of manna which fall on us day after day with a wonderful continuity on your part. They are really strange and charming to me, wonderfully annihilating time and space between us, bringing you and your whereabout vividly home to us as in a magic glass. It is little to say of them that I have had no such epistolary pleasure for the last eight years. If I could command or expect such a thing, I should say *Encore, encore*, do not cease while I live! but, alas, that is not in my power; and while the reciprocity is all on one side[1] such a thing in nature is not to be expected. Go on at any rate, so long as it is not a bother to you, and know always that nothing you can do is more certain of a grateful welcome. I think we have had eight Letters since I wrote to you last, and now that you are going or gone to Perugia and we are soon to be driven out of London by the fervent heat, I write again to apprize you as far as possible when we are going whitherward, both of which points, especially the latter, are still somewhat involved in haze.

As to the time, it seems certain enough that we are still to be here for ten days; so that there is still room for a Letter or two, if you will stand good, not to say for three or four wh. could be safely and immediately forwarded to Froude's in Wales (J. A. Froude, Esq., Crogan, Corwen, Merionethshire);—and should we even sail to Lerwick, where we suppose my Brother John to be, diligently looking out for bathing quarters, there is a daily post to that Scandinavian locality with only an addition of two days or perhaps of only one to the distance between Cheyne Row and you. Go on therefore for at least ten days hitherward and for ten more Froude-ward. Before the latter period expire you shall have another despatch concerning our ulterior movements; and so enough, on that poor time-table head.

Mary and I turned up and punctually perused, & with great attention, all chapters and passages of Scripture appointed you in childhood, by one now sacred to you; nor did we omit the recent passage of

<hr>

Letter 150. MS: Rylands, English MS 1191/7. Pbd: Sanders, p. 233.

[1]Sanders (p. 233) adds that this Irish phrase was "Coterie speech in the Carlyle household. Mrs. Carlyle had found the expression very amusing and had used it often." Carlyle's earlier reference to "the last eight years," is to the year 1866, of course, when he last received a letter from his wife.

Jeremiah's Lamentations; but cannot any more than yourself ascertain *who* the "them" and "they" especially are. As to the rest, I found them one and all beautifully significant and maternally fit; indeed in nearly all of them I was struck by a kind of divineness of piety, intensity, and perfect sincerity not to be found in any other Book; ever wonderful old Jews! In three or four of the pieces, I forget now which, there was speech about Wisdom, of its dwelling with the Lord before anything else existed, of its being the essence and foundation of all that does or ever will exist; nay, of its being almost the Lord himself, which struck me very forcibly with a light quite new, as words springing from the very deepest region of man's soul, and being eternally the truth for the soul of man,—for me at this day as for the ancient Hebrew that penned them in his remote wilderness, thousands of years ago, thrice wonderful old Hebrews, sunk now to Baron Grant[2] and his scoundrel Resuscitations of the Fine Arts in Leicester Square!— Under this head, too, I may as well mention that your earnest and eager enquiry twice repeated, 24th and 27th June, about my notions on Abbot Samson's religion on King Frederick's, Cromwell's and my Mother's have been often present to me; and at first gave me some surprise at finding you think I had still something more to tell you on that subject; though of late the surprise has gone, for I can now bethink me of almost nothing I have ever hinted, even in the obscurist way, on that point, if it be not one transient, but to myself significant allusion in *Past and Present* apropos of that duel *apud Radingas*[3] (at Reading) where a sinful caitiff, desperately fighting for his life, sees the gigantic figure of St. Edmund, looking doomful and minatory upon him in the splendor of the evening sun, and falls down as if dead, but is brought to life again by the monks and lives as a monk many years afterwards absolved from the world. There followed that a little word or two which had much much [*sic*] meaning to myself; but I now see can have had none to anybody else. I would gladly write on that subject, were there left in me, without fingers, the smallest power of writing, but it will be better that we first talk of it, as you propose, which I shall long for an opportunity of doing.

[2] Albert Grant, known as Baron Grant (1830–99). His real name was Gottheimer, and he was known as a free-wheeling "company promoter." In 1873 he had purchased unused land in Leicester Square and turned it into a public garden, with statues of Newton, Shakespeare, and others.

[3] See *Past and Present*, book 2, chapter 14. The duel was between Henry of Essex and Robert de Montfort, youngest brother of Simon de Montfort, mentioned by Ruskin in the previous letter. The "little word or two" that followed is in *op. cit.*, *Works*, X, 108–9.

Froude is bound for the Cape of Good Hope and generally for the Colonies on an earnest mission from Lord Carnarvon[4] and the government to look into that colonial problem with his own eyes, and to advise what, in his own best judgement, can by wise Government be done or attempted. He is to leave Southampton for Cape Town on the 23rd August; to be away many months, so that, probably, I shall never see him again. But the whole world, and all British men in the first place, may fairly expect to get some good of it, and in the end a boundless quantity of good by this adventure; and to himself in his silent sorrow it seems to me of all enterprises the most promising and wholesome. Everybody that I hear speaking of it warmly approves of the project & of the man selected for it. For my own part I feel well enough what I shall lose by the affair and how sad and solemn the adieu is. Of course I must see him on whatever terms for a few days before we part.[5]

I had much to say about the last *Fors* and things relating to yourself but my unfortunate ethereal part is so crushed down into the foul mire by this intolerable heat and feebleness of nerve and muscle that I must forbear it all till a better time. I tell you only two things; *first*, that I think and have long thought that you are dreadfully in error as to the German people and the genius of Germany; which (including England & its Shakespeares, wh. are radically German) I place far above the genius and characteristics of any other people ancient or modern; very especially above whatever can be called French; and truly I wish you

[4] Lord Carnarvon, colonial secretary under Disraeli, sent Froude on an unofficial visit to South Africa to investigate the possibilities of federation in that colony. Froude's account of this voyage is in his *Short Studies on Great Subjects*, Third Series (1897), pp. 343–400.

[5] In 1873, Carlyle had turned over to Froude large numbers of his and his late wife's personal papers and letters. He entrusted Froude with the decision of whether many of these papers should eventually be published as a memorial record of his wife's life, but by 1874 Froude had not yet made his decision. On July 10, 1874, six weeks before leaving for South Africa, Froude wrote a touching letter to Carlyle concerning these papers. "I should like to hear something of your plans that I may see you again before I go," he said. "You must give me directions about the sacred letters and Papers which you have trusted to my charge.— whether you wish them to be returned to your custody during my absence—or whether they shall be locked up in a sealed parcel in Onslow Gardens, with instructions, in case I never come back, to be placed in such hands as you will desire. If God so orders it, I will fulfill the trust which you have committed to me with such powers as I have.— No greater evidence of confidence was ever given by one man to another,—and in receiving it from you I am receiving it from one to whom no words of mine will ever convey the obligations which I feel. . . . I hope we may both live till I can relate my experiences to you, and witness, I trust, some effect produced which you will recognize as good. The thought of you will still be with me wherever I go to encourage, guide and govern me." (MS: Folger Shakespeare Library.)

could get to understand how poor an affair, if you deducted those *Franks* out of it who are purely German every fibre of them, and not the best of German, la belle France, with all its boundless self-conceit, and even its pretty tailoring and cooking and ingeniously filigreeing talent, would be.

The second thing I had to say is but a repetition, namely of the dreadful shock you have given to the Fine Arts here, especially to the Architectural, by your refusal of the Gold Medal to be presented by the Queen & the tittering and *tee-hee*ing of many sober minded and ingenious people by your dreadful offer to sit willingly in sackcloth and ashes with any respectable body of Fine-Artists that will invite you for such a purpose. Oh joy! Was there ever such cruelty heard of! How well deserved, I and the ingenious people do not now say.

Adieu, dear Ruskin, many kind adieus. Mary adds her kind regards and best wishes to mine.

Yours ever,
T. Carlyle

151. *Ruskin to Carlyle*

Perugia, 17th July, 1874

My dearest Papa,

I've been in a somewhat wo[e]ful state, for this week past, The Root of bitterness is failing in my drawings or not being able to finish them,—the sense of—that German word you quote from Goethe, meaning weakness in one's craft,[1]—being indeed worst of all to bear. But on this root, the sense of the vileness of the whole population about me,—and not less of my own, according to my better opportunities I want to lead strongly now, in this Fors movement, for I see it must be done, not said, and I am so luxurious and dependent on all that I say people should be independent of.— However, I don't doubt but that things will clear themselves to me as I get nearer them. It seems to me the first thing I have to do, next term at Oxford, is simply to make a present of my fine rooms, with their Titian, Turners, and Gothic MSS, value—at most temperately calculated market price, thirty thousand pounds within the oak door—to Corpus Christi College itself as a part of their library, and myself to take up a proper student's establishment, on the scale of a great Earl of Essex, (Froude

---

Letter 151. MS: NLS, 556.87. Hitherto unpbd.

[1] Probably *unkraft*. See *Sartor Resartus*, book II, chapter 7, "The Everlasting No": "'The painfulest feeling,' writes he 'is that of your own feebleness (*Unkraft*)'" (*Works*, I, 131).

Short studies, last series, p. 330)[2]—but I don't feel much inclined to
do this, yet awhile—and at all events, will come and have a chat over it
with Papa first.— You need not be frightened and think I'm getting
excited and wrong headed. I never was more lazy or less enthusiastic—but one can't preach simplicity of life with one's room-furniture
worth 30,000; and I've got to preach simplicity of life, if *any*thing.

Ever your loving   J. R.

152. *Ruskin to Carlyle*

Perugia, Sunday
19th July, '74

My Dearest Papa,

I have your lovely letter,[1] so full of pleasantness for me; chiefly in
telling that I give you pleasure by putting you in the place of the poor
Father, who used to be *so* thankful for his letter, and content with so
little. "If only I would date accurately," said he: (and he never got me
to do it!).[2]

What *is* the use of that terrible law of Nature that one knows all
that is best to know, too late. But it is a great comfort to me to think
that *you* also will be glad to see the postman stop sometimes. Your
reading all those pieces that my mother chose is very wonderful and
helpful to me. To think she should be able to give some new thoughts
even to you!

I will note with extreme fidelity and care all you tell me of Germany
and France.

I want mainly to ask you to give my love to Froude when you next
see him. I will write some morning letters to him also, now—for the
little while before he leaves. I am glad he is going on any mission in
which he is interested, and thankful that his words are of weight with
government in any matter. But what Colonial problem can there be,
soluble by any formula, until the Home problem has become—I
do not say soluble—but even intelligible? When your emigration is
nothing but the over-boiling of a neglected pot—what sort of problems can one have out of the fat in the fire? Our modes of dealing with
the Aboriginies [*sic*] may indeed be looked into with advantage. I
heard, and have no doubt of the truth of the hearing, from the daugh-

---

[2] I.e., Froude's *Short Studies on Great Subjects*, Second Series (1871), p. 330. The
essay is on "Education."

Letter 152. MS: NLS, 556.88. Pbd: Ruskin's *Works*, XXXVII, 123–24.

[1] Letter 150.

[2] See, for example, Letter 146, where Ruskin gives the wrong year.

ter of the Bp. of Natal,[3] that our treatment of the Caffres[4] had been as cruel as dishonourable, and that the effect of it was now remediless.

I am drawing angels carrying buckets of roses here—with peacocks eyes in their wings.[5] Absolutely alone with them in the gallery today; till they seemed real. But to think that only one monk, out of the hosts, should have been able to draw such! and now that they're drawn—I don't know anybody who really cares for them, but myself.

Love to Mary, & thanks for her pretty writing. Ever, my dearest Papa, Your affect.

J. Ruskin

153. *Ruskin to Carlyle*

Florence, 26th July, '74

Dearest Papa,

This is only to say where I am,—or where the shell of me is—for the kernel is nowhere—got all black & damp like a bad walnut with biliousness and sulkiness, the two reacting on each other wonderfully when I find 12th century churches being knocked down to build barracks, and billiard-rooms, which is the course of improvement here and elsewhere.

There's nobody in Florence and only one room in the inn, not under "restoration." That room is twelve of my paces by thirteen and a half, my pace being about a yard, it has three tall windows, and six tall doors— Over every door is a chandelier with five candles in it, and in the middle of the ceiling a chandelier with 62 candles in it—at least I count thirty-one on this side as I sit, the furniture is scarlet & gold, the paper green and gold, the doors, all double-folding, hidden by crimson curtains—a landscape good enough to sell to an American for a Salvator,[1] hangs opposite the windows, & the marble chimney piece is

[3] Frances E. Colenso, daughter of the famous missionary bishop, J. W. Colenso. See Letter 163.

[4] Or "Kaffirs." Kaffir tribesmen were given nominal rights in South Africa, but were generally subjugated by white rule and by their ignorance. One of the things Froude was to investigate, for instance, was the case of a Kaffir chief who had been imprisoned by the lieutenant governor of Natal, Sir Benjamin Pine, after a mock trial. Bishop Colenso, a constant friend of the natives, interfered on behalf of the chief, and Lord Carnarvon eventually recalled Pine to England.

[5] Fra Angelico's *Madonna of Perugia*. See *Works*, XXXVII, 124n.

Letter 153. MS: NLS, 556.89. Pbd: Ruskin's *Works*, XXXVII, 124–25.

[1] Salvator Rosa (1615–73), Neapolitan painter, etcher, poet, actor, and musician. Rosa was an academically trained court painter who proclaimed his specialty to be portraiture and historical views; the nineteenth century chiefly admired his vivid, tempes-

finely sculptured with vine leaves and a nymph going to sacrifice a goat.

The general sense of being in one of the deepest holes of Dante's inferno which this room produces on me, after my cell at Assisi, is very unpleasant, this Sunday morning. And so that's where I am—and what I am; and now I must stop, for I'm behindhand with my letter to the landlords,[2] and it's about the right room to get on with it in.

Love to Mary.

Ever your affectionate
J. R.

I've been reading Froude's Calvinism—State & Subject—Colonies—Progress,[3] carefully this last week. What a trick he has of knowing everything and then polishing himself off to nothing.

154. *Carlyle to Ruskin*

5 Cheyne Row, Chelsea
30 July, 1874

Dear Ruskin,

Thanks again and again for these little showers of manna immediate from the skies, which do not wholly cease but still come to us now & then,—last night from Florence, for example, and some nights before from Perugia: wonderful things for us amid the dusty tumult of London in our little cell at Chelsea here.

The gorgeous splendour of your room at Florence, and, alas, your wild gloom of mind while lodged in it, as if it were the blackest nook of Malebolge;[1] that is a strange but not unaccountable phenomenon, such as easily occurs in this wicked perversity of a world! But we can expect a still more emphatic and scorching *Fors* from you on that account, which is some benefit of good out of evil.

On the whole, is it not evident for one thing, that the Italian sum-

---

tuous landscapes, which he himself considered to be his lesser work. His own vigorous and rebellious life and the atmosphere of his landscapes won for him the reputation of a precursor of the Romantic age among Ruskin's contemporaries; but his draughtsmanship was, in essence, as classically severe as that of his contemporaries, Claude Lorrain and Nicolas Poussin. Ruskin's reference to landscape here reflects the record prices Rosa's paintings in that genre were fetching in the 1870's.

[2]Letter 45 of *Fors Clavigera*. See Letter 155.

[3]"Calvinism," "Reciprocal Duties of State and Subject," and "The Colonies Once More," in Froude's *Short Studies on Great Subjects*, Second Series (1871).

Letter 154. MS: Yale University Library, 24. Pbd: Sanders, p. 236.

[1]The eighth circle of Dante's *Inferno*, mentioned by Ruskin in the previous letter.

mer is getting far too hot for you; that in practical truth you ought to bundle up your notebooks and come home, or nearer home? I really think so, but must not take upon me to advise. If at the "tomb of Simon de Montfort," in more tolerable air (in France, as that may well be), you could pick up for us any vestige of clearer evidence or intelligibility about that notable and to me inconceivable man, it would beyond doubt be a welcome thing. But wasn't he clearly cut down and chopped into mince meat, flesh and bones, at Eavesham [*sic*]; how then can he have got buried near Paris?[2] Furthermore, have you not heard that his Son was "The blind Beggar of Bethnal-Green"?[3] What a Dark-Lantern is history, or worse, even, a Lantern of darkness; absolutely tenebrific, instead of illuminative!

The one real object of this Letter is to tell you that we are still here, & likely to be so for at least a fortnight longer, hungry therefore for your immediate missives if you will have the charity still to send such. Froude is expect[ed] here Saturday (the day after tomorrow), stays for three weeks, and in the course of the first, must settle many small but important things with me, in case we should not meet again in this world.[4] I am confident he will do real good in his colonial expedition; good, even in the emigration line, in spite of the pot boiling over. These things go on at an inconceivably *slow* rate; a century, nay ten centuries, representing what would actually be but a minute in a real pot, dashing its fat into the fire. Patience, my Friend, patience; we must have patience.

Before leaving Florence I must ask you to take another look at Michael Angelo's Statue of David and explain to me a little (on your return) how it is that the gigantic plaster cast of this Figure (in our

[2] Simon de Montfort (see Letter 150) was killed in battle with Prince Edward, later Edward I, at Evesham on August 4, 1265. He was interred immediately in an unmarked grave in the close of Evesham Abbey by the monks there, though his head was struck off and sent to Wigmore for exhibition.

[3] Henry, Earl Simon's second son by his marriage with Eleanor, sister of King Henry III, was killed in battle at Evesham with his father. The legend that he survived to become the "blind Beggar of Bethnal-Green," whose identity was revealed when he provided a rich dowry for his daughter, can be traced to a two-part Elizabethan ballad, "The Beggar's Daughter of Bednall-Green," printed in Percy's *Reliques of Ancient English Poetry* (series II, book ii, number X). The legend was enlarged considerably when it formed the plot of *The Blind Beggar of Bednal Green*, written in 1599 and acted in April 1600, by Henry Chettle (1564?–1607?) and John Day (1574–1640?), the earliest known work of the latter. James Sheridan Knowles (1784–1862), a cousin of R. B. Sheridan, produced a successful play on the same subject in 1834.

[4] Since 1871, Carlyle had been making arrangements with Froude for the eventual publication of his biography and reminiscences, as well as the letters of Mrs. Carlyle. He had given Froude all the private papers and manuscripts necessary for such tasks, and Froude had already begun work on them. See Letter 150.

Brompton Boilers here) is more impressive to me than any statue I have ever seen.[5]

Not a word more; there is an intrusion jingling at the door, peremptorily saying cease. Mary sends her love.

Yours ever, dear Ruskin,

T. Carlyle

155. *Ruskin to Carlyle*

Lucca, 2nd August, [1874]

Dearest Papa,

I have been forced to get to my Squireen Fors,[1] in before breakfast times, this week past, and have had no sense to write during the day, under curious vexations—which have ended in my resolving to stay till Oxford term time, here in Tuscany, and do my best against its modern ways. The good of which plan is, (first, at least) that my letters can be secure, and that if you or Froude have any word to say to me, if addressed Hotel d'Arno, Florence,[2] it will come safe & quickly.

Any scattered grain you may either, have sent me, to former addresses, I shall gradually gather.— Having only today finally resolved on this, I send you first word of it. I shall get the Squireen Fors sent off to printers tomorrow with orders to send Froude a proof. I want him to see that one can get into hot water out of Africa, if one chooses.

I'm not going to speak of *colonies* in Fors at all.— I do hope that Froude will take up the subject on his own and gradually concentrate his influence on some practical matter which will lead on to the truth. In haste today. Ever your and his affectionate.

J. R.

[5] A copy of the *David* of Michelangelo exhibited in the Victoria and Albert Museum, South Kensington. See Letter 157.

Letter 155. MS: NLS, 556.90. Hitherto unpbd.

[1] Letter 45 of *Fors Clavigera* (*Works*, XXVIII, 145–66). It is dated "Lucca, August 2nd, 1874," and is entitled "My Lord Delayeth His Coming. The British Squire." Throughout it, Ruskin holds the British landed gentry, or "Squireens," up to judgment before God and the poor, and finds them wanting.

[2] The Hotel d'Arno, later the Royal Grande Bretagne e d'Arno, was located on the north bank of the river whose name it bears, between the Ponte Vecchio and the Ponte S. Trinità, at Lungarno Acciaioli 8. It was then a fashionable hotel with about a hundred rooms. Ruskin chose it perhaps because of the immediate proximity of Santi Apostoli, a vaulted Tuscan-Romanesque basilica of the eleventh century with a High Renaissance facade.

156. *Ruskin to Carlyle*

Lucca, 5th August, '74

Dearest Papa,

I was out among the vines and maize last night, across the Serchio—now only a mountain stream, running among long banks of shingle, and *almost* clear;—but with no voice, like Tweed or Liddel. I shut my eyes and listened, to find if by any imagination—or honest defiance of imagination—I could fancy myself listening to Tweed at Melrose. But no—utterly shallow and empty—the Italian stream in voice, as an Italian opera song to the fullest of Burns, in thought. The reasons were clear enough, on looking. The shingle was as wide as Tweed's, but was of dull limestone instead of ringing quartz—and for twenty *round* pebbles, lay one square stone. The water flowed past, silently instead of tinkling *through.*— In the second place,—there were no deepcut channels through enduring rock, to give gush, and hollow tone—the bass to the pebble-trebble. Nothing but waste of stones and sand—the signs of the folly and misery which left the river to overflow the plain in winter.

I went on, through winding lanes between maize and vine—sunset turning into little nimbuses the bunches of white filaments at the ends of the ears of maize—the peasants at work, of old Etruscan feature, bidding me good evening rightly and quietly. At last at the turn of a path, I met a pretty dark-eyed boy of eleven or twelve years old. He knelt down in front of me quickly, silently, like a dog ordered to do so, on both knees—holding out his cap. There was no servility in the action any more than would be in the dog's—great beauty in it—and in the entirely quiet face, not beseeching, but submitting its cause to you. I never saw such a thing before. The real root of it is in Etruscan religion, and the Ghibelline training of the old town, in Castruccio's time, & before.[1] But, if Castruccio had forseen it!—in fields of his own Lucca—as he went out on his triumphal march at Rome!

Ever your loving

J. R.

Letter 156. MS: NLS, 556.91. Pbd: Ruskin's *Works*, XXXVII, 126.

[1]Castruccio Castracani degli Antelminelli (1281–1328), Ghibelline leader and ruler of Lucca from 1316 until his death. The entrance of the Emperor Henry VII into Italy saw a resurgence of Ghibelline power in northern Italy under Uguccione della Faggiuola, aided by Castruccio. They occupied Lucca in 1314, and two years later Castruc-

157. *Ruskin to Carlyle*

Lucca, 16th Aug, '74

My Dearest Papa,

I only got your lovely letter of 30th July this moment at breakfast, having been kept here by unlooked-for difficulties in work, and *delights* in the neighborhood.

I underline that word, because I want you to be assured I don't write to you in mere *bilious* misery. I've plenty of that, and know it well. But I never allow it to alter my thoughts of things. I was wretched in the Florence room, because I knew it to be English Nidification in Florence, and the Sum of English Influence there. And that it was pure Hell fire—in the midst of what I have here, every evening;—a country of Marble rocks—of purple hills, and skies of softest light—under which *still* dwell a people who labour, & pray. You like the "David" because—it is the only piece of true Tuscan sculpture you have been able to *see*. Its colossal size rescues it from the Kensington lumber—you cannot see any *other* piece of Florence work but in its place.— I am at work here on the statue carved in the olden times, "Lady Gladness" (Ilaria) of Caretto¹—it lies on her tomb quite open—at the cathedral wall, as if she had been carried in, and laid there while they sang the burial service. Thirty years ago, a modern radical—one of the school of that Florence drawing-room—put his hat on the face of it as he was talking to me, thinking it would answer handily to keep said hat from the dust.

As I was working there, last week, two of the Lucca countrywomen came in, and stopped at it suddenly,—then knelt down—and kissed the hem of its robe. "Yes, she deserves your kiss," I said. They opened their great black eyes wide, half frightened, like pretty wild animals. "Che santo é?" ["what saint is it?"] said the bravest of them, at last.

---

cio was made captain-general of the city for a term of six months. This appointment was continually extended until, in 1320, he received the office for life. At the same time Frederick of Austria, emperor-elect, made him imperial vicar of Lucca, Versilia, and the Lunigiana. In 1327 the Emperor Louis IV gave him Lucca as a hereditary duchy, but Castruccio's further rise was cut short by his sudden death in Lucca on September 3 of the following year.

Letter 157. MS: NLS, 556.92. Pbd: Ruskin's *Works*, XXXVII, 130–31.

¹The tomb of Ilaria del Carretto (d. 1405), second wife of Paolo Guinigi, lord of Lucca. The monument, executed in 1406 by Jacopo della Quercia (1374–1438), is in the left transept of the cathedral of San Martino at Lucca. It had captured Ruskin's attention when he first saw it in the spring of 1845. See the catalogue of Ruskin's drawings in *Works*, XXXVIII, 258, nos. 862–65.

These are the people whom Froude is leaving to be crushed to death—to breed Englishmen on black pepper.[2] (He had better give them gunpowder at once—for permanent diet—and then set them to,—fire eating.)— And you, Papa, preaching *patience* to me!

I happen, by Fors care, to have under my hand two leaves of an old lecture,[3] cancelled and kept to be worked up farther—perhaps Mary won't mind looking over the second before reading it to you. I don't, so she must.— Mind it is *sighting*, not *fighting*.

Ever your loving filius.— more tomorrow about Montfort. see 4th page. Love to Mary—I couldn't answer a difficult bit in her letter, tell her, about the Bible but I'll try to do so.

I must have made a mistake, I *meant tomb* of Coeur de Lion—*Forts* of Mont*fort*.[4] I believe Evesham to have been the fatallest battle ever fought in Europe[5]— But can't say why today.

J. R.

158. Ruskin to Carlyle

Lucca, 17th Aug. [1874,] morning

My Dearest Papa,

I've just been reading the prayer of Judith—(Judith IX). (If Froude is with you still, tell him I do so wish he'd stop from his Missionary business, and write a *Philistine's* history of Delilah.)— But how glorious those 8th and IXth chapters are.

[2] A reference to Ruskin's disagreement with Froude over English emigration policies. In a letter to Froude on July 27, 1874, Ruskin told him: "You have taught me . . . what an Englishman is, and here you are deliberately acting as if you could grow one on pepper & squash. You must grow Englishmen in England." (Waldo H. Dunn, *James Anthony Froude: A Biography 1857–1899* [Oxford, 1963], p. 355.)

[3] The pages are printed in full in a note to this letter in *Works*, XXXVII, 130–31. They begin by describing Michelangelo's *David* as a view of "The entire personality of David as a youth under Divine inspiration," and then describe a modern "somewhat clever study of David imagined at this same moment by I suppose a young student—at all events an inexperienced one—and catalogued under the title of 'David *sighting* Goliath.' The youth's mind being probably fuller of rifle practice than of his art, he would not regard the contest otherwise than as a momentary question of handling the thong and pebble. . . ."

[4] The reference to the tomb of Coeur de Lion is almost assuredly to the great Romanesque abbey of Fontevrault, wherein are buried not only Richard I (1189–99), but also his parents, Henry II (1154–89) and Eleanor of Aquitaine (d. 1204). The reference to "Forts of Mont*fort*" is more difficult. Possibly it is to the ruins of several Norman castles to be found within the appanage of the counts of Montfort in the medieval epoch, since Montfort-l'Amaury seems to be ruled out.

[5] See Letters 150 and 154.

Letter 158. MS: NLS, 556.93. Pbd: Ruskin's *Works*, XXXVII, 132.

It is no wonder you disbelieve in Art, papa. Of the history of John the Baptist, and of Judith, the practical Sum and substance, to the British and other public, is two pretty girls carrying two bloody heads,—which is what the Painters & Sculptors as a Body have seen, in these matters, with the utmost of eyes they had—the Italo-French schools giving further flavour to the apocryphal story by scornfully sniffing at Judith's report of the way she passed the night.[1]

Yesterday was the loveliest day I have seen in Italy this year.— I was up after dinner 1500 feet on the hills to the south, in a little stubble field, hedged with chestnut and wild bay; the field itself terraced out of the steep hillside in banks about four feet high—which lay, like a line of steep bastions—green—successive—fragrant, with all manner of herbs—relieved against the blue mountains of Carrara, twenty miles away.

Have you ever noticed how steady I am to my purpose of terracing the Apennines like this—everywhere on their soft ground, and catching all the rain. The spear into the sickle—the Bastion, into banks like this. But I scarcely hope to see it with my own eyes.

I must get to my work. Ever your loving Filius.

159. Ruskin to Mary Aitken

Lucca, 18th Aug[t] [1874]

My dear Mary,

I'm greatly pleased with your pretty note, and account of your uncle, and of the Thames' future prospects, and of Mr. Elwin's house,— the last, to me, most interesting, but in a way you won't guess,[1] though you may find out by chance some day, but I won't tell you.

I've been thinking so often of your last letter, and the difference between the education of thoughtful young persons, fifty years ago, and now. What puzzles me, is how you all take things so quietly—and rest content in doubt, and perpetual questioning—with no answer. "He said he would come back again and tell us all about it, and we waited, and waited, but he never came," said my old German courier to me, tonight, (as he carried my hammer for me up a glen in the intensely

---

[1] See Judith 8–16. Ruskin elaborates upon this thought in *Works*, XXIX, 187: "So again, all aim that is fraudful is viler than that which is violent; but the venal fraud of Delilah is not to be compared with the heroic treachery of Judith." Carlyle had also referred to Judith as "heroic" in *Latter-Day Pamphlets* (see *Works*, XX, 65).

Letter 159. MS: NLS, 556.94. Hitherto unpbd.

[1] See Letter 161.

hard Etruscan marble which needs a doubly heavier one than any rock I know)—of himself and his seven brothers and sisters after their father's death.

It is mainly my sense of this calamitous mystery—less and less thought of *as* a calamity—which keeps me from putting Fors into more practical form. I can't get my foundation on *any* faith.

I am tired tonight and intensely stupid—but would not sleep before acknowledging your second letter, and am ever

Your affectionate friend,
J. Ruskin

I had written friend, with an r so very subordinate, that the word didn't *look* friendly, by any means.

160. *Ruskin to Carlyle*

Lucca, 19th Aug^t., '74

My Dearest Papa,

Yesterday evening I was climbing among the ravines of marble to the south; and came on a cottage like a Highland one—for roughness of look—only the mountain path winding round beneath it, went under a roof of vines trellised from its eaves, and opened before it entered the darkness of green leaves, into a golden threshing floor—the real "area" of the Latins. That so few people past [*sic*] that the people could make their threshing floor of the path, was the first deep prettiness of it. Then, they *had* been threshing and winnowing—the little level field was soft with chaff. The marble rocks—bright gray—came down steep into it, as at Loch Katrine[1] the rocks into the water below, on the other side, the hill went down steep to the blue plain of Lucca—itself (the hillside) one grove of olive—but—as I saw—without fruit—or nearly so.

I crossed the threshing floor, and met the peasant under his vines, looking pale and worn—the Lucchese "Good even Signoria, [*sic*]" given with more than usual gentleness. I said to him what I thought of his happy place,—as well as I could. Yes, he said, but it was a "very dry" country. "The olives had no fruit this year—see—the berries had

Letter 160. MS: NLS, 556.95. Pbd: Ruskin's *Works*, XXXVII, 134.

[1]Loch Katrine is about nine and a half miles long and is separated by a ridge from the larger Loch Lomond, to the southwest. The topography Ruskin describes is characteristic of the eastern end of the loch, which is also the site of "Ellen's Isle," made famous by Scott in *The Lady of the Lake*, which is set in this region.

all fallen, withered for want of rain." For want of *water*, yes, I said—why don't you catch it on the hillside, before it runs to the Serchio and the sea? In short, I found him able to hear, and think— He was actually building a cistern behind his house to catch the rain. "From the *roof*"! (And the Roof from which he ought to receive it rose above him—1500 feet of pure marble!)— I had a long talk—I examined the place; and though I've got to go to Florence today to hunt down St. Dominic,[2] if I don't come back to do a little bit of engineering beside that man's threshing floor—it will be, not my fault, God willing.

I've written a shabby little letter to Mary,—but couldn't help it.

[J. R.]

161. *Ruskin to Mary Aitken*

Florence, 28th Aug. '74

My dear Mary,

In looking over your letter again yesterday, I found a little note of admiration which I had not observed before, after Mr. Elwin's name.[1]

I do believe, under that grave little face of yours, there lies hidden as hearty a love of mischief as ever any young lady or kitten, or other charming juvenile animal was blessed with—and that you knew very well what you were about.

Well, I'll forgive your mischievousness, in thanks for your having read Fors—even to the notes.[2]— And now, seriously, remember that a life may be entirely *exemplary*; yet entirely selfish.

[2] A reference to the *badia* ("abbey") of San Domenico di Fiesole, near Florence. The monastery was founded in 1028 on the site of an earlier cathedral of Fiesole and was first a Benedictine congregation. Later, after 1445, it fell into the hands of the Augustinians. It was entirely rebuilt in 1456–66 after plans by a pupil of Brunelleschi under the patronage of Cosimo de' Medici, *Pater Patriae*. Under Lorenzo the Magnificent, Cosimo's grandson, this harmonious set of buildings was a frequent meeting place of the Platonic Academy, and Giovanni Pico della Mirandola resided here for some time. In Ruskin's time the ruins of the printing establishment of the Florentine scholar Francesco Inghirami filled the site, but two years after this visit the Padri Scolopi ("Brothers of Christian Schools") established one of their institutions in the edifice. See the catalogue in *Works*, XXXVIII, 251, numbers 676–80. A note in Ruskin, *Diaries*, III, 806, says that he "got pretty sketch of San Domenico of Fiesole, in calm sweet evening."

Letter 161. MS: NLS, 556.96. Hitherto unpbd.

[1] Rev. Whitwell Elwin (1816–1900), a former editor of the *Quarterly Review* (1853–60). In 1871 and 1872 he published five volumes of his edition of the works of Pope, with notes both biographical and critical. The edition was finished by W. J. Courthope during the years 1881–89.

[2] Ruskin had been an admirer of Pope since his early youth. Mary Aitken's "mischievousness" must have come from her knowledge that Ruskin had already attacked Elwin in print. *Fors Clavigera*, letter 32, for instance, contains Ruskin's resolution, made in August 1873, to "at least rescue Pope from the hands of his present scavenger

I have no doubt that Mr. Elwin *enjoys himself* more, with his charming and well brought up family, his swallows in church, his—no doubt excellent—sermons, and his very learned and accurate biography of Pope, than he could in any other life.

Meantime, while he is proving that the most intelligibly moral poet of England lied about his letters, Mr. Elwin goes up into his pulpit every 7th day, to tell his congregation that such and such things are so, concerning God and his ways.

Now, if he tells them one word more, positively, than Pope has written in his universal prayer— He tells them—what is in all probability a lie—at least what no man living can prove to be true—and he tells them this, assuming to be a messenger from God. Which, think you, is the worst Liar—Pope—or the self-styled God's messenger with no credentials?

But that is not all.

He is perfectly happy with his children and his swallows. So could I be, with my pictures and nightengales [*sic*]—if I liked—and perhaps something else than a nightengale, in a cage.— Well, I could perhaps even get *that*, if I looked for it;— But, I choose to consider whether other people are happy—Bill Sykes and Nancy[3]—shall we say?

And I enquire, why Bill Sykes and Nancy are not happy.

And I find—briefly—that it is because people listen to Mr. Elwin, instead of to Pope, whose one couplet,

> "Never elated,—while one man's opprest,
> Never dejected, while another's blest"[4]

—is worth all the Sermons, taking the best of them, and leaving out the lies, that I've heard since I was born— And I've heard better than Mr. Elwin's, I can tell you.

Ever my dear Mary, your affectionate

J. Ruskin

Love to Papa, and tell him to keep *you* in order.

---

biographer" (*Works*, XXVII, 586). The "Fors" that Ruskin thanks Mary for reading may be letter 40, written in April 1874. It has a long note defending Pope against Elwin, and its argument follows the one expressed above (*Works*, XXVIII, 76): "He [Pope] cringed—yes—to his friends; . . . to how many more than their friends do average clergymen cringe? . . . and for lying—any average partisan of religious dogma tells more lies in his pulpit in defence of what in his heart he knows to be indefensible, on any given Sunday, than Pope did in his whole life. Nay, how often is your clergyman himself nothing but a lie rampant. . . ."

[3] Characters in Dickens' *Oliver Twist* (1837–39).

[4] See Pope's *Essay on Man*, IV, 323–24.

162. *Mary Aitken to Ruskin*

[Chelsea, August 1874]

. . . your little account of Michael Angelo's David. I don't know if it is to be returned but in any case it is quite safe.

I am somewhat alarmed at the size this letter has grown to! Of course I don't want you to answer it; not indeed if it is too much trouble, even to read it at all.

Uncle who is reading beside me sends his "love and the very best prayers he can form for you."

Dear Mr Ruskin

Yours respectfully and affectionately,

Mary Carlyle Aitken

163. *Ruskin to Carlyle*

Florence, 13th Sept. '74

My dearest Papa,

I have not been writing lately, a great overpress of new discovery having kept me at work, even at night, vainly trying to set the things down. They show themselves to me and then vanish, and I can't keep up with the story of the magic lantern.

But I *must* send you the enclosed which I have no doubt is wholly trustworthy.[1] I hope Froude will see through it all, and be indignant. I have known it has been going on for years.

My chief discovery here is that the old Etruscan race has never failed and that Florentine art is *all* Etruscan—Greek—down to the 15th century, when it expires in modern confusion.

Ever your loving

J. R.

Letter 162. MS: Yale University Library. Hitherto unpbd. The MS is that of only the last page of the letter, the rest of which is missing. Internal evidence—especially the reference to the *David*—suggests the date of August 1874 for the letter. It is also probable that the letter was sent from Chelsea during the last two weeks of August, since Carlyle and Mary went to Scotland at the end of that month.

Letter 163. MS: NLS, 556.97. Hitherto unpbd.

[1] A letter is enclosed from Frances D. Colenso, daughter of Bishop Colenso, to Ruskin, describing how her father had been "fighting, almost single-handed, against falsehood and wrong" and "the amazing falseness of the people in power" in Natal. The letter is dated July 15, 1874, and therefore is relevant to Ruskin's letter of July 19 (Letter 152).

164. *Ruskin to Carlyle*

Corpus Christi College, Oxford
28th Oct. [1874]

Dearest Papa,

I find it must be Saturday, not Friday, when I come to see you: my lecture is, (to my own surprise) on Friday instead of Thursday.— I do hope Saturday will not be an inconvenient day for you,—but if it mischances to be so I shall be up again next week only I want to get into the way of coming to see you every week,[1] if I can.

Saturday then at 2, if I may.

Love to Mary
Ever your affectionate
J. Ruskin

165. *Ruskin to Carlyle*

Corpus Christi College, Oxford
Friday evening,
[November 28, 1874]

My dearest Papa,

I have been hindered from getting up to town this evening; and must dine at Balliol tomorrow, so that I fear the cold double journey in this snowtime, and must resign myself to the loss of my happy hour tomorrow with you; I was going to have brought poor Rosie to see you, but she is too ill to bear coming out just now[1]—next Saturday, at all events, I shall keep tryste, if I'm well; my lectures will be over, and I shall be free-hearted.

I expect a report soon from Mr. Merritt on John Knox:[2] but he is displeased with me for not going to see *him*, and may be dilatory.

Letter 164. MS: NLS, 556.99. Hitherto unpbd.
[1]Ruskin had already paid one visit to Carlyle, on October 25, and the visit mentioned in this letter was made on October 30. It is described at some length in *Praeterita* (*Works*, XXXV, 460) as a pleasant visit in which Carlyle talked about his early life and the death of his sister Margaret. Ruskin's diary records further pleasant visits made to Carlyle on November 7, 21, and 24. For Carlyle's description of these visits, see his letter to his brother John on November 6, in the Introduction.

Letter 165. MS: NLS, 556.100. Pbd: Ruskin's *Works*, XXXVII, 148. The MS has "Post Mark 28 Nov., 1874" in another hand.
[1]Rose La Touche was, in fact, only a few months from death. In January 1875, Ruskin wrote in *Fors Clavigera* (letter 49) that she was dying. See *Works*, XXVIII, 246.
[2]The "Somerville" portrait of John Knox, at the National Portrait Gallery in South Kensington, was currently the subject of Carlyle's study, and was to be discussed by him

Three of my men have asked leave to come to talk—or learn—about St. George's Company.[3] I've asked them to breakfast on Monday.

Love to good little Mary.

Ever your affectionate

J. Ruskin

166. Ruskin to Mary Aitken

Corpus Christi College, Oxford

[December 7, 1874]

My dear Mary,

I send you a "revise" of our card[1]—they stupidly used only one name. If you are pouring thee yourself any day you will find my old servant Lucy very thankful for a little chat, and the chat with her not unpleasant. Dearest love to my papa—I thought him so sweet and dear and well the other day.

Ever your affe

J. Ruskin

Perhaps Papa may like a bit of enclosed scrap. He sent the girl a word of advice which she *took*—seven or eight years ago.[2]

---

in his "Essay on the Portraits of John Knox," published in *Fraser's Magazine* in April 1875. Henry Merritt's report on it is printed at the end of this essay. See also Letter 167.

[3] Ruskin's rustic, communal society, for which *Fors Clavigera* was written. See Letters 108 and 176. For Carlyle's opinion of the organization, see the Introduction.

Letter 166. MS: NLS, 556.101. Hitherto unpbd. The MS has "P.M.^{k} 7 Dec^r, '74" in another hand.

[1] Ruskin had opened a tea shop on Paddington Street in London, designed to supply his customers with pure tea at a very low price. He put it in the care of two of his mother's old servants, and debated on the color of the shop sign at great length in *Fors Clavigera*, letter 48 (*Works*, XXVIII, 246). In this letter to Mary Aitken, Ruskin enclosed a business card, which reads "Mr. Ruskin's Teashop, kept / by Lucy and Harriet Tovy / ~~Tea and Coffee Dealer~~ / 29 Paddington Street, W." The shop did little business, however, and finally closed when one of the old servants died.

[2] Ruskin here sends part of a letter from Blanche Atkinson (see Letter 130). "I think of that grand old Carlyle," she says, "it's his birthday again on Friday. How glad we ought to be that we have him still among us! It vexes me so, that the whole nation does not show its pride and delight in him, before he is gone. We have still a king in the earth, and we take no notice of him. . . ." The "word of advice" may be found in *Good Words*, XXXIII (1892), 460, where a letter from Carlyle to Miss Atkinson, written on October 29, 1866, is printed. In it Carlyle advised her that "a young lady's chief duty and outlook is not to write novels . . . but . . . to be queen of a household."

V

MY SOUL CLEAVES TO THE DUST

"And yet day by day, my soul cleaves to the dust—or—rather the
dust to what soul I had."
Ruskin to Carlyle, May 6, 1875
Letter 170

LETTERS 167-199

January 2, 1875, through December 1879

Ruskin tours northern England. Death of Rose La Touche. He continues *Fors Clavigera* letters, Oxford lectures, and work on St. George's Guild, until his first attack of insanity in early 1878.

Carlyle publishes *Early Kings of Norway* and "An Essay on the Portraits of John Knox." He celebrates his eightieth birthday. Last visit to Scotland in 1879. His death in 1881.

167. Ruskin to Carlyle

2 January, [1875]

Dearest Papa,

The enclosed opinion from Merritt,[1] though it does not go far, is pleasant, it seems to me, as far as it does go. I do not doubt our being able to get nearer the picture when the Secretary is better.

I have been terribly languid and idle, in reaction from exacting work, and worse than work. Often thinking of you and Mary; but with nothing nice today, except how faithfully I am, your loving

John Ruskin

168. Ruskin to Mary Aitken

Brantwood, [January] 13th, 1875

My dear Mary,

It was not your uncle's fault. He is never inaccurate. It was entirely mine, I supposing, and not listening, that there was only one place where portraits were shown, and that blunt "Kensington" was enough.

I am as much delighted as I ought to be by the interest of the reports by Mr. Merritt on the true picture—and am still happier to be able to assure you that I never did mention, nor could have mentioned the name of Porbus [*sic*];[1] for—though I have often in my life heard it—I never by any chance recollect it—but confuse it with Phoebus, & thus get rid of the taste of it as soon as I can.

To [*sic*] Mr. Merritt's testimony is crystal-clear from all prejudice or adulteration.

I've had ten days of unbroken black fog, and can't get up in the morning.

Letter 167. MS: NLS, 556.102. Ruskin has erroneously dated the letter 1874. Hitherto unpbd.

[1] Ruskin encloses a letter from Henry Merritt concerning the "Somerville" portrait of Knox (see Letter 165). Merritt explains that the picture is "far out of reach" at the National Portrait Gallery, and that the illness of the gallery's secretary has prevented his seeing it better. He adds that it "looks to belong to the period of Knox, when Anthony More and Lucas Deheere practiced portrait painting in England. . . ."

Letter 168. MS: NLS, 556.104. Hitherto unpbd.

[1] Franz Pourbus the elder (1545–81) was thought to be the painter of the "Somerville" portrait of John Knox, but Merritt's opinion, as well as that of others, was that the portrait was only a copy of one done in the time of the elder Pourbus, who worked exclusively in the Burgundian circle. Pourbus never got further away from his birthplace in Bruges than Antwerp. See Carlyle's *Works*, XXX, 365–67.

I can always be at my work in winter at seven if—between seven and eight—I see the blue of dawn. But to get up at seven when one is to breakfast by full candlelight at nine, beats me.

That's why papa has had no letters. The little light between nine or ten goes in my day's work and leaves me—too disgusted to speak, and ashamed of myself, Coniston, and the Universe—but ever faithfully and affectionately Papa's and yours

J. Ruskin

169. *Ruskin to Carlyle*

Corpus Christi College, Oxford
4th March [1875?]

Dearest Papa,

May I come and see you tomorrow?— and will two be nice time— just send me word by bearer how you are and if I may come.

Ever your loving,
J. R.

With love to Mary, and all thanks to her for help to St. George.

170. *Ruskin to Carlyle*

Corpus Christi College, Oxford
6th May, '75

Dearest Papa,

The book found me today,[1] more than usually helpless and, earthy. How should it be so, when you say—what you have said in your gift— and feel me to be anything to you. And yet day by day, my soul cleaves to the dust—or—rather the dust to what soul I had.

—Absolute illness though not serious, alters my thoughts just now, and I will not grieve you by telling you how needful your precious words were.

—I had but begun glancing at the book, deeply thankful for the Northern History in this consummate form.— I must try to get stronger, that I may not feel too poor to live, in the presence of such creatures.

Letter 169. MS: NLS, 556.121. Hitherto unpbd.
Letter 170. MS: NLS, 556.105. Hitherto unpbd.
[1] Carlyle's *The Early Kings of Norway: Also an Essay on the Portraits of John Knox* (May 1875). The book was dedicated by Carlyle "to dear, ethereal Ruskin, whom God preserve."

—I shall see you again next week, unless it may be, I can't shake off the cold without some change of air. But I'll write to you—if I go anywhere it will be to see one of my best pupils at Arundel.[2]

Love to Mary. Ever your affect^e &—far more than grateful

John Ruskin

171. Ruskin to Carlyle

Corpus Christi College, Oxford
4th June, 1875

Dearest Papa,

I have had so little to say of myself, pleasing to a Papa's ear, that I neither wrote nor came when I was last in London—for the rest, the Academy work[1] involved much weariness. I had just got it done, with other worldliness, and was away into the meadows to see buttercup and clover and bean blossom, when the news came that the little story of my wild Rose was ended,[2] and the hawthorn blossoms, this year—would fall—over her. Since which piece of news, I have not had a day but in more or less active business, in which everybody congratulates & felicitates me, and must be met with civil cheerfulness. Among the few rests or goods I get indeed—the reading of the Knox's portraits has been the chief. I never saw a more close, inevitable piece of picture criticism; and the incidental sketches of Wishart and Knox are invaluable.

I am coming to town in a week or ten days now.[3] What possesses Froude to go away again so soon? Love to Mary.—

Ever, dear Papa,
Your affectionate
J. Ruskin

[2] Ruskin was a charter member of the Arundel Society, founded in 1849. Its purpose was to provide instruction on works of art, especially those that were fading or crumbling away and had not been described, identified, or copied. See Letter 149.

Letter 171. MS: NLS, 556.106. Pbd: Ruskin's *Works*, XXXVII, 167–68.

[1] Ruskin's *Notes on the Royal Academy, 1875.* See *Works*, XIV, 260–306.

[2] Rose La Touche died on May 29, 1875.

[3] Ruskin describes a visit with Carlyle in a letter to Mrs. Severn dated June 26, 1875 (in *Works*, XXXVII, 169). On this occasion, Carlyle took Ruskin to see the sculptor J. E. Boehm, who did a bust of Carlyle and was to do one of Ruskin as well. For additional details see Letter 133, n. 3.

172. *Ruskin to Carlyle*

Brantwood, Coniston, Lancashire
[July 12, 1875]

Dearest Papa,

Please let Mary read enclosed to you and send it back to me and send me a line to say how you are.

I've had a pleasant journey here, *but for* weather. Now I'm at work on the flowers—& they get blown to pieces before I can gather them, sometimes.— Oh me, if Spring would last—and one's strength, and one's time— What one could do!

Ever your loving
J. R.

173. *Ruskin to Carlyle*

Brantwood,
21st [July 1875]

Dearest Papa,

I would fain write to you every morning, but am at present so depressed, and so overworked, inevitably by the mere interests and thoughts of the passing spring days, so few of them—so full of cloud and flower sight or question, now—as it seems to me—only to be rightly or at all dealt with by the knowledge and feelings which I have only gained in declining life, and, by warnings too clear, know cannot last but a few years, if that, in available strength—what obscure stuff I am writing!— I mean, that every cloud on the hills is a problem to me, every weed on the banks; every sentence I read of old books, has new force to me, and I want to begin all work over again, with a boy's strength.

I wonder how far you have this same feeling, increased by the sorrowful quiet in which you now stay;—surely—age should not, to those who have laboured so nobly, be sorrowful; and yet, my own sorrow certainly is rooted in the sense of inability to work, for ever.

You see *I* can't write, neither— Indeed, I would write beautifully and legibly to you, if I could, but I scrawl so much—it can't be. Mary sent me such a lovely bit of yours about books.— please thank her for it and for her letter.

Ever your most loving and faithful
J. Ruskin

Letter *172*. MS: NLS, 556.107. Hitherto unpbd. The MS has "12 July, 1875" in another hand.
Letter *173*. MS: NLS, 556.108. Hitherto unpbd.

174. *Ruskin to Carlyle*

Keswick [September 1, 1875]

Dearest Papa,

How often I have thought of you, you won't believe,—how much I rejoice in hearing from Allen,[1] first of your enjoyment of peace, and then, of your kindness to Allen, and then, of your having been pleased with my new books[2]—you will I trust believe—most totally.

I am in confused helplessness of overwork, which I only carry through by resolved quietude for some piece of the morning—so *very* short lately, inevitably, that even my letters to you have become impossible. I *must* find some way out of all this turmoil, but can't today say more than how I love you always and am your affectionate God-son in the most solemn sense.

J. Ruskin

175. *Ruskin to Carlyle*

[Oxford, November 27, 1875]

Dearest Papa,

I'm just putting the notes together for my last of 12 lectures.[1] Here's a nicish little bit just concocted. I rather like it—I hope it'll make you laugh,

English Constitution

The rottenest mixture of Simony, bribery,
sneaking tyranny, shameless cowardice, and
accomplished lying, that ever the Devil chewed
small to spit into God's Paradise.

I must write it fair to be sure it's given without a slip of the tongue. They say my lectures have been rather an impression this term.

Letter 174. MS: NLS, 556.109. Hitherto unpbd. The MS has "September 1, 1875" in another hand.
[1] George Allen, Ruskin's publisher. See Letter 143.
[2] The "new books" could be *Mornings in Florence, Deucalion, Notes on the Royal Academy, 1875,* or any of the letters of *Fors Clavigera,* numbers 49 to 56—all published before September 1875. Just how pleased Carlyle was with them is questionable. See his comments in his letters to his brother John on September 9 and October 26, in the Introduction.
Letter 175. MS: NLS, 556.110. Pbd: Ruskin's *Works,* XXXVII, 186. The MS has "PM^k Nov. 27, 1875" in another hand.
[1] The "Studies in the Discourses of Sir Joshua Reynolds," delivered throughout the month of November at Oxford. For the "nicish little bit," see *Works,* XXII, 507.

Oh dear, I mustn't go on, the morning is the only time I can find things rightly in my head, and I've two lectures today, the closing one here, and one at Eton.[2]

Ever your loving

J. R.

176. *Ruskin to Mary Aitken*

Corpus Christi College, Oxford
4th Feb., '76

My dear Mary,

You should before now have received Ulric der Knecht,[1] and I cannot tell you how very happy I am in the thought of your translating it, with occasionally a flash of guidance or sprinkle of salt from your uncle.— It will give three times the value to the book that it has been so done; and the character of Frenel deserves it, no less than of the housemistress.

I think it would be well to keep the German Knecht in our title, and call it, "Ulrich the Knecht,"—this will serve to lead us to another kind of knighthood.

For, in our company,[2] the title of Servant is to be the highest!— There are to be three orders of companies;—namely (lowest) C. Retainers, who though taking the vow, are paid as labourers: clerks, & Companions simple; who are paid nothing, but attend more to their own business than the Company's, giving the tenth of their income however, always,—and Companion-Servants who devote themselves wholly to the Company's work. They will write themselves

C. R. of stGeorge

C. of stGeorge

C. S. of stGeorge, which will be equivalent to the Knighthood in other orders.

---

[2] A lecture on the Spanish Chapel in S. Maria Novella in Florence. See Cook, II, 269, for a glimpse of the "impression" this lecture, and Ruskin's lectures at Oxford, made upon his hearers.

Letter 176. MS: NLS, 556.111. Pbd: Ruskin's *Works*, XXXVII, 192.

[1] *Uli der Knecht*, a novel by Jeremias Gotthelf (Albert Bitzius). See Letters 97 and 182.

[2] In July, Ruskin had finished drafting the constitution of his St. George's Guild, which was granted a license by the Privy Council in 1878. The poet William Allingham, in his diary for March 6, 1876, mentions a conversation with Carlyle about "St. George's Society, which Carlyle thinks an absurdity, and gives nothing to" (*William Allingham's Diary*, introd. by Geoffrey Grigson [Carbondale, Ill., 1967], p. 245).

The book has perhaps been sent to Broadland,[3] by mistake, but will soon come.

Dearest love to Papa,
Ever your affectionate
J. Ruskin

I've told the printers to send you a revise of the preface to Xenophon's Economist which begins the series.[4]

177. Ruskin to Carlyle

Corpus Christi College, Oxford
[March 6, 1876]

Dearest Papa,

Was it a sparrow, or robin, I forget, that you were watching the little eyes and ways and pleasures of, when the sense of its having been a bit of yellow jelly not a year before, and the miracle of it, came on you so? I wish I could recollect what you called the egg aspect of it—perhaps Mary can? it was infinitely better than any "bit of yellow jelly"—yet I can't think.

I've been looking at Humboldt.[1] I see he "defines" the vital force as "that which prevents the original affinities from acting." Not at all which acts itself! What a lovely and cheerful view of life! (Mortal and other). God—as the Preventor of Original Affinities from acting—an omnipotent Drag upon Originality? *isn't* it nice?

Ever your loving Filius,
J. R.

Isn't my French-Revolutionary shell in last Fors[2] rather nice too?

---

[3] Broadlands was the home of Ruskin's Irish friend, Mrs. Cowper-Temple, whom he had recently visited.

[4] *Bibliotheca Pastorum*, a projected series of books chosen by Ruskin to be put into a special library for the use of the people of St. George's Guild. Both Xenophon and Gotthelf were to be part of this series, though the latter was later excluded. See Ruskin's *Works*, volumes XXXI and XXXII.

Letter 177. MS: NLS, 556.112. Hitherto unpbd. The MS has "Post M^k. 6 March, 1876" in another hand.

[1] Baron Alexander von Humboldt (1769–1859), a German naturalist, traveler, and statesman. Ruskin refers in this letter to Humboldt's *Kosmos* (1845–62), a description of the physical universe.

[2] In *Fors Clavigera*, letter 63 (*Works*, XXVIII, 553), Ruskin speaks of snail shells and mentions "a French snail, revolutionary in the manner of a screw."

178. *Mary Aitken to Ruskin*

5 Cheyne Row, Chelsea
7 March, 1876

Dear Mr. Ruskin,

My Uncle's little friend is a sparrow. I did not hear him tell the story about it on Sunday, but when I did, a day or two before, he said "it had been only a small speck of *slobber*"! He, too, thinks this is the word he used.

We have a good many birds here,—robins, sparrows, & some blackbirds; and last summer a nightingale used to make his "tender and strong" note heard quite close to us; a little robin built her nest in a tool house in the garden adjoining ours. Our neighbours left the window open so that she could always be free even when the door was closed, and thence she sent out nine little redbreasts to the world. They are disposed to be very friendly but we never become intimate because of the cat who usually follows me into the garden. If the poor little things reason about a personal devil, I am sure they must think of our cat and have no doubt about his existence.

My Uncle was much interested in what you said about Humboldt. He had missed the passage which you refer to.

My Uncle sends his love & I am always, dear Master and Teacher
Yours affectionately & respectfully
Mary Carlyle Aitken

179. *Mary Aitken to Ruskin*

June 6, 1876

Dear Mr. Ruskin,

I take the liberty of sending with this a note that has come tonight from Lady Lothian,[1] who, as you will see, is anxious to have a nomination to the Blue Coat School, for a boy she is interested in. I do not know whether the lady is right in supposing that you have the power of nomination,[2] but if you had and were willing to give the required

---

Letter 178. MS: Frederick W. Hilles. Hitherto unpbd.

Letter 179. MS not located. Pbd: Ruskin's *Works*, XXXIII, 344.

[1] Lady Victoria Alexandrina Montagu Douglas Scott, wife of Schomberg Henry Kerr, ninth Marquess of Lothian. They had been married in 1865 and succeeded to the title in 1870. The marchioness died in 1938.

[2] The "Blue Coat School" was Christ's Hospital, of which Ruskin was a governor. See *Time and Tide* (*Works*, XVII, 418), where Ruskin discusses the nature of people who send him such "anxious" letters.

promise for next year, you would be doing a kindness to one of the hardest-working and most self-denying people in the world.

I hardly know how to put into words the awful fact I have to communicate. I have failed utterly and ignominiously in any attempt to translate Uli into English.[3] I have tried over and over again and can't get on at all. It is written in cramped, foreign German,[4] largely interspersed with Swiss words, which no dictionary will explain. My uncle has goaded me on with cruel jibes; but he read the book himself, and says now that *he* could at no period of his life have translated it. I need say no more, except that I am much grieved to find what would have been a great pleasure to me so far beyond my very small powers.

You will be sorry to know that my uncle has been very weak and poorly of late weeks. He is, however, getting a little better as the weather improves.

He sends his kindest and best love to you; and I am ever, dear Mr. Ruskin,

Yours affectionately and respectfully,
Mary Carlyle Aitken

180. Ruskin to Mary Aitken

Brantwood, 18th June '76

My dear Mary,

A strange and to me most blessed, continuance of truly natural & sweet summer weather has kept me out nearly all day long,—though always with your letter in my breast pocket, to be answered,—"tomorrow, at latest".— Had my presentation been free I had answered at once but it was given away months ago. The Ulrich is a more important matter. There is no reason whatever for your translating it from the German. If you can do it from the French; with notes on any German word you happen to know, it will be all I want. I am greatly set on having it done by you, with your Uncle's help.

Your report of his health troubles me, but I think the change from that bitter weather to gentler, *seemed* at first weakening to us all. I had a week when it first came fine—of extraordinary & helpless lassitude.

---

[3] Gotthelf's *Uli der Knecht*. See Letter 177. The translation eventually was done by Mrs. Julia Firth, and was published as *Ulric the Farm Servant: A Story of the Bernese Lowland*, in nine parts, from July 1886 to October 1888, with a preface and notes by Ruskin. See *Works*, XXXII.

[4] A note by Mrs. Firth (*Works*, XXXII, 344) adds: "This must have been a dialect edition; the one I used was in ordinary German with occasional patois."

Letter 180. MS: NLS, 556.113. Hitherto unpbd.

Write me word soon again how he is, and whether you are both sick
of Ulrich, or will try the French.

Ever your grateful

J. R.

Dearest love to my Papa. Tell him I'm on Frederick again now.[1]

181. *Ruskin to Carlyle*

Venice, 9th Sept. '76

My dearest Papa,

I am so thankful to hear from Mary that you are better. I have not
been writing because I thought you would scarcely care to hear of my
many failures and languid progresses; or of my "scientific" museum
work,[1] slowly organizing itself; but I think it will please you to hear
that I have good hope now of recasting the Stones of Venice[2] into a
book such as you would have a pupil of yours write. I shall throw off
at least half of the present text, and add what I now better know of the
real sources of Venetian energy,—and what I—worse—know of the
cause of Venetian ruin,—with some notes on modern Italy which I do
eagerly hope you will be satisfied with. Only we must keep clear of
Barbarossa![3]

And I trust you will like a bit of preface I'm writing for an edition of
Sir Philip Sidney's Psalter,[4] bearing on the psalms before and after Leu-
ther [*sic*], and on sundry other musical "performances"—not paid for
by spectacular managers. I have a great deal to think out about Scotch

---

[1] Ruskin was rereading Carlyle's *Frederick the Great* in preparation for the "Notes on
Frederick the Great" he was to publish in *Fors Clavigera*.

Letter 181. MS: NLS, 556.114. Hitherto unpbd.

[1] The St. George's Museum in Sheffield.

[2] Ruskin was in Venice to gather material for a new edition of his *The Stones of Venice*, which was originally published in 1851–53 (see Letter 1). The new edition was finally issued in 1879–81.

[3] A reference to Frederick Barbarossa's wars in Italy. Carlyle, in his *Frederick the
Great*, volume I, book ii, chapter 5 (*Works*, XII, 82), called Barbarossa "the greatest of
all the Kaisers of that or any other House. . . . A magnificent magnanimous man." Ruskin, in *Fiction Fair and Foul*, no. IV (*Works*, XXXIV, 355), says "My own estimate of
Frederic's [Barbarossa's] character would be scarcely so favourable; it is the only point
of history on which I have doubted the authority even of my own master, Carlyle."

[4] *Rock Honeycomb: Broken Pieces of Sir Philip Sidney's Psalter, Laid Up in Store for
English Homes* (Orpington, 1877). It was volume II of the *Bibliotheca Pastorum* series.
See *Works*, XXXI.

music, and song; partly with the help of Mary's book,⁵—as soon as I get a clear proof I'll send you one.

I shall be here for a month at least, but hope to see you before going to Oxford in November.— And do not think, however seldom I *can* now see you, that I am less your loving,

John Ruskin

182. Ruskin to Mary Aitken

Venice, 9th Sept. '76

My dearest Mary,

I've no paper but this tonight, and will not put off till tomorrow my thanks—I am just beginning some drawings and other work requiring some cheerfulness to do it well; and your letter with better news of your uncle just comes to cheer me,—besides its pleasant holding out of hope that you will still do Ulrich for me.

I had nearly come to see you in Scotland; but I lost so much time in the fine weather, merely in drinking light and air that at last I found all the summers tasks had to be done in a fortnight, and I was bound by most religious promise to be here this autumn.

Will you please give the enclosed line to Papa. I have less and less power, somehow, continually to say how much I regard him, but I am ever faithfully his & yours,

J. Ruskin

I've put Papa's note in a separate envelope to avoid double folding.

183. Ruskin to Carlyle

Venice, 15th Nov. '76

My dearest Papa,

I have been much too sad to write, lately, but am so thankful to hear of you today from Joanna that I cannot but tell you so. I am so very lonely now, missing the father and mother more and more every day, and having no more anything to look forward to here, but the gradual

---

⁵ *Scottish Song: A Selection of the Choicest Lyrics of Scotland* (1874), compiled and arranged by Mary Aitken. On the verso of the half-title page the edition is marked "Golden Treasury Series."

Letter 182. MS: NLS, 556.115. Hitherto unpbd.
Letter 183. MS: NLS, 556.116. Hitherto unpbd.

closing in of all, and feeling, for you, with continually increasing respect & love, more and more sorrow as I felt myself also entering with you the time of waiting, that what comfort I might otherwise have taken in telling you what I was doing quite left me. Also, I have been failing so utterly in keeping up to my plans, or fulfilling my promises,—so many things "gone to water" with the work done for them, that I have little heart for giving account of myself. I have an immense quantity of notes made for the life of Scott;[1] and I had done much work in gathering the pieces I wanted of Frederick;[2] and now here is another year gone, and nothing got into form, and new claims on me, it seems, from my own old work. For, coming here only to put myself into some temper of fancy, in recasting the Stones of Venice, I have got a new clue, utterly unseen by me when I wrote it, which will give, and ought to give me, many hours of added toil; but I believe I shall now leave the book a sound piece of work, and connect it with a short history of Venice for the schools of St. George[3] which I am not without hope will give you pleasure. I have sent a little piece to be printed, and will send you the first revise in any readable state. I shall keep close at it all this winter.

Also, concluding now the sixth year and volume of Fors, I am going in the seventh year, to gather it all into connected force, and drive it home, not any more enigmatically; but with literal and quiet advice to the men, what to do. First of all I shall take up the organization of food supply, then of clothes;[4] getting actual answer or question from the Sheffield operatives on all principles. I have sent, through my secretary Mr. Tyrrwhitt, (Rev^d R^stJ),[5] a formal and careful interrogation to the Bishop of Manchester, whether he means to answer my challenge or not; and the same to Mr. Fawcett,[6] and their replies shall be kept in the Sheffield Museum.

[1] The biography was never written, but the notes can be found in several of the *Fors Clavigera* letters. See *Works*, XXVII, 564–601 and 606–21; XXIX, 541–45.

[2] See Letter 180.

[3] Published in 1876 as *St. Mark's Rest: The History of Venice, Written for the Help of the Few Travellers Who Still Care for Her Monuments*. See *Works*, XXIV.

[4] See *Fors Clavigera*, letter 73 (*Works*, XXIX, 13–29), which deals with these problems, and which is dated November 20, 1876.

[5] Reverend Richard St. John Tyrwhitt (1827–95). Ruskin here misspells the name "Tyrrwhitt." Besides being connected with Ruskin and the church, Tyrwhitt was well known as a writer on art and as an artist, especially at Oxford. See the doctoral dissertation by Jay Wood Claiborne, "Two Secretaries: The Letters of John Ruskin to Charles Augustus Howell and the Rev. Richard St. John Tyrwhitt," the University of Texas at Austin, 1969.

[6] For Ruskin's interrogation of Dr. James Fraser, bishop of Manchester (1870–85),

I must send this poor note to day. My love to Mary. Posta in Firma [?], Venezia, will always find me, if she has word of Ulrich to give me.

Ever your loving
John Ruskin

184. Ruskin to Carlyle

Venice, 1st December, 1876

Dearest Papa,

I am so thankful to hear from Mary that you are yourself again, and bright, and reading Shakespeare to her. What a blessed girl that is, to have you and another uncle to "do for," and to be able to do for them!—and to be witty and insighted besides; and have her uncle liking to read Shakespeare to her.

There is something left in "the Present" still, if we can get the mischief of it quieted—cocks not to crow except on properly far off dunghills, & so on.[1]

Then it's so nice having your beautiful letter to read. I didn't mean to stay out this winter, and I've no Carlyle with me—not a bit—and I've been reading French novels instead with no benefit in the change.

All the same, I think if you will glance over two stories in an English-French one, which I told Joanna to get and will tell her to send to Cheyne Row—"Our New Bishop" and "A Hero of the Commune,"[2]—you will find some good in them.

I'm very unhappy in my work here—I don't want to write about Venice, now, but about Sheffield; and yet I think I ought to finish rightly what I have done so much of, and dot all the i's. I get in a fury, because whenever I come to the original statement of anything it's always a reference to an MS. in the Vatican—or the like.

Fancy, papa, what times you and I should have had if those beasts of aristocrats, instead of spending all their money in horses, had set up

---

see "Usury; A Reply and a Rejoinder," in *Works*, XXXIV, 405–25. For Ruskin's private challenge to both Fraser and Professor Henry Fawcett concerning usury and interest, see *Fors Clavigera*, letter 78 (June 1877), in *Works*, XXIX, 136.

Letter 184. MS: NLS, 556.117. Pbd: Ruskin's *Works*, XXXVII, 213–14.

[1]The allusions are to Carlyle's *Past and Present* (1843) and the nuisance caused by cocks crowing beside Carlyle's window in London. See Froude, IV, 135, for a discussion of Carlyle's complaints about this noisy incident. Ruskin, in a letter to C. E. Norton on August 28, 1886 (*Works*, XXXVII, 569), comments with grim humor: "How many wiser folk than I go mad for good and all . . . like poor Turner at the last, Blake always, Scott in his pride, Irving in his faith, and Carlyle because of the poultry next door."

[2]See *French Pictures in English Chalk*, by E. C. Grenville Murray (1876).

printing presses, and printed all the first documents of their own history (the worthless dishwashings that they are)—and nice Indexes!

Please give my love to Froude, and impart the above idea to him. I'm a little proud of it, because it's the first time it ever occurred to me what printing was good for.

Love to Mary, and thank her for her letter, and say, I rather like that notion of the bursting bubble—only I fear it's more like a bursting balloon—with small chance for the car.

Forgive my ill writing. I've tried so hard to do better but it's not in me.

Ever your loving and faithful
J. Ruskin

It is very dear of you to revise Ulric for me.

185. Ruskin to Mary Aitken

Venice, 9th Jan., '77

Dear Mary,

All good and dear wishes are with you and your uncle from me, always—but so much has been happening I can't tell you, yet awhile, but it will interest your uncle much I think. Enclosed little note will perhaps please him. I write this only to enclose it, not for your Christmas letter.

Your grateful & affectionate
J. Ruskin

186. Ruskin to Mary Aitken

Venice, 16th Jan., '77

My dear Mary,

I am so very glad of your letter, and laurel leaf.— It comes with benediction to me—for truly, the horses of St. Mark's are I think putting on their harness for me,—and I do hope your uncle will like some of the harness-bronze, in next Fors.[1]

My dear love to him. I'm so thankful you've taken poor Alice home again. Nobody, you will find, can do him, but—great and simple people— Not that you're very "simple" neither! I'm very glad to hear of

Letter 185. MS: NLS, 556.118. Hitherto unpbd.
Letter 186. MS: NLS, 556.119. Hitherto unpbd.
[1] See *Fors Clavigera*, letter 75 (*Works*, XXIX, 55).

the Elwins.[2] But my dear, I will answer your question in a word—"No one should ever write a biography, or paint a picture in Hatred."

I do not intend to write a biography of John Stewart [*sic*] Mill, nor should Mr. Elwin have written one of Pope. He has done quite limitless mischief to the cause of all truth. How he was so Godabandoned as to do it, he will find out some day, being good at heart as you tell me.

Ever your grateful and affectionate
J. R.

I do not mask or deny Turner's sins,—nor do I wish any one who understands Turner to be ignorant of them. But not to know the sins without the Virtues.

187. *Ruskin to Carlyle*

Venice, 10th May, '77

My dearest Papa,

This was my dead Papa's birthday, and he will like me to write to you. I should, often, if I were in good heart; but my work here is full of discouragements keeping me silent. Also I've rather been expecting some little compliment from you on something or other in Fors, and have been chilled by getting none; lastly, I have been reading Frederick right through, with care, and am a little vexed;—I don't like him as well as I did. His treatment of his brother after the Zittau business seems to me quite brutal[1]—and I am *entirely* vexed at finding him always speaking of himself and Prussia, never of the *interests of Silesia.* I am very thankful for your letter in Times on the "Interests of England."[2]

—That Pottery, field *chiefly*, the buildings very shabby I believe— I've never seen it!!!—is—and will be, mine.

The enclosed note will admit your friend I doubt not.

Love to Mary always,

Ever your devoted
John Ruskin

[2] See Letter 161, n. 1.

Letter 187. MS: NLS, 556.120. Hitherto unpbd.

[1] See Carlyle's *Works*, XVII, 202–15. Frederick's brother, Prince August-Wilhelm, was bombarded and trounced by Prince Charles of Lorraine and the Austrians at Zittau. Frederick then wrote him an angry letter accusing him of treasonable cowardice, and the prince died soon afterward—of a broken heart, it was rumored.

[2] "On the Crisis," in the *Times*, May 5, 1877. This letter, on Disraeli's foreign policy, was Carlyle's last public word.

188. *Ruskin to Carlyle*

Corpus Christi College, Oxford
Sunday afternoon, [late July 1877]

Dearest Papa,

I send this by my good framemaker—or his man whom you may entirely trust to remove the encumbering frames from the dining room.[1] I will write as soon as I get home—here I am very dismal somehow, and have nothing to tell or say, except that I am your faithful and devoted son, in the Florentine sense.

J. Ruskin

My very true regards to Mary.

189. *Ruskin to Carlyle*

Herne Hill
Tuesday, 6th Nov. [1877]

Dearest Papa,

I send my gardner only to ask for you—myself captive here to printers and what not—I can't get over to Chelsea till four, tomorrow. I have an hour then of quiet. Is it your resting or walking time, or sleeping:—just send verbal message if I'm to come—I must get away to Oxford rail after & chat—but I shall be soon in town again.

In hope of hearing at least that you are well.

Your lovingest
J. Ruskin

Letter 188. MS: NLS, 556.123. Hitherto unpbd.
[1] An entry in Ruskin's diary for July 14, 1877 (*Diaries*, III, 965) may have some relevance here. "Stopped at Oxford," he says, "and found . . . Carlyle's last gift to me—the portrait of Knox."
Letter 189. MS: NLS, 556.122. Hitherto unpbd. Although Ruskin used letterhead stationery from Corpus Christi College, Oxford, for this letter, it was actually dated at Herne Hill.

190. *Ruskin to Carlyle*

Corpus Christi College, Oxford
5th January, '78

Dearest Papa,

Might I come to see you tomorrow about ½ past one? or at any hour after that you would like better? Merely send out *word* yes, with the hour, if changed, or No, if it cannot be.

Ever your faithful & loving
John Ruskin

191. *Ruskin to Carlyle*

Hawarden Castle, Chester
15th Jan. '78

Dearest Papa,

I am going home today, but I think it will be only to bid the servants good New Year, and that I shall be quickly up in Oxford again; and the more that I want to see you again, soon, and not let you say any more "how long?"

Also, I want to bring with me to your quiet presence-chamber a youth who deeply loves you;[1] and for whom the permission to look upon your face will be strength and memory in the future, much help-ful to the resolution and the beauty of his life,—and to please let Mary write and say that I may bring him—and give *me* also better will to return to my Oxford duty from the Calypso woods of Coniston. And so believe me ever your faithful and loving son,

J. Ruskin

192. *Ruskin to Mary Aitken*

Brantwood, Coniston
17th February 1878

My dearest Mary,

It *is* so kind of Papa to let me bring Mr. Lyttelton, but it may be a little while yet—and please—I want to know how Ulrich is going

---

Letter 190. MS: NLS, 556.124. Hitherto unpbd.

Letter 191. MS: NLS, 556.125. Pbd: J. Ruskin, *Letters to M[ary] G[ladstone] and H[elen] G[ladstone]* (New York, 1903), pp. x–xi; and (with omissions) in Ruskin's *Works*, XXXVII, 237.

[1] Alfred Lyttelton, a nephew of Gladstone, whom Ruskin was visiting in Hawarden at the time. Lyttelton describes his visit in Wilson, VI, 423. Carlyle, he says, at first "groaned and sighed a good deal, receiving kindly enough, however, Ruskin's kiss, most tenderly given." See also Introduction.

Letter 192. MS: NLS, 556.126. Hitherto unpbd.

on—or anything else you are about. I've never time to say a word when I'm there. Write me a nice long letter—there's a dear.

Ever your loving
John Ruskin

193. *Ruskin to Carlyle*

Brantwood, Coniston
17th February 1878

Dearest Papa,

I know you don't care quite so much as foolish I do for Walter Scott— But please don't think it saucy of me then, to write you this with his pen, which the Master of Harrow D. Butler[1] has lent me.— It's to thank you for—ever so many things—but lastly for bringing that youth to see you, (the Hon^e Alfred Lyttleton, of Trinity, Cambridge)— I can't come yet for ten days or so, but then, I shall be so happy to be by the fireside again. And now, please, for this is my chief business, make that sweet Mary tell me a little of what you would have me say in next Fors—of *anything*.

Ever your faithful and loving servant, & son,
John Ruskin

194. *Ruskin to Carlyle*

Brantwood, Coniston
23rd June, '78

My dearest Papa,

I have not written to you, because my illness broke me all to pieces, and every little bit has a different thing to say,—which makes it difficult in the extreme to write to any one whom one wants to tell things to, just as they are, and who cares very truly whether they are right or wrong. It was utterly wonderful to me to find that I could go so heartily & headily mad;[1] for you know I had been priding myself on my peculiar sanity! And it was more wonderful yet to find the madness made up into things so dreadful, out of things so trivial. One of the most provoking and disagreeable of the spectres was developed out of the firelight on my mahogany bedpost[2]—and my fate, for all futurity,

---

Letter *193*. MS: NLS, 556.127. Hitherto unpbd.

[1] Dr. H. Montague Butler, then headmaster of Harrow School. Ruskin had given a collection of minerals to Harrow in 1866.

Letter *194*. MS: NLS, 556.128. Pbd: Ruskin's *Works*, XXXVII, 248–49.

[1] Ruskin suffered an attack of delirium from February 23 until early June. Wilenski and many others agree that he suffered from a form of manic-depressive psychosis that had been building for years.

[2] See Introduction.

seemed continually to turn on the humour of dark personages who were materially nothing but the stains of damp on the ceiling. But the sorrowfullest part of the matter was, and is, that, while my illness at Matlock encouraged me by all its dreams in after work,[3] this one has done nothing but humiliate and terrify me; and leaves me nearly unable to speak any more except of the natures of stones and flowers.

I have regained great part of my strength, and am not in bad *spirits*,—on the condition, otherwise absolutely essential, that I think of nothing that would vex me. But this means a very trifling form of thought and direction of work, throughout the day.

Nevertheless, I am working out some points in the history and geography of Arabia[4] which I think will be useful, and reading you, and Gibbon! alternately—or Mahomet! I am going to stigmatize Gibbon's as the worst style of language ever yet invented by man—its affectation and platitude being both consummate. It is like the most tasteless water-gruel, with a handful of Epsom salts strewed in for flowers, and served with the airs of being turtle.[5] Has Mary done any more Gotthelf—I never read him without renewed refreshment.

By the way, *you* are very unsatisfactory about Mahomet's death,[6]— which I want to know all that may be known of; and also, in re-reading *Frederick*, the first book I got to, after I got my natural eyes again, I was worried of questions in his life—how far it was good for Silesia to be Prussian or Austrian—whether Silesia itself is Prussian or Austrian-tempered—and how its geography marks its relations to south and north. I might make out this from detached passages; but the great impression left on me was, how blessed it would have been for Silesia, Prussia, and Austria, if all their soldiers, generals, & Princes had been made at the first outbreak of the war one grand auto da fe [*sic*] of, in the style of—my recent scenic effects deduced from damp in the ceiling.

I can't write more today, but am ever your lovingest

J. Ruskin

---

[3] See Ruskin's *Works*, XXII, 445–47; and Letter 111, n. 2.

[4] See *The Bible of Amiens*, Ruskin's *Works*, XXXIII, 92–97.

[5] Later, in 1880, when Ruskin was amending Lord Avebury's list of the "Best Hundred Books," he crossed out Gibbon's name. See *Works*, XXXIV, 582–88.

[6] See Carlyle's *Heroes and Hero-Worship*, *Works*, V, 72.

195. *Ruskin to Carlyle*

Herne Hill
10th July, '78

Dearest Papa,

I got pleasantly up from Brantwood yesterday, and shall be most thankful to hear from Mary that I may come and see you, if I may, and what time now you like best for people to come.

Ever your lovingest
J. Ruskin

196. *Ruskin to Carlyle*

Arthur Severn's, Herne Hill,
Friday [March 28, 1879]

My dearest Papa,

I couldn't come today—it was so cold in the train, yesterday, it took all the life out of me; and I've been forced to rest—and now I've no day till Tuesday, when I can come, I hope, whenever you would like me.

I am fairly well and can do much, yet—if I keep myself quiet; but if I read *papers*, or try to talk, I get excited and weary very soon, so that my days are passed either in my wood, or my library, and I dare not come up to London. The lawyers forced me just now.[1]

I won't say how it grieves me never to see you,[2]—or would, if I could now let myself grieve. But I am ever

Your faithful and loving
John Ruskin

197. *Ruskin to Mary Aitken*

Brantwood, Coniston
[June 1879]

Dear Mary,

So many thanks for your letter—long expected—now, today at least unanswerable before post time. Dearest love to Papa.

Ever your affe
J. R.

Letter 195. MS: NLS, 556.129. Hitherto unpbd.
Letter 196. MS: NLS, 556.130. Pbd: Ruskin's *Works*, XXXVII, 278.
[1] In a letter to C. E. Norton, February 27, 1879, Ruskin speaks of "being summoned to London to give evidence on a charge of forgery" (*Works*, XXXVII, 276).
[2] For Carlyle's explanation of Ruskin's absence, see Introduction.
Letter 197. MS: NLS, 556.131. Hitherto unpbd.

198. *Ruskin to Mary Aitken*

Brantwood, Coniston
6th June, '79

My dear Mary,

I haven't it in me to write you a word, yet I am very thankful for all you tell me,—for your uncle's blessing, very solemnly, for I need it.

I hope all possible good for him and you, in what Heaven has brought about thus.[1]

Ever your affectionate
J. Ruskin

199. *Ruskin to Carlyle*

Herne Hill
December, 1879

My dearest Papa,

And did you come here—yourself—actually—you dearest, kindest papa—to see your poor unfilial prodigal?— Oh me, I'm always being routed about by the pigs—(not that I mean that, I mean by pigs everything that's bad)—and can't get away. I've been working—as I never thought to do again—against time lately—and have been writing letters to my clerical friends—e.g., grey pamphlet[1] sent with this I hope—and a quantity of talk besides—as useless probably—about pictures, which you'll get on Monday, and I hope to go over myself early in the week to get some forgiveness and blessing from you.

Very good it was of Froude to come too—after what I've been writing to him[2]—but certainly the Devil's got into him lately—though he's still himself all but that contents.

Love to Mary.— Ever your faithfullest & lovingest
J. Ruskin

Letter 198. MS: NLS, 556.132. Hitherto unpbd.
[1] Mary Aitken married Alexander Carlyle, son of Carlyle's brother Alick, in the summer of 1879.
Letter 199. MS: NLS, 556.133. Pbd: Ruskin's *Works*, XXXVII, 303–4.
[1] The first edition of *Letters to the Clergy*, privately printed in October 1879. See *Works*, XXXIV, 179. For the "talk about pictures," see *Notes on Prout and Hunt*, *Works*, XIV, 369–452.
[2] Ruskin's remarks to Froude remain unknown, but six weeks later, in *Fors Clavigera*, letter 88 (February 8, 1880), he remarked of Froude that "year by year his words have grown more hesitating and hopeless." He then added further derogatory remarks about Froude's Protestantism and belief in progress. See *Works*, XXIX, 387.

INDEX